O9-BTO-002

THIS OLD MAN

ALSO BY ROGER ANGELL

Let Me Finish

Game Time

A Pitcher's Story

Once More Around the Park

Season Ticket

Late Innings

Five Seasons

The Summer Game

A Day in the Life of Roger Angell

The Stone Arbor

THIS OLD MAN

Roger Angell

All in Pieces

DOUBLEDAY

New York   London   Toronto   Sydney   Auckland

Copyright © 2015 by Roger Angell

All rights reserved. Published in the United States by Doubleday,
a division of Penguin Random House LLC, New York,
and distributed in Canada by Random House of Canada,
a division of Penguin Random House Canada Ltd., Toronto.

www.doubleday.com

DOUBLEDAY and the portrayal of an anchor with a dolphin
are registered trademarks of Penguin Random House LLC.

Owing to limitations of space, permissions to reprint previously
published material appear on page 304.

Grateful acknowledgment is made to the following for permission to reprint
previously published material: Pearson Education, Inc.: Foreword by Roger Angell
from *The Elements of Style,* 4th Ed., by E. B. White and William Strunk, copyright
© 2000. Reprinted by permission of Pearson Education, Inc., New York, NY.
Tilbury House Publishers: Foreword by Roger Angell from *One Man's Meat* by E. B.
White, copyright © 1997. Reprinted by permission of Tilbury House Publishers.

Jacket design by John Fontana

Library of Congress Cataloging-in-Publication Data
Angell, Roger.
[Works. Selections]
This old man : all in pieces / Roger Angell.
pages   cm
ISBN 978-0-385-54113-8 (hardcover)—ISBN 978-0-385-54114-5 (eBook)
1. Angell, Roger. I. Title.
PS3551.N46A6 2015
818'.5409—dc23
[B]   2015018255

MANUFACTURED IN THE UNITED STATES OF AMERICA

1   3   5   7   9   10   8   6   4   2

First Edition

FOR LAURA AND LILY AND CLARA AND EMMA

CONTENTS

THIS OLD MAN

INTRODUCTION

Dogs start the day with a spoonful of Alpo or some other canned meat on top of a heap of patented, vitaminized kibble. In no time the meal is gobbled down and the dish licked clean and, like as not, poked noisily about the kitchen like a hockey puck, amid waggings. But I can recall another era, when every dog took a quick first look into his dish, to see what was in there. It was different each morning, but might contain a last chunk of pot roast or ham hock, plus gravy, from the previous night's dinner table, a scraping of scrambled eggs, a slice or two of stale bread, leftover lima beans or spinach, a fresh but limp carrot, a splash of milk, and a half-bitten doughnut. It went down just as fast and probably did no harm, but what I'm getting at here is the old phrase "a dog's breakfast," because that's what this book is. A mélange, a grab bag, a plate of hors d'oeuvres, a teenager's closet, a bit of everything. A dog's breakfast.

Most of these entries are *New Yorker* pieces of mine that appeared in the magazine over a span of decades; many of them are short and light, and a majority quite recent. Longer pieces include book reviews and Profiles of heroes of mine, now departed. There was plenty of old stuff for me to look over when I was getting this meal together, and every selection had to pass a sniff test. Readers are invited to do the same, and to skip about, make a grab, turn back. There are swatches of old letters and some obituaries, but not much mourning. There are Talk of the Town pieces and Comment pieces and sidebars and online posts. Also verses and scribbled notes and family doggerel. A photograph of me, at ten, pitching a softball to my mother. A photograph of me in front of an assemblage of Hall of Fame ballplayers delivering an address at Cooperstown in July, 2014. There's more baseball, sometimes in the form of blogs, and often on reassuringly familiar topics: Big Papi, Derek Jeter, postseason pain.

There's a rough chronology to this, but the book can also be seen as a portrait of my brain at ninety-four: a different serving, with good days and bad days in there, some losses and recurring afterthoughts right next to a midnight haiku, a fugitive great movie, a party conversation reborn. A later piece, which has provided my title, presented itself unexpectedly one morning, and ran in *The New Yorker*'s anniversary issue in 2014. It has brought a rush of personal and posted mail, a prize, and more kindness than anything else I've written. That was a good day.

HORSE TALK

Horses once abounded in New York, with a hundred and twenty thousand of them still in residence in 1908, when a reporter called them "an economic burden, an affront to cleanliness, and a terrible tax upon human life." Their numbers declined precipitously thereafter, trailing off into art and sentimentality—who doesn't remember the Steichen photograph of a misty, soft-edged Flatiron Building, with the silhouetted horse cab and plug-hatted cabbie in the foreground? Horsepresence took another hit last month, when the ancient Claremont Riding Academy, on West Eighty-ninth Street, closed its doors, reducing our equines to that redolent line of tourist-pullers on Central Park South. A few older city types (this writer among them) can remember cloppier times. The appearance of flower vendors, with their brilliantly hued horse-drawn wagons of blooms, was once a certain sign that another city spring was at hand. Taken along to the theatre by your parents, and in among the dressed-up, perfumed, and excited hordes in the West Forties before curtain time, you were watched over by godlike city mounties, unmoving atop their enormous steeds. (At school, ambivalently, you heard that these same Cossacks sometimes dealt less sweetly with political demonstrators in Union Square. Want to lift the embargo on Spain? Want to free the Scottsboro Boys? Bring along a handful of marbles to drop on the pavement: police horses *hate* marbles.)

Back to the stage: when the musical "Annie 2" opened, in 1989, the dog playing Sandy several times missed a bark cue in the second act: a vital bit of business in the plot. Quizzed urgently by the director and producers, Sandy's handler said that the one thing that always made his thespian mutt bark was the sudden sight of a horse. At the next performance—and then at every performance thereafter—an assistant stage manager donned a full-sized horse head and stepped into sight in the wings on cue, producing the *arf.* Back to cops: when the mounted-police stable in the Squadron A Armory, on East Ninety-fourth Street, was closed, in 1966, a woman (it was my wife) alighting from a Madison Avenue bus at twilight was almost knocked flat by a riderless police horse, stirrups flying, which came wildly past her on its way home to its old barn. A minute later, a cab pulled up and an embarrassed policeman in jodhpurs got out, shaking his head, retrieved his animal, and trotted off toward their new stable, way across town.

Something's sad about horses, and not just Barbaro. Who ever expected that they would be not just less frequent on the Central Park bridle path but gone for good? I walk my dog, Harry, on the path every day, and now it turns out that the end of horseback riding in New York is my fault, along with global warming. The recent proliferation of dogs and joggers and baby strollers on the broad, stony old bridle path had led to the dwindling numbers of Claremont customers. Some days you never saw a horse at all. A week before the shutdown, Harry and I were close to the giant plane tree on the northeast bend near Ninety-seventh Street when a clockwise equestrienne came walking toward us on a gray horse. She wore jodhpurs, black boots, a black top, and a black helmet, set straight on her head. She sat up tall, her spine strong, her heels tilted back, her hands at rest with the reins, her crop held at an angle. She looked straight ahead. Everything exactly right.

Harry, a smooth fox terrier, watched the horse and horsewoman with his usual extreme interest, giving this horse the attention it deserved. Here it came, five yards away, picking up its stonelike, clomping feet. Huge black holes for nostrils, legs knobbed like furniture, ears aloft, and the curved, satiny, massive rear end lifting and putting down the great package with springy ease. The nearer eye, straight above us, took us in and rolled away. The smell of the great animal—nothing else is like it—arrived and then went by. I don't always know what my dog is thinking but this time I did: Holy *shit*!

Talk, May, 2007

LINEUP

The ballpark in this treasured spring-baseball photograph is a stretch of meadow or rough lawn in Bedford, New York, an upper-Westchester exurb where my mother and stepfather found a modest spring-and-summer rental in the first years of their marriage. Judging by the post-blossoming young apple tree just down the third-base line, this opening day fell on a mid-spring Sunday in, let's say, 1931. Since the photo is undated, I base its time on the size of the pitcher, who is me, at ten and a half. The batter is my mother, Katharine White, and the tweedy, cautious catcher is my seventy-nine-year-old grandfather, Charles Spencer Sergeant, a retired executive of the Boston Elevated Railway. Not a great athlete, perhaps, but a man with a strong conceptual awareness of foul tips.

I can't take my eyes off my mother. Her uniform, which appears a tad formal, is a well-cut suit skirt and a silk blouse, both in keeping with Sunday-outing styles of that time. Despite a certain wariness in her gaze and upper body, her stance is excellent—her weight mostly over the slightly flexed back leg, her front foot stepping boldly forward in preparation for the swing, which will initially

take the bat up and back, then swiftly down into the reversing pivot and full-body turn that precede and accompany her Tris Speaker–esque, closed-stance cut at the ball.

My pitching form is O.K., too. Yes, I look more like a center fielder trying to cut down a speeding baserunner at third base or home, but give me a break, guys. By the looks of me, I go about eighty-two pounds here, and the angle of my arm shows an instinctive understanding of the physics of the fling. Only the greatest athletes seem to have this somewhere within them, an elegant je ne sais quoi that marks the Mathewsons and Mayses of each era and warms the hearts of even the idlest, most distant onlooker. The photographer, who is my stepfather, E. B. White, has snapped the softball in first flight, only a blurry yard or two out of my grasp, and this good fortune, taken with the tilt of my follow-through, allows us to supply the invisible arc of the sphere, a combined heater and changeup that will parallel the lower profile of the apple tree and, descending, cross the plate hem-high: a pitch taken by my mom for a called—called by me—strike one.

Way to go, kid.

Post, March, 2014

THE LITTLE FLOWER

Like every other New York kid who came into his teens in the nineteen-thirties, I had President Roosevelt by heart (chin, cigarette, Groton accent, T.V.A., soak the rich) but felt much closer to Mayor Fiorello La Guardia. Stubby under his operatic black hat, hilariously busy, looking by turns indignant, disbelieving, and delighted, the Little Flower had piercing dark-brown eyes and a thick jaw that looked punishing when he was talking about fat-cat landlords or Tammany bosses but often fell into an engaging, half-open smile. He ran New York for a dozen years like a manic dad cleaning out the cellar on a Saturday afternoon. The La Guardia voice was high-pitched, excitable, and whiny—I should know, because I listened to it, from the next room, for the better part of nine hours one January day in 1936, while I waited for our interview. Well, maybe not "our"—it's not as if he knew I was coming.

Home from boarding school on Christmas vacation, I had taken the subway down to City Hall with my friend David Maclay, each of us being in need of a celebrity interview as part of the tryout for a school newspaper. We weren't competitors—David's new school was in Pennsylvania, mine in Connecticut—but we were emboldened by our eight prior years together as classmates at the progressive Lincoln School, on West 123rd Street, a fountainhead of juvenile overconfidence. Mulling potential interviewees, we had rejected Fred Astaire (too far away) and Joe Louis (too scary) before settling happily upon the Mayor, who was just then winding up his second year in office. Arriving at eight-thirty in the morning, notebooks in hand, we presented ourselves before the Mayor's secretary in City Hall—a youngish, not unfriendly fellow whose name I have forgotten.

"Press," I announced.

"Here for a—uh, interview," David said.

"No appointment, I take it," the secretary said. He carefully wrote down our names and the names of our publications, and showed class by not asking our age, which was fifteen. "Take a seat, boys," he said. "It may be a while."

We had expected this, and had come prepared with magazines but not lunch. Eagerly, patiently, wearily, we sat and watched and listened as politicos and petitioners, City Council members, women in hats, editorialists, judges, commissioners, and real-estate magnates arrived, were greeted within, reappeared, and took their leave. Even when the tall door to La Guardia's office was closed, we could hear the ceaseless mayoral yammer, rising in impatience or laughter, cajoling and caressing in argument, like an offstage tenor in a bad opera. Longer than an opera. Noon came and went, the light crept across the dusty windows of our chamber. Noticing us at last, a motherly looking woman on the Mayor's staff brought us a couple of chicken sandwiches and an Oh Henry! bar. We sat on. Dark had fallen outside when the secretary, emerging from a brief exchange with Hizzoner, beckoned us forward. "You're on," he said, "but make it snappy."

I can remember La Guardia's dishevelled black hair, and the tough gaze that flicked over us while he gestured us toward a couple of chairs. He was in shirtsleeves. The mayoral feet, below the mayoral leather chair, did not quite touch the carpet.

"Reporters—right?" he said. "What'll it be, fellas?" Whatever it was, it didn't go well. We had some questions about the transportation system, I think—the Mayor had been promising to take down the El lines along Sixth and Ninth Avenues—and maybe about his campaign against smutty burlesque shows.

"But I'm on record about all that," he said, breaking in. "What else?"

"Is Tammany Hall about to—" David began.

"Nah!" he said, holding up one hand. "Not a chance!"

We weren't quite done. "Sir," I said, reading from lines that David and I had put together during our long wait, "each of us is in the ninth grade in a really good private school. Do you believe that there are any students in the New York public schools who are getting the kind of education we are?"

"What!" he cried. "What was that?" Nuclear fission had not yet been discovered, but the explosion before us now mounted and thickened abruptly, darkening around its whitish inner fires, and drooping foully along the top. Rumbling and squeaking by turns, waving his arms, the Mayor unloaded his full package. Why, the New York public-school system was the envy of the entire United States—no, the envy of the free world. Boys and girls of all races and origins and from every neighborhood came to it, flourished and grew wise, and were set free. Didn't spoiled kids like us know anything? Look at Billy Rose! Look at Justice Pecora, Eddie Cantor, Elmer Rice—New York public-school kids all. Borough President Lyons. Jimmy Cagney. Ira Gershwin, Ethel Merman. What about his own wife, Marie La Guardia, who had gone to school on the Lower East Side? Why, he himself, born on Sullivan Street but exiled to distant outposts in his youth (the Mayor's father had been a United States Army bandmaster), had passed his boyhood yearning only to come back and go to public school in New York. Scrawling excitedly, flipping pages, underlining, David and I tried to capture fragments of the oratory on our narrow notebook pages. Famous city schools abounded, the Little Flower went on—Erasmus Hall, Curtis High, Stuyvesant. Art and music instruction flourished here, as in Athens. Had he mentioned Eddie Cantor? By the third grade,

talented city kids were already playing on municipal violins and
clarinets, not to mention enjoying a nutritious and delicious hot
lunch every day. High-school swimming pools! Foreign languages!
Chess clubs! Greek and Latin, even! Football. Calculus— There
was a pause, and we looked up to see the Mayor staring at us.

"Hold on," he said. "Wayddd a minute! Did you two . . . ?" He
pointed a finger. "Why, you kids set me up, didn't you? You got me
going—right?"

David and I exchanged guilty smiles. My face was hot.

The Mayor threw up his hands. "Ya got me," he said. "I'll be
God-damned—I can't believe it." He shook his head. "Good night,
boys," he said, picking up some papers. "You got a hell of a story."

Yelling and gabbling, David and I crowded onto the rush-hour
I.R.T. and rode home in triumph. Each of our La Guardia stories
subsequently saw print, and each of us made the paper. Was it that
same week or later on, I wonder, when our exploit began to gnaw at
me? Why should it have stayed with me all this time? All we had
done was to strike an ugly pose, tell a trifling lie, in order to chivy
some quotes out of an obliging public figure. How could we have
let him down this way? We had behaved like little wise guys, just
to get a story. We had become reporters.

Talk, February, 1999

ME AND PREW

The U.S. Open tees off again Thursday, at the Congressional Country Club, in Bethesda, Maryland, and just the other day the *Times*
had a piece revealing that during the Second World War Congressional's svelte green layout and florid Italianate clubhouse had been
the secret training grounds for commandos operating under the
Office of Strategic Services, a predecessor of the C.I.A. War and

golf are strange partners, but not to me. As an Army Air Corps sergeant stationed at Hickam Field, outside Honolulu, in 1944 and 1945, I soon discovered that the private Waialae Country Club, the best course in Hawaii, was reserved for Army enlisted men over the weekends. No officers allowed. I was an editor with the Seventh Air Force G.I. magazine *Brief,* a lively weekly with a westward beat of about two million square miles. We closed late on Friday night; Saturdays were workdays, but early Sunday often found three or four of us desk guys back at Waialae, where decent rental clubs and open tee times were miraculously available. The course, still the site of the Sony Open on the P.G.A. tour, nestles along the shore near Diamond Head, and it offered windblown palms, stunning surf and skies, and a chance for us to work on our hackers' games without embarrassment. The left-hand side of one of the outbound holes was weirdly occupied by a spacious fenced-off zoo, and I can still recall setting up for my 7-iron recovery from another drive hooked into the weeds while under scrutiny by an adjacent kudu or giraffe.

Back to the war—or ahead, rather, about nine years, to a Rockland County movie theatre, where, a civilian again and a suburbanite, I am watching an early run of the classic Fred Zinnemann film of the James Jones novel "From Here to Eternity," which, of course, is all about the regular Army in Oahu before and just after Pearl Harbor. My war, I think to myself. Yow, this time they got it right. Burt Lancaster is just like my old First, minus the gut. Those are the Schofield Barracks balconies. Here are the beaten-down Maggio and Prewitt, a.k.a. Frank Sinatra and Montgomery Clift, down on their knees on another chickenshit fatigue duty; here are Burt Lancaster and Deborah Kerr making out on the sand in swimsuits; here's the sadistic Fatso knifed in the belly; here come the Japanese planes. And here's Prew again, AWOL and on the lam, bravely trying to rejoin his company under the cover of night, now that we're at war. It's a day-for-night scene, actually, with palm trees and a shorefront, and Diamond Head out beyond in silhouette. "Halt!" cries a soldier in a tin hat. (Wisely, our guys are guarding the shore against potential saboteurs.) The soldier raises his rifle and fires. Prew dodges.

A burst of machine-gun fire. Prew, hit, clutches himself, spins, and disappears over the rim of a little knoll.

"My God!" I say, rising in the Nyack dark. "That's the first hole—I was there, I was there! I've been in that trap a hundred times!"

Post, June, 2011

PAST MASTERS: E. B. WHITE

FOREWORD TO THE 1997 TILBURY HOUSE EDITION OF "ONE MAN'S MEAT" BY E. B. WHITE

Modest in its size and presumptions, engaging in tone, E. B. White's "One Man's Meat" has resisted becoming historic, even after a non-stop run of fifty-five years in print. Perhaps now, with this fresh edition, we should allow the laurel to descend, although we may be certain (the moment we open its pages) that the author would wince at the ceremony, or simply not attend.

First published in 1942 and reissued in expanded form two years later, the book was unweighty by design, being not a sustained single work but a compilation of the writer's monthly columns for *Harper's* (which he had begun writing in 1938), along with three casual essays first published in *The New Yorker*. Because of this format and the format of the author's mind, the book has always had the heft, the light usefulness, of a bushel basket, carrying a raking of daily or seasonal notions, and, on the next short trip, the heavier burden of an idea. (The image owes much to White himself, whose remembered easy, unstriding walk across a pasture or down the shore road of his Maine farm remains unique, as does his touch with the homely utensils of prose.) Strewn with errands and

E. B. White in the 1940s

asterisks, farming tips and changes of weather, notes on animals and neighbors and statesmen, "One Man's Meat" is too personal for an almanac, too sophisticated for a domestic history, too funny and self-doubting for a literary journal. Perhaps it's a primer: a countryman's lessons that convey, at each reading, a sense of early-morning clarity and possibility.

When White first removed, with his wife and young son, from a walk-up duplex on East Forty-eighth Street, in Manhattan, and went to live on a saltwater farm in North Brooklin, he seemed almost eager, in his early columns, to detect even the smallest signs of awkwardness in himself in his fresh surroundings (as when he found himself crossing the barnyard with a paper napkin in one hand), but the surge of alteration that overtook him and swept him along over the full six-year span of the book quickly did away with these little ironies. Despite its tranquil setting, this is a book about movement—the rush of the day, the flood and ebb of the icy Penobscot Bay tides, the unsettlements of New England weather, the arrival of another season and its quick (or so it seems) dispersal, the birth and death of livestock, and the coming of a world war that is first seen at a distance (White is shingling his barn roof during the Munich crisis), then sweeps across Europe (he is fixing a balky brooder stove during the German spring drive in the Balkans), and at last comes home (he mans a town plane-spotting post and finds a heron) to impose its binding and oddly exuberant hold on everyone's attention.

Another change, though we don't pick it up at first, is in White

himself. Early effusions about the beauty of the egg, some Thoreau-
vian phrasings ("It is not likely that a man who changes his pursuits
will ever succeed in taking on the character or appearance of a new
man"), or a *New Yorker*ish dying fall about a faded wooden croquet
set give way to more direct and more satisfying stuff about the way
to build a dry-mash hopper, the obligations of freedom, and useful
stratagems against cold weather. He had grown up (he turns forty
in mid-book), and he was too busy around the place to be a full-
time stylist. I think "One Man's Meat" was the making of him as a
writer. Freed of the weekly deadlines and the quaintsy first-person
plural form of the *New Yorker*'s Notes and Comment page, which
he had written for more than a decade, he discovered his subject
(it was himself) and a voice that spoke softly but rang true. "Once
More to the Lake," his 1941 account of a trip with his son back to
the freshwater lake where he had vacationed as a boy, is an enduring
American essay—and could not have been written until its precise
moment. "Stuart Little," "Charlotte's Web," and ten other books
and collections were still ahead, but the author had found his feet.

What also becomes plain in the book is that Andy White was
a born farmer—not so much an agriculturist as a handyman. He
relished the work and he was good at it. He laughs at his prepara-
tions for taking on a cow (the first time he leads her out into the
pasture he feels "the way I did the first time I ever took a girl
to the theatre—embarrassed but elated"), but he is no gentleman
farmer. While reading the late chapters "Winter Diary," "My Day,"
and "Memorandum" (a list of some two hundred chores around the
place that demanded immediate attention), you envy him the work
but even more the sensual pleasure of its details and the workman's
hoard of expertise. Not much escapes his eye, whether it lights on a
loose tailboard or a dopey moment in a movie, the bloated appearance of late-model automobile fenders or some fashionable and ugly
trends in thought he finds afloat at the moment when the Nazi

armies are overrunning France, but his powers of observation somehow go deeper the moment he concentrates on something small
and at hand—the little running sea on the surface of the hens'
watering fountain on a windy morning; the dainty grimace of the
dachshund, Fred, as he licks up a fresh-fallen egg on the cellar floor.

Because White is such a prime noticer it is a while before a
reader becomes aware of how much he has chosen to leave out of the
book. There is very little here about his wife, Katharine—who was
pursuing a demanding job of her own as an editor-by-mail with *The
New Yorker* all this time, as well as running the household—and
not much more about their schoolboy son, Joel. The ineffable Fred
almost has a larger part in the daily drama, as does the neighbor
lobsterman, Dameron. Nor do we hear about the help required to
keep an operation of this sort afloat: the full-time hired man and
his occasional assistants, and a cook and a housemaid indoors. These
gaps have been commented upon in critical and biographical writings about White, but it is not my memory that he was any more
heedless of those around him than most authors are; neither was he
uneasy or apologetic about the comforts of his multi-income, triple-
profession household. The omissions arise from his instinctive,
lifelong sense of privacy—a dated, almost Victorian consideration
in these confessional times—and must also be attributed to the
writer's sense that this story, however it turned out, was not going
to be about the enveloping distractions of family life. The privacy
was extended to himself, as well; there is more of Andy White left
out of his writings than was ever put in.

EVEN AS THE WAR engaged the full energies of the Whites'
farm—among his production goals for 1942 are four thousand
dozen eggs, ten pigs, and nine thousand pounds of milk—news of
it remained thin, by today's measurements. The engrossing events

from Europe and Washington, arriving by radio and mailed newspapers, did not take up much of the day, and the writer, to judge by his pieces, responded by thinking more and more about the world at large and his place in it. Engaging himself in long colloquies about freedom and the chances of world federalism, once peace came, he goes one on one with his government, even as he accedes to its demands on his time and supports its immense gatherings and expenditures of men and matériel. People of my generation are often asked now what it was like to live in a nation engaged in a popular, all-encompassing war, and "One Man's Meat" provides a vivid answer. White covered the war—at bond rallies, at civilian-defense centers—but also noticed that the passionate new love of Americans for America was a patriotism that would have to be relinquished, at least in part, if the world was ever to achieve a lasting peace. Elsewhere, he wrote that the hardest thing about the war was to maintain a decent sense of indignation about its deadly details.

Much of this, perhaps most of it, sounds naïve to us now, in our time of instant access to bad news everywhere and surly apathy about it all. If truth be told, White's passionate essays on world government sounded idealistic and simplistic even in their time—he was not a pundit by nature—but what we can honor him for, then and now, is his clear conviction (no one was ever clearer on the written page) that he is qualified to think about freedom, all on his own, and to address his reader as one citizen to another about such urgent business. Who among us can be certain that when another time as vivid and dangerous sweeps us up we will find an E. B. White somewhere, to talk to us in these quiet and compelling tones?

April, 1997

FOREWORD TO THE
FOURTH EDITION OF "ELEMENTS OF
STYLE," PEARSON/LONGMAN

The first writer I watched at work was my stepfather, E. B. White. Each Tuesday morning, he would close his study door and sit down to write the Notes and Comment page for *The New Yorker.* The task was familiar to him—he was required to file a few hundred words of editorial or personal commentary on some topic in or out of the news that week—but the sounds of his typewriter from his room came in hesitant bursts, with long silences in between. Hours went by. Summoned at last for lunch, he was silent and preoccupied, and soon excused himself to get back to the job. When the copy went off at last, in the afternoon R.F.D. pouch—we were in Maine, a day's mail away from New York—he rarely seemed satisfied. "It isn't good enough," he said sometimes. "I wish it were better."

Writing is hard, even for authors who do it all the time. Less frequent practitioners—the job applicant; the business executive with an annual report to get out; the high-school senior with a Faulkner assignment; the graduate-school student with her thesis proposal; the writer of a letter of condolence—often get stuck in an awkward passage or find a muddle on their screens, and then blame themselves. What should be easy and flowing looks tangled or feeble or overblown—not what was meant at all. What's wrong with me, each one thinks. Why can't I get this right?

It was this recurring question, put to himself, that must have inspired White to revive and add to a textbook by a Cornell English professor of his, Will Strunk, Jr., that he had first read in college, and to get it published. The result, this quiet book, has been in print for forty years, and has offered more than ten million writers

a helping hand. White knew that a compendium of specific tips—
about singular and plural verbs, parentheses, the "that"-"which"
scuffle, and many others—could clear up a recalcitrant sentence or
subclause when quickly reconsulted, and that the larger principles
needed to be kept in plain sight, like a wall sampler.

How simple they look, set down here in White's last chapter:
"Write in a way that comes naturally," "Revise and rewrite," "Do not
explain too much," and the rest; above all, the cleansing, clarion "Be
clear." How often I have turned to them, in the book or in my mind,
while trying to start or unblock or revise some piece of my own
writing! They help—they really do. They work. They are the way.

E. B. White's prose is celebrated for its ease and clarity—
just think of "Charlotte's Web"—but maintaining this standard
required endless attention. When the new issue of *The New Yorker*
turned up in Maine, I sometimes saw him reading his Comment
piece over to himself, with only a slightly different expression than
the one he'd worn on the day it went off. Well, O.K., he seemed to
be saying. At least I got the elements right.

THIS EDITION HAS BEEN modestly updated, with word processors and air conditioners making their first appearance among
White's references, and with a light redistribution of genders to
permit a feminine pronoun or female farmer to take their places
among the males who once innocently served him. Sylvia Plath
has knocked Keats out of the box, and I notice that "America" has
become "this country" in a sample text, to forestall a subsequent
and possibly demeaning "she" in the same paragraph. What is not
here is anything about e-mail—the rules-free, lower-case flow that
cheerfully keeps us in touch these days. E-mail is conversation, and
it may be replacing the sweet and endless talking we once sustained

(and tucked away) within the informal letter. But we are all writers and readers as well as communicators, with the need at times to please and satisfy ourselves (as White put it) with the clear and almost perfect thought.

1999

MOOSE TALES

At lunch yesterday, a friend of mine said she'd almost run into a moose last weekend, on a back road in the Berkshires. It wasn't till later that I remembered a moose tale told to me by a college class-mate, along about 1940. Heading home to Maine on the evening before Thanksgiving, he'd been riding in a local Bangor & Maine passenger car, up in Hancock County, when there was a bang and the train came to a halt in a stretch of silent woods. They'd hit a moose. It took almost forty-five minutes before the crew could get the carcass off the track, and they started up again. Twenty minutes later, the train stopped again, for another twenty minutes or so, then resumed its leisurely journey to Ellsworth.

When the conductor came through, a little later, my friend asked why there'd been a second halt, and the conductor said that by state (or maybe it was county) law they were required to inform the local game warden about the dead moose, and that the engineer had waited until he spotted the lights of the first nearby farmhouse before he stopped once again. He, the conductor, had then walked across the field, knocked on the door, and conveyed the news by phone. My friend asked why he couldn't have done this at the end of the line, and the conductor smiled and told the rest of the story.

Another state or county law specified that any fresh meat taken from animals accidentally offed on the right of way went first of all to residents of the nearest state poor farm, but after that it was first come, first served. The warden he'd reached said that the institu-tion in question had only two residents at present, and that their teeth were not in great shape. They'd get some bits of tenderloin, all right, but the rest of the moose would now be divided up between the train crew, the farmer with the telephone, perhaps the warden, and also the nearest butcher, who was probably already headed for the scene.

"We'll be picking up our shares, cut and wrapped, on this same run, come Friday," the conductor said. "Don't happen often, but it's always nice when things work out."

Happy Thanksgiving!

Post, November, 2010

FAMILY LINES

When my mother, Katharine White, in her sixties, had to spend a Christmas Day confined in the Harkness Pavilion of Columbia Presbyterian Hospital, I tried to cheer her up with a fresh version of the hoary Clement Moore jingle. She enjoyed it, even while exclaiming, "But they told me to avoid any laughing!"

THE NIGHT AFTER CHRISTMAS

T'was the night after Christmas in the Pavilion called
   Harkness:
The patients were lying in pain and in darkness;
The interns were nestled all snug in their beds
While visions of catheters danced through their heads;
And Mama in her traction and I with my piles
Had just settled our heads for a night of brave smiles,
When down through the airshaft there came such a whining
From an ungrateful patient they were trephining,
Away to the window I flew like a gull—
Tripped over the bedpan and fractured my skull!
And what should appear in response to my curses
But a miniature quack and six surly nurses—
Miss Frowner, Miss Jouncy, Miss Middle-Aged Pixie,
Miss Coldhands, Miss Sphincter, Miss You-all from Dixie.
Their smiles were so starchy, so plain their frigidity

That I almost smiled back, despite my rigidity.
They said not a word but went straight to the task,
Took sputum and fluids and blood in a flask;
"Any record of madness, TB, croup, or others?
Give names and birthdates of both your grandmothers."
The doc checked my Blue Cross, the girls checked reflexes
By chanting a mantra to my solar plexus.
More happy surprises! More cries *a cappella*
When they tapped out some sambas upside my patella.
The doctor then sighed and gave his diagnosis:
"This poor fellow's suffering mild acidosis
I foresee some CCs of antibiotic—
Let's try this free sample, it looks quite exotic."
He bade me farewell as he smoothed my pajamas:
"They'll fax me your look-see in the Bahamas."
And ignoring the clots on the back of my head
The Nightingales bundled me back into bed.
They turned out the light with a cheery last warning:
"Be ready for bed-baths at five in the morning!"

My lawyer father, Ernest Angell, was chairman of the board of the American Civil Liberties Union from 1950 to 1969. When he stepped down from the august post the A.C.L.U. gave him a festive dinner. One of the entertainments was my rewrite of W. S. Gilbert's "I Am the Very Model of a Modern Major-General," from "The Pirates of Penzance," bravely performed by a chorus of staffers, law professors, and judges.

I AM THE VERY MODEL OF A CIVIL LIBERTARIAN

I am the very model of a civil libertarian,
I favor equal rights for Capricorn and Sagittarian.
I am a big defender of each gender in the picket lines,
I like to see some G.O.P. in dirty-movie ticket lines.

I'll fence the board that's evidenced creationist proclivities;
I'm wise to guys with cries of un-American activities
I tout the outed Seminole or fallen seminarian,
For I'm the very model of a civil libertarian.

I am a bold upholder of American amenities,
I cede the budding playwright's need to write in pure
    obscenities.
I know the lowly portion of the Mexican agrarian;
I share your rage at wages of the sexagen librarian.
I'll read you your Miranda in a minute, but, more latterly,
I gotta spring this Dalton kid caught reading "Lady
    Chatterley."
I'll fix your nanny's visa in a style egalitarian,
For I'm the very model of a civil libertarian.

There were two or three more stanzas, but this brief is running long.

LONG GONE

WHO WAS *THAT*?

As I went into our local Korean fruit store on a recent evening, the man just coming out—gray, trim, shockingly handsome—was Paul Newman. My gaze crossed his, the city moment passed. When I got home with my bananas and seltzer water, I told my wife, Carol, about it. "How'd he look?" she said. "Great," I said. That was about it, except that my mind, repeatedly and oddly returning to this non-event, has been telling me that celebrity-spotting, like other New York amenities, has actually been in a long decline. That seemed a curious development in our phone-in, paparazzified time of megacelebrity, but the old New York street-meet always had its own protocol of strict privacy: one looked and then looked again at the passing diva or statesman but did not speak. One smiled in recognition, and sometimes got back a tiny gleam or nod of acknowledgment. It was enough. We told our friends about the moment, and they said "No!" or "Wow!" in the manner of an exchange between dedicated bird-watchers, and then we tucked the specimen and the circumstances away in some mental life list. Now we want more—an autograph, a handshake, a posed digital snap, perhaps even a conversation designed to close the six (or sixty) degrees of separation between us and them. What we get, unsurprisingly, is a glimpse of a famous ankle disappearing into a black-glass limo, and miles of crowded avenues and side streets almost devoid of the sudden exciting face. Our loss.

I've lived in New York all my life, and a quick refresher rundown of my own sidewalk sightings yields up Walter Cronkite, Babe Ruth, Vladimir Horowitz, Greta Garbo, Eleanor Roosevelt (gray chiffon wing bars), Fay Wray (Fay Wray!), Harry Truman, Uma Thurman, Yves Montand, James Mason, Jacqueline Onassis, Rex Harrison, Richard Nixon (yeeks!), Ezio Pinza, Alexander Calder, Ethel Merman, Sigourney Weaver, Benny Goodman, and more. Some of these were glimpsed more than once. Horowitz, who lived right across the street from our old walkup on Ninety-fourth, took regular afternoon strolls in the neighborhood. Beaky and elegant, he sometimes gave the impression that he was checking me out to make sure he'd been noticed; some days, helping out, he wore a silk bow tie with a piano-keys motif. Then there was the afternoon when Callie, a grownup daughter of mine, took her five-year-old brother, John Henry, out for a spin on his bike in Central Park; a very recent soloist, John Henry waveringly preceded her up the sidewalk toward Fifth, on a path that relentlessly converged with that of a frail, black-swathed woman coming from the other direction, who paused, made a small dodge, and then caught boy and bike in both hands. My daughter hurried up, appalled, and the woman said, "Dangerous, aren't they?" Garbo.

The Truman-meet began after lunch one day in the middle fifties, when he emerged from the front door of the *Times,* on West Forty-third Street, as I was walking by, and took up an eastbound path just to my left. I figured he'd been lunching with his son-in-law, Clifton Daniel. He was several years out of office, but had the same dapper, energetic look. No Secret Service men were in view; he appeared to be wholly unaccompanied.

"Say something, dummy," I muttered to myself. Breaking the

rule, I managed a little sidewise bow and said, "We miss you, sir."
He responded graciously and, a good politician, quickly asked my
name and found out where I worked. He asked if I knew John
Hersey (who had written a Profile of him for *The New Yorker*), and
I said yes—a little. "My wife gets *The New Yorker* every week and
reads it," he said. "I read it, too, when she's done." We walked
together, crossing Broadway—"Hey, it's Harry!" yelled a cabdriver,
and the President smiled and waved—and continued another full
block together while we chatted about the burdens of the Presi-
dency ("It's a job nobody can do entirely right") and the burdens of
the Mayor of New York ("Nothing in the world could persuade me
for *that* job!") and more. Midway, a man I knew named Harding
Bancroft—a *Times* executive, in fact—spotted me and my companion as we came toward him, and performed a double take worthy of
the late Oliver Hardy. I cut him dead.

Nixon encounters were almost commonplace for anyone cov-
ering baseball in New York in the early 1980s, after the post-
resignation Prez had become a fellow Gothamite. He would turn
up unexpectedly at mid-season games at Yankee Stadium, where
he would visit the clubhouses and offer strategy to the manager and
coaches. This was at the old Stadium, where the only passageway
between the press dining room and the Yankee clubhouse was a
narrow, low-ceilinged corridor, with a couple of bends in it. Here,
in mid-turn, I would sometimes come face-to-face with President
Nixon, five or six feet away and scary smile attached. "Yow!" I cried,
each time, to which he nodded in friendly fashion as he passed by,
with a murmured "How are you?" The experience was the same
as the moment I remembered from boyhood visits to Coney Island
fun houses, where you rode through inky passages in your bumpy
little car and a suddenly illuminated ghost or skeleton would drop
before your face.

These tales, like my life list, have an old-time flavor, I know, and though I stay alert as I walk New York nowadays, I no longer expect such moments. Celebrities are only a click away all day long now, on my phone or home TV, accompanied by their posses, and the rest dead or in the Hamptons. But we, too, are missing—we, the other street-strollers, the other half of the compact, deep into our Facebook and Pulse and Twitter and Instagram, scarcely on the same city block with anybody. What I miss isn't just that flash of face and name but the accompanying terrific compliment I once sensed in these innocent encounters: if I was walking on the exact same stretch of sidewalk as some worthy or glittering personage, then it was plain that each of us had chosen absolutely the right time and place in which to live. What a city!

Paul Newman, to be fair, was seen quite often in my neighborhood over the years, often with his wife, Joanne Woodward, and a couple of small dogs. Even now, he turns up again in urban legends, including the Paul Newman ice-cream-cone story. Lady stops at a roadside ice-cream stand in Greenwich, and after ordering her single-scoop sugar-cone chocolate ripple notices that the midsized customer standing next to her is Newman's own self. Now just be cool, the woman reminds herself. She pays for her cone, takes a fast, delicious gander, and walks away. Back in the car, still not staring, she reaches for the ignition but then realizes that she has no ice-cream cone. What? She climbs out again, looks under the seat, looks under the car—nothing. She goes back to the counterman for help: Uh, I was here just a minute ago, chocolate ripple—I paid, etc., etc., and realizes that Paul Newman is watching *her.* "I believe it's in your pocketbook," he murmurs.

I've actually been introduced to a few celebrities, down the years, and interrupt our street-meet theme to trot out Judge Learned Hand, the bygone jurist of the Federal Court of Appeals, who was a friend of my father's. Judges are meant to be elderly and distinguished in appearance, and Hand, who was born in upstate New

York in 1872, filled the bill in every particular, with alert blue eyes, a shock of thick white hair, and a permanent aura of curiosity. Best of all was that name: *Learned Hand*—a creation worthy of Trollope or a Hollywood publicist. An older cousin of his, Augustus Hand, became a celebrated federal district judge in his own right, thus creating a little buzz or chord in the better circles whenever the anatomical handle came up. Also if you go to Saratoga for the races in August you can order a Hand melon for breakfast: a delicious regional cantaloupe developed by an agrarian in the same family, and said to be too juicy to survive export to the downstate markets.

Hand was a celebrity of a special order—a hero not known to great numbers of his countrymen but almost fiercely treasured by those who came within his presence or his legal arena, or who had read his 1944 book, "The Spirit of Liberty," with its disarming and oft memorized central lines ". . . the spirit of liberty is the spirit that is not too sure that it is right; the spirit of liberty is the mind which seeks to understand the minds of other men and women." He appeared to represent us at some higher level, I mean, making you feel that moments of clear thinking might always be within your reach.

At my father and stepmother's dinner parties, there was always a little scuffling among the ladies for a seat next to Judge Hand in the living room, and at dinner he actually listened, even to me as a burning young opinionist in my teens or early twenties. "Interesting, Roger," he would murmur to some political or literary blathering of mine. "And particularly that you would think so."

I fell into silence—not from awe but because he had answered without irony. He had taken me seriously, a terrifying compliment.

Because of his influence, Judge Hand was sometimes called the "tenth judge" on the Supreme Court that he never attained, but ponderousness was not in him. He was well along in his eighties when he and my father had dinner in Midtown New York one night—this was in the late 1950s—and afterward walked up Sixth Avenue together. It was a warm summer evening, my father told me later, and the street was full of young strolling couples. Here and there, lightly dressed lone females lurked in the shadows. "Ernest," the judge said unexpectedly, "do you think there's as much fucking going on as there was when we were younger?"

My old man gave the matter his attention, as he did to all of Hand's inquiries, and said, well, on the whole he thought probably there was. Yes.

"So do I, so do I," Hand replied. "Good."

And here come two last name-drops, each one a Nobelist, though met many decades apart. A woman at V. S. Pritchett's house in London, in 1995, began talking about her old friend Bertrand Russell, who had lately celebrated his ninety-fifth birthday. She asked if I'd ever met him, and I said that as a matter of fact I'd been sent to interview him once in the fall of 1939, when I was a sophomore trying out for the *Harvard Crimson*. Russell was in Boston to deliver a lecture, and he and I had tea together at the Ritz, where he quickly must have realized that I knew nothing about him except that he proclaimed to have some unusual views about sex. Unoffended, he carried the conversation, saw to it that I got my interview, and—alone that night, for some reason—asked if I might also be free to stay on and join him for dinner as well. He was as easy to take as Judge Hand, it turned out, and perhaps surpassed him in the Great Hair department. Like the judge, he unsettled me in retrospect when I realized that he'd been more interested in the contents of my mind than I was.

In London, the woman who knew Lord Russell—she was Constance Wells, then the wife of A. J. Ayer, the logical positivist Cambridge philosopher—told me that she'd helped get up the celebratory birthday lunch for the ancient philosopher, and then placed herself to his right in the table seating. Planning ahead, she had also come up with a question for the great man, which she put to him over the soup. She reminded him that he was not only the world's best-known atheist but now also perhaps the world's oldest atheist. What would he say, she wanted to know, if, when the moment came, it turned out that he'd been wrong all this time and now found himself standing before the Pearly Gates? Russell's eyes lit up, she told me, and he replied with eagerness. "Why, I should say," he cried, in his high, thin voice. "I should say, 'God, you gave us insufficient evidence!' "

At home at our Brooklin, Maine, summer cottage in the mid-seventies, we received a late-morning visit from our friends Stephen Dixon and Anne Frydman, he a prolific fiction writer and a Johns Hopkins English prof and she a translator of Russian literature. They'd brought along a younger couple, out-of-town friends up here for a long weekend: the woman a striking blonde Italian lady who spoke only a few words of English (I've forgotten her name), and he a thin, intense, fortyish Russian, new to our country but now safely ensconced as a visiting poet at the University of Michigan: Joseph Brodsky. We invited them all out to our sunny porch, where Carol produced iced tea, and the conversation flowed along easily enough to turn the occasion into lunch, a little later. Brodsky, in a thin cotton summer suit, smoked incessantly and could not take his eyes away from his date. In time, though, he asked if he could walk around a little, and vanished in the direction of our adjacent granite point on Eggemoggin Reach, which offers panoramas of seaweedy shoreline and, across the waters, Deer Isle. He was away almost half an hour, and when he reappeared he was excited.

"I have found moossels!" he cried. "Moossels everywhere!" And so he had: every pocket of his pants and his jacket now bulged with damp live mussels he had plucked from the crevices and crannies of barnacled ledges, now exposed at low tide. We often sat down to the same backyard provender, steamed and dripping with wine and butter, with friends at dinner, but Brodsky, an exile, understood things differently. This was his next meal, packed and ready to go.

We saw him now and then after this, back in New York, where he was a vibrant presence at dinners given by our friend and near neighbor Eileen Simpson. He was a world-class conversationalist, with flowing ideas and a smoky laugh. He died in 1996, at fifty-five: a shock to the world. Another New York celebrity, of course, and almost a friend of ours. Now he has become a companion, ever since I started memorizing poetry as a prop to my declining brain, and came upon his "A Song," which first appeared in *The New Yorker* in 1989. Each of its four stanzas begins with "I wish you were here, dear." The third one goes:

> I wish you were here, dear,
> I wish you were here.
> I wish I knew no astronomy
> when stars appear,
> when the moon skims the water
> that sighs and shifts in its slumber.
> I wish it was still a quarter
> To call your number.

Shouts & Murmurs,
February, 1993 / September, 2013

PAST MASTERS: HAROLD ROSS

MAN OF LETTERS

Harold Ross, the founder of this magazine, in 1925, and its uniquely attentive shaper and editor until his death twenty-six years later, has achieved a niche of fame and obscurity that would appear to keep him mercifully safe from the attentions of a fresh biographer. Exempt from the yappings and shin-bitings that have greeted recent memoirs centering on his successor, William Shawn, Ross stands upon a farther hill like a Martin Van Buren of American journalism: a good man of whom one knows just about enough. In truth, Ross himself was patronized and misrepresented in posthumous books about him and his magazine written by celebrated colleagues. James Thurber's "The Years with Ross" (1959) managed to suggest that Thurber himself, not Ross, had been mainly responsible for the magazine's reputation, while Brendan Gill's "Here at *The New Yorker*," published in 1975, savaged him for his boorishness and limited education, and diminished him by anecdote. These lingering hurts were put away in 1995 by Thomas Kunkel's "Genius in Disguise," a foursquare, fully researched biography that cleared up some paradoxes about the man (Ross the gap-toothed Aspen rube as one of the founding sophisticate members of the Algonquin Round Table; Ross the habitual "Goddamn"er and "Oh Christ"er who wished to protect young women on his staff from the sight or sound of the shorter expletives; Ross, the publisher of Nabokov and Edmund Wilson, asking "Is Moby-Dick the whale or the man?" and so on). Ross is also a central figure in the balanced and useful new "About Town: *The New Yorker* and the World It Made," by Ben Yagoda, which draws upon six decades of archives while assessing the magazine's fortunes during its accumulating editorships and extremely various eras.

No serious reason remains, then, for anyone but scholars or obsessives to take up still another book about Ross and his "fifteen-cent comic paper," which suggests that the latest entry, "Letters from the Editor: *The New Yorker*'s Harold Ross," should be read simply for pleasure, in which it abounds. The collection comes from Thomas Kunkel, a grateful biographer, who notes in his introduction that Ross, who never wrote a word for the magazine, "was, with the possible exception of the protean Edmund Wilson, the most prolific writer in its history," if one counts the letters. Prolific in this case doesn't necessarily mean lengthy. "I hope your God-damned stomach is better since you've quit writing," Ross writes to E. B. White (whose furlough was temporary). To the poet William Rose Benét, he is encouraging and corrective, in thirteen words: "We like your stuff, God knows, but this verse, damn it, is obscure." To James Thurber, he notes, "While bathing this morning, it came into my mind that what that dog is doing on your New Year's cover is winking, dog winking. I'm not exactly clear on how a dog winks but it's probably as you've drawn it." In 1930, the unknown young John O'Hara receives "I don't know of any job and I'm not likely to hear of one, but if I do, I will let you know. Maybe the only thing for you to do is to keep on writing and become a writer." O'Hara complies, and then some, and hears a different tone fourteen years later: "Dear John: I regret to report that there is nothing doing as to the proposed $3,200 advance. I formally put it up to the big-scale fiscal man and the result was a laugh, in which, in the end, I joined."

These are excerpts, but almost every letter in the book's four hundred and eighteen pages contains similarly brusque and entertaining clarities—the Rossian nub—which makes this a read-aloud, or read-across-the-room, sort of book. One-sentence mailings turn up as well, even in the daunting condolence form: "White: Was very sorry to hear about your father, and send my sympathy, which is about all I have to say, except that after you get to be thirty people you know keep dropping off all the time and it's a hell of a note."

Ross wrote letters all the time, frequently logging several hours at it in a single day. Some were handed over to secretaries for correction and retyping, but surviving *New Yorker* editors and writers who recall the steady thrash of Ross's old Underwood upright emanating from his nineteenth-floor, West Forty-third Street office have told me that they looked forward to perhaps receiving something from the daily outpouring of inquiries and encouragements or afterthoughts. The messages, pristine in type in the book, actually arrived in an imperfect rush of grimy black lines on yellow copy paper, with hurried X-ings out and pencilled-in corrections; sometimes Ross would produce an opening three or four lines of gibberish—it looked like code—before noticing that in his hurry he had placed his fingers on the wrong deck of keys. Ross often stalked the halls, hunched and scowling with the burden of his latest idea, but these in-house letters, conveying the same urgent and dishevelled impression, also appeared to bring him into your office, so to speak, and nearly in person. When Brendan Gill took exception to the sense of intimidation his boss sometimes conveyed, Ross wrote back, "I don't try to scare anyone, although occasionally I don't give a damn if I do probably."

The notes, in any case, got passed around, and, as Kunkel has observed, were often tucked away for posterity, in spite of their dashed-off informality. Salutations are curt and pauses for throat-clearing or attitude-seizing absent. The man was too busy for bonhomie or style. He hid very little and knew what was on his mind—an ever-increasing burden that he groaned and complained about even in the act of dealing with it—and amazingly shortened the distance between his thoughts and their departure. He always sounded like himself, which is the whole trick.

Ross had a full-scale life away from the magazine as well, and one finds him making a backgammon date with Bennett Cerf, firing off a reminder to Noël Coward that he has tickets to take him to the circus, offering to sell Jimmy Cagney a used tractor for four hundred and ninety-nine dollars and twenty-five cents, and imploring Ambassador Joseph P. Kennedy to help with a wartime shipment of Haig & Haig to Chasen's restaurant, in Hollywood, of which he was a backer. His divorce from his first wife, Jane Grant, and the arrangements for her support become a clenched-teeth obbligato running through the book, once producing a letter to her lawyers which he famously signed, "Very truly yours, Ross, Ross, Ross, Ross & Ross, sgd / H. W. Ross, B. H. W. Ross." But there is no levity within the position papers, ultimatums, and near-resignations that follow the trail of his lurid struggles with Raoul Fleischmann, the publisher and co-founder of the magazine, whom he mistrusted (with some reason) and in the end despised.

Kunkel calls Ross an "organic complainer," which is another way of saying that he was victimized by his insistence on quality and clarity in his magazine, and by the natural scarcity of editors and writers who could produce it. When the irreplaceable Whites moved to Maine—E.B., his prime stylist and the writer of the weekly Notes and Comment page; and Katharine, a formidable fiction and all-purpose editor (here fully disclosed as my stepfather and mother)—Ross somehow suppresses outrage. "If you will do a very little bit of timely Comment it will help out," he says to White (who had begun

writing his longer "One Man's Meat" columns in *Harper's*). To Mrs.
White, who continued editing from long distance, he writes, "As to
your sharp-shooting of the issues, and your recent memo about this,
I say do it your way. I deplore your way, but since you can't do it
another way, I'll settle on it."

The loudest outcries went to writers of humor, on whom he
was almost pathetically dependent. "I have come to expect little
from writers, including writings," he grumbles to Frank Sullivan,
a friend and funny man, whom he often addressed more directly.
"I cannot refrain from urging you to write a piece. If you don't do
one, you are a little bastard" comes at the conclusion of a 1941 note
that began, "Dear Frank, old fellow." He is still at it in 1946: "GOD
DAMN IT, WRITE SOMETHING! As ever, Ross." He would not have
used the capitals to a writer of less ability.

His health and his teeth weren't good ("Honest to Christ, I
am more dilapidated at the moment than Yugoslavia," he writes to
White), and office troubles had begun to compound themselves in
wartime, when so many editors and artists and staff writers went off
to the service that he found himself at his desk seven days a week,
and seriously considered scaling down to two issues per month. But
Ross loved the work, there's no getting away from it, and a tinge of
enjoyment sifts into a summary whine of his, to Alexander Wooll-
cott: "I am up to my nipples in hot water, what with half of the
staff going off to war, a limitation of fifty-seven gallons of gasoline
for six weeks, the Holy Name [Society] demanding that we stop
printing 'son of a bitch,' and so on. This war is much harder on me
than the last one."

ROSS WAS NEVER SUNNY, but his powers of attention lighted
him up, particularly when he was dealing with writers and their
copy. One of his notorious query sheets turns up here in a 1948

letter to Thurber about a casual of his, "Six for the Road"—a routine (for the magazine) sort of notation in which Ross lists fourteen items worthy of the author's immediate attention. No. 11 is typical—"Very unexpected to learn at this late date that there's a bar in this place. Not mentioned before, and the definite pronoun has no antecedent"—but No. 3 brings Ross to near-frenzy: "This mixing up of a dinner party and an evening party that begins in the afternoon baffled me for quite a while, and I have come up with the suggestion that the party be made a cocktail party with buffet dinner. I think this is a brilliant suggestion. You never later have the people sitting down to dinner, nor do you take any notice whatever of dinner," etc., etc. One can almost hear Thurber's cries of irritation, even from this distance, but he has been poked or maddened into a tiny but perhaps useful fix, which was the main idea.

It's surprising that Ross never saw himself as a writer, or succumbed to the notion that he was growing into one. I think he sensed instead that he was a genius appreciator of clear writing and strong reporting, and understood that the care and comfort of those who were good at it required full-time attention. When the first-rate Profiles reporter Geoffrey Hellman decided to go to work for the better-paying *Life* (it was a temporary aberration), Ross goaded him with "What is the temperature over there? Do you need any pencils?"

He is almost fatherly in a mini-crisis with the touchy Whites that blew up when a one-letter typo slipped into an E.B.W. proof— "hen" had become "her"—and he could always sound unfeigned appreciation for a writer's best, even in a rival magazine. In 1940, after White had published a piece in *Harper's* on the meaning of freedom, Ross wrote to him, "I think it is a beautiful and elegant thing, probably the most moving item I've read in years and worthy of Lincoln and some of the other fellows that really went to town." And he concludes, "Knock me down anytime you want."

Ross's *New Yorker* got better and deeper near the end of his tenure (he died in 1951), and the editor who had once expected so little of his contributors must have been startled by what was happening. Writing to John Hersey, whose account of the atomic-bomb destruction of Hiroshima had been given an entire issue, in 1946, he says, "Those fellows who said 'Hiroshima' was the story of the year, etc., underestimated it. It is unquestionably the best journalistic story of my time, if not of all time. Nor have I heard of anything like it." And when Rebecca West, who had written some notable pieces for the magazine, dedicated her book "The Meaning of Treason" to him, he was astounded—"just overflowing with gratitude and goodwill to you. . . . I consider that I have now crashed American letters, which gives me much amusement."

ROSS KNEW HIS OWN value, but his tenure at the magazine, to hear him tell it, was all about process. He didn't give a damn what people thought about him or how he would be weighed; he just wanted to get the stuff right on the page. "It's all right for people to say that we are too fussy, that ten or twenty slightly ungrammatical sentences don't matter," he writes, "but if (from where I sit) I break down on that the magazine would break down all along the line." Similarly comes the confession "I still find journalism glamorous," in a long and uncharacteristically personal letter to the editor of *Current Biography,* in which he recounts, among other things, his departure from high school after two years, in favor of full-time newspaper work on the Salt Lake City *Tribune.* And, writing to the artist Gluyas Williams in 1934, Ross says, "I'm employed by *The New Yorker . . .* largely as an idea man. That's what I regard myself as, at any rate, and what I think my chief value to the magazine is." This city-room angle on the world elates the old sourpuss again and again in this refreshing and unironic anthology. Who gets the royalties to "Happy Birthday to You"? he suddenly asks a Talk editor. To the actor Fredric March, he declares, "The belief that 'none' is a singular pronoun is an old American legend which grew out of an error made in a common-school grammar many years ago." To E. B. White, an accomplished countryman by now, he takes up a dictionary exploration of "compost," both verb and noun, which must have required three or four pages out of his Underwood. And in a memo to Shawn, his most valuable discovery, he wants additions to a coming June Talk piece that will explore more fully the story behind the home-plate umpire's little hand brush, and the ball capacity of his pockets. "Are these brand-new balls, or are they balls that have been played with some, and been knocked foul?"

For Ross, the invention of his magazine was just another good story. *"The New Yorker* is pure accident from start to finish," he wrote to George Jean Nathan. "I was the luckiest son of a bitch alive when I started it. Within a year White, Thurber, Arno and Hokinson had shown up out of nowhere. . . . And Gibbs came along very soon, and Clarence Day, and a number of other path-finders I could name if I spent a little time in review. . . . And Benchley was alive, for instance." They were lucky, too.

Books, February, 2000

OFF WE GO

Yesterday brought a foggy morning to Brooklin, Maine—"Imagine that!" said our presiding chairman and speaker, Richard Freethey, striking the lone note of irony of the day—or so it seemed at 8:50 A.M., when the Brooklin Band (white shirts, tan pants) struck up with "America the Beautiful," and the last seats in the double row of folding chairs reserved for veterans and creaky elders filled up, while arriving families of every size walked in from their cars, parked along Route 175, and stood beside and behind them. The Fourth in Brooklin is always celebrated with a 10 A.M. parade— floats and fire trucks, Model Ts and shined-up ancient roadsters, and kid- and Lab-laden pickups—that forms on Steamboat Road and beyond, and, honking all the way, streams slowly along past householders waving from their aluminum lawn chairs, makes the turn between the Brooklin General Store and the Friend Memorial Library, and heads out along Naskeag Road. This year was differ- ent, beginning as it did with the earlier dedication of Brooklin's Veterans' Memorial—a sizable new chunk of gray granite, with a tilted, bronze, message-bearing face, standing in front of three daz- zling white flagpoles and, farther back, the modest Brooklin Town Hall, once known as the Brooklin School. The Veterans' Memo- rial arrived only after a great deal of dedicated local planning and fund-raising, but it was also something of a catch-up, as Freethey reminded us, since several other local towns got theirs up shortly after the Civil War.

But never mind. Everything about this event—the flag-raisings,

The Fourth of July, Brooklin, Maine, 2014

the Pledge of Allegiance, the Dedication, and the rest, was perfect and perfectly unsurprising, unless you count Ms. Eleanor Tarr's sweetly unadorned, dead-on soprano rendering of the Anthem, or young Nicholas Bianco's poised delivery of "Taps," gently echoed by Aaron Glazer's more distant trumpet from a patch of grassland not far from the Brooklin Cemetery. There had also been a moment when Freethey introduced seventeen surviving Brooklin veterans of the Second World War and the Korean War.

None of this, perhaps, would be worth noting so carefully if you didn't happen to be one of the old guys there who had doffed his baseball cap when his name came along, and felt his heart beating oddly. At ninety, I belong to the generation that was called into service almost en masse, sixteen million of us, in 1942 and 1943, and went off to war. We had to go, no two ways about it, and, bitching and groaning, we left school or quit our jobs, said goodbye to our parents and wives or girlfriends, and went and got the great bloody, boring thing done, and came home again, most of us. Mine was an easy war, and I've always felt a bit awkward with that Greatest Generation wreath that Tom Brokaw generously draped on us. Not for me, thanks, if you please, except on this particular holiday morning. Sitting among elderly serviceman friends and neighbors—among them Henry Lawson, who ran the engine division of my brother's boatyard for so many years; Russell Smith, whose wife, Madeline, used to keep one of his discarded work boots out on their porch, full of petunias; and Steve Parson, a longtime summer pal of mine, who went to Guadalcanal in his teens and never talked about it afterward—I saw the crowd swell to a hundred or more as groups of folks and their amped-up, flag-bearing kids stopped by on their way to the parade. The sun, I noticed, had begun to get the best of the fog, just as we knew it would, and I felt, well, yes, thank you, thank you very much.

Post, July, 2011

Memory of this sweet Fourth of July morning, now almost four years past, remains clear, but the questions it raises and almost answers about "the Greatest Generation"—my generation, that is—may be slipping into irrelevance. We veterans of the Second World War are about to disappear. Eight hundred and fifty-five thousand of us remain, out of the original sixteen million, and five hundred of us are dying every day. We're the last five per cent; next year, two per cent. With an effort, I can bring back a memory of myself, at fourteen, watching a few bent, white-haired veterans of the Grand Army of the Republic turned out in their shabby blue uniforms for another Memorial Day in the mid-nineteen-thirties; I can't recall anything I felt about them. The two distances—each a seventy-year removal from a famous bloodletting—are identical, and there's barely the shadow of a difference between us now: wasn't I at Antietam?

When my war comes up in a conversation, people around me seem startled if I say that I was in it, I took part; then they smile and look at me benignly. I am great and somehow good, they're thinking. The talk shifts and goes elsewhere, but I am a little uneasy now. You've won, Tom, and thank you: yes, mine is the Greatest Generation, but despite the compliment, the people who are really feeling good about that aren't us old guys, I notice, but everybody else, anybody who's younger. If we're great, then they're a little great, and America itself is great all over again.

Something's missing here, and it eats at me, and may explain why thoughts about my own war have been persistent. In March, 2003, on the eve of the Iraq war, I wrote a *New Yorker* Comment piece in which I named more than a dozen friends or school or college classmates of mine and told how they had died in my war and how and where it happened, and listed some others who had been wounded, and still others I knew who were killed in later wars. I mentioned a brother-in-law, Neil MacKenna, now deceased, who got blown up at Belfort Gap, in eastern France, and walked with a cane after that; later in his life he needed two canes. I also wrote about a close friend, Gardner Botsford, also departed, who as an infantry officer landed on Omaha Beach on D-Day, fought in Normandy and at the Bulge and Aachen and the Hürtgen Forest, was twice wounded, and received numerous decorations, including the Croix de Guerre. He remained silent about all this until his seventies, when he wrote a memoir that touched on some of it but never with pathos. "He is suave and unflappable," I went on, "but when there's a thunderstorm passing over his house in the Berkshires he turns pale and wears a different look."

Later on, I noted, "The slim roster of people I've known who died or nearly died in old wars is not something I run over in my mind, any more than I make myself think about the much longer list of strangers far away (it's up in the millions) who have died or suffered in wars in my lifetime, but these old names have come back. Sometimes I think it's wrong to mention the friends I had who have died in the service, because I was luckier than they were and had an easy time of it, all in all; my list is only a sliver compared with ones that could be drawn up by combat veterans of my age. But then there's a shift and I feel that as long as I can hold on to these names and glimpsed faces, their bearers will not be relegated to the abstract status of heroes or the honored dead. Maybe some of them *were* heroes, but what I feel toward them, I find, is an extreme civility due them because they have stayed young."

I was back on my case the following year, with a Comment piece about Errol Morris's riveting documentary "The Fog of War," a feature-length interview or history lesson or moral travelogue by the documentarian, who previously gave us "The Thin Blue Line" and "Mr. Death." In it, the eighty-two-year-old former secretary of defense Robert S. McNamara is rarely off-screen, stubbornly vis-à-vis in a close-up that stops at the knot of his necktie. He is still energized by war, gesturing and jabbing his finger at us, then pausing with jaw ajar as he contemplates what he must next bring forth about the Cuban missile crisis or the firebombing of Tokyo or the Quaker protester Norman Morrison, who immolated himself outside McNamara's Pentagon office (he was there) in 1965, in reaction to the escalating American devastation of the Vietnamese countryside.

For older audiences, among which I place myself, McNamara's testimony cuts deepest when he goes back to the Second World War firebombing of Tokyo by the American Twentieth Air Force, whose high-altitude B-29 bombers, redeployed at five thousand feet, rained down incendiaries that killed at least eighty-five thousand civilians on that single night. The relentless subsequent B-29 bombing campaign, which was continued almost in secrecy against lesser targets, is accompanied here with a thrumming score by Philip Glass. Morris transforms the clustering names of the burnt-down wooden Japanese cities into equivalent American towns, with the percent of residents killed attached: thirty-five per cent of Chicago, fifty-eight per cent of Cleveland, ninety-nine per cent of Chattanooga, forty-two per cent of Toledo, and so on. Sixty-seven Japanese cities were firebombed by the B-29s in the spring of 1945 and three hundred and fifty thousand civilians burnt to death—and the war in effect won—well before Hiroshima. McNamara, then an Air Force colonel and the chief statistician to General Curtis E. LeMay, the superhawk commander of the campaign, almost puddles up when he talks about the tactic, then recovers to say, "I was part of a mechanism that in effect recommended it." He quotes LeMay's perception that both of them would be prosecuted as war criminals if the war were to be lost. The age-freckled McNamara stares out at the camera and into himself through all this while he talks about the hundred and sixty million people who died in wars during his lifetime. He is less the star than the soul of "The Fog of War," and he sweeps us into his anxious, reconsidering purview.

As I've been saying, that war has almost slid out of memory, and it takes an unexpected work of art like this to look at it head on, even for one who was around at the time—I was an editor with a G.I. Air Force weekly in the Pacific which reported extensively about the B-29s and their work. And who among us can remember, before that, a world where such a war could not have been imagined? Today, thanks to our sleek modern weaponry, Americans will probably never again have to kill civilians in indiscriminate numbers in wartime, and can despise and fear enemies who hold to the idea that anyone can be targeted for death in the name of a fervent cause, even while we do the same thing, in our own more technical fashion and from a safe distance. What is disquieting about old Robert McNamara—who at times appears to stand in our path with the bony finger and crazy agenda of a street saint—isn't his conscience, which he keeps private, but his consciousness, which we share and would just as soon do without.

One of *The New Yorker's* greatest war accounts was a three-part Reporter at Large story by St. Clair McKelway, "A Reporter with the B-29s," that ran in the magazine starting on June 9, 1945. It's a vivid, first-hand, inside account of the entire B-29 program, from its beginnings to its massive and then still ongoing huge daily fire-bombing raids on Japan. It's the magazine's single greatest news-beat and the strangest *New Yorker* story ever. McKelway, an upper-level editor and then a notable writer of Profiles and fact pieces for the magazine, had joined the Air Force as a captain in 1943, and was soon made chief public relations officer of the budding B-29 program. It was a significant post, in which he rose to the rank of colonel and, once in the Marianas, became an intimate daily companion of the Twentieth Air Force's top generals—Major General LeMay, Brigadier Generals Emmett (Rosy) O'Donnell and Haywood S. (Possum) Hansell, and some lesser brass. He had been on overseas duty for twenty-three months and would have still been there, hard at work, had he not suffered a jarring mental breakdown that suddenly had him firing off cables from Guam that accused Admiral Chester W. Nimitz, then the commander of all Pacific operations (including the Twentieth Air Force), of treason and attempted obstruction and sabotage of the B-29 campaign. McKelway, who had suffered from bouts of manic depression in civilian life, had flipped out. He was relieved, and, gently taken in hand, sent back to Washington, where he received a brief medical examination and was given an extended furlough. He hurried to New York, took a room at the Ritz Hotel, and, still on his bipolar high, wrote the twenty-thousand-word piece in less than two weeks.

In an article I wrote about all this for the magazine in 2010, I said that Mac's writing (everyone called him Mac) in that series was not crazed or rushed but seizes the reader with its energy and precise presentation of events. There was also a glow of romance that surrounds McKelway's war, and shows itself in his heroic portraits of the Twentieth Air Force's commanders and in his longing for the pioneering early days and sights on Saipan in the campaign's début. There are moments when he describes the B-29s' "red and green flying lights" as "those colored necklaces of faraway railroad trains that run through American childhood."

But something even more bizarre comes over Mac when he writes about the ground personnel closely involved in LeMay's campaign and its rush of successes. He mentions the sleeplessness that accompanies the days and nights of hard work of those times, and a tenseness and quickening of tempo in the performance of tasks. Messengers walk faster, jeep drivers take care of their jeeps and never run out of gas. For all of them, whether airmen or ground crews or adjutants and their clerks, "the mind, the body, the spirit, the whole being seemed free and ready for anything and confident of success. It was not elation so much as it was a knowledgeable acceptance of maturity. . . . Good men were better. Men who had seemed mediocre became good." Describing LeMay himself (the two are sitting in a jeep, waiting for the B-29s to return from their enormous Tokyo raid), he says, "Here was a representative, I thought, of a great many men in all ranks who are better men than they have ever been before."

McKelway loses his perky tone when he writes about the first time he got to look at the intelligence photographs, back from Tokyo and elsewhere, and began to think about what they meant, and I have pretty well decided that these photographs and those scarifying, not quite exact large numbers are what made him insist, oddly but perhaps not insanely, that our men in the Marianas were good. And I believe this is exactly the same ascribing of goodness that overcomes us all when we force ourselves to think about (or resolutely not think about) the numbers we have seen before and then must sum up: a hundred and forty thousand dead at Hiroshima; eighty thousand dead at Nagasaki. Three hundred and forty thousand dead in the other, extended fire raids. Five hundred and sixty thousand civilians dead, more or less. Old Robert McNamara, who was there, too, ultimately claimed the number was over nine hundred thousand.

This is how we won that war, and how we'd do it again in a "Groundhog Day" replay. The Japanese enemy had pulled their remaining planes and ground forces and weaponry back to the mainland and would have exacted an enormous toll of blood and death had we been forced to invade Japan. We exacted the toll and avoided invasion and won. Killing more civilians than the other side is what war makes you do, but reaching the decision and then acting on it doesn't make you good or great. It makes you tired and it keeps you awake at night, still crazy after all these years.

May, 2015

CONGRATULATIONS! IT'S A BABY

"I always look at the cartoons first," everyone says. So do I, and I've had practice. When I say that I grew up looking at *New Yorker* cartoons, I do not speak in metaphorical terms. My mother, Katharine Angell—later Katharine White—became an editor for the newborn magazine in 1925, the year I turned five, and because she was involved in the art as well as the prose of Harold Ross's little enterprise there were always photocopied drawings (with the captions typed on the back) and covers, along with fiction galleys and Talk of the Town pages, all over the house. I went for the cartoons right away. It's odd to look back on this precocious diet and wonder what I made of Ralph Barton's gin-raddled nineteen-twenties weekenders or the florid fake engravings by John Held, Jr., which spoofed everything Victorian. I passed them over, I suppose—storing them away in memory until my sophistication quotient caught up a little—and ate up the rest: the covers, which were so much brighter and livelier than my children's-book jackets, and, inside, Rea Irvin's plump paired cops tooling around in tiny roadsters; Peter Arno's thin young men in tails crowding into speakeasies; and engrossing multi-part strips, like O. Soglow's Little King running away to join some Gypsies; the dusty cross-town peregrinations of a restaurant hard roll, from bakery to diner's plate, as delineated by Al Frueh; and Irvin's boldly inked parson rushing over hill and dale, in full ecclesiasticals, to bless the fox after he has blessed the hounds. The first *New Yorker* cartoon to become famous may have been

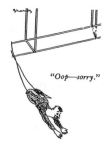

"*Oop—sorry.*"

George V. Shanks's circus mishap—the butterfingered trapeze artist apologizing, and his dropped partner glaring back up from the bottom of the page. I got that right away.

I can't remember myself often asking for help with a caption or a situation. One exception was Helen Hokinson's American lady in a Paris back street shyly asking, "Avez-vous 'Ulysses'?" A book banned in this country; I was told, and, uh—well, it's hard to explain. I was still only ten. I never said anything about an earlier, darkly brooding Reginald Marsh drawing of a bored, vulturous cleric, from a 1929 issue, which my mother had put up, matted and framed, in a corner of the hallway, but I kept stopping to look it over. "Let us pray," he is intoning into a basket-like nineteen-twenties radio microphone just under his chin: a biting joke back then, when radio was so new—and still disturbing now. I don't think Pat Robertson would put it up in his hallway, I mean.

Just lately, I've been looking at Gluyas Williams's splendid full-page 1928 drawing captioned "A Little Bird Reveals the Facts of Life to the Editor of the New York *Times*," and imagining the intense twenty minutes' study I must have given to that situation: the Editor, an ancient gent in Dundreary whiskers, sitting stunned; the birdie flying out the window; the horrified editors and press-men recoiling at the door. But what were "the facts of life," and why didn't the editor of the *Times* know them? Within a year or two, I must have spotted the scene again, in one of the early *New Yorker* albums, and understood it better. It doesn't matter now, because the joke is still strong and alive. Art waits for us to catch up, and never goes out of date.

I had modern parents—my mother used to take me to lunch at speakeasies—and although they certainly didn't agree about every-thing (they were divorced), there seems to have been no debate between them about the notion that kids should be left on their own when it comes to reading. I was a bookworm, and was terrifi-cally lucky to be growing up in a place where funny drawings and brilliant, hardworking artists were taken seriously. When Arno and Hokinson and James Thurber and Mary Petty and Richard Taylor and William Steig and Saul Steinberg and Whitney Darrow and George Price and Charles Addams and the rest began to flourish, in the thirties, every other *New Yorker* reader got lucky, too.

Cultural historians who offer explanations for this sudden flowering of the *New Yorker* cartoon seem to share an owlish tone, and cite the same roster of names and sources in their accounting: the old *Punch,* Charles Dana Gibson, Frank Crowninshield's *Vanity Fair, Life* (the old *Life*) and *Judge,* Prohibition, H. L. Mencken and George Jean Nathan, the Depression, the genius of Harold Ross and the genius of his art editor, Rea Irvin. I can't disagree, but I have a different conclusion. I think it was a miracle. It was an accident of history: something in the drinking water; sunspots; the conjoining of Aquarius and Herbert Hoover in the third house. Nobody knows what happened; we only know that it hasn't happened again. Something very much of the same order was going on with *New Yorker* writers at this same moment, when Robert Benchley, Frank Sullivan, Ogden Nash, James Thurber, E. B. White, Russell Maloney, Wolcott Gibbs, and S. J. Perelman were all writing for the magazine. Ah, *New Yorker* subscribers must have thought, what a funny bunch we Americans are. Just think—all these writers and artists, every week like this, from now on! Well, no. That coming together was a time too good to last, and somebody else will have to explain why. I'm just glad I was around.

THE SUMMER I TURNED fifteen, my mother and my stepfather, E. B. White, were startled one evening at the dinner table when it came out that I could remember every single drawing and every caption that had appeared in the magazine in its first decade. My claim was tested on the spot and it held up, and I can recall my mother briefly worrying about whether I'd been wasting my time. It was too late, in any case, because *The New Yorker* surrounded me on every side. The magazine was talked about endlessly, all day long, and then some more over the weekends. Frank Sullivan or James Thurber or the Robert Coateses turned up on Sundays sometimes, and we all played word games and Kick the Can. I took on Thurber at Ping-Pong; he could still see then, and he was

excitable and scary-wild across the table. After I went off to boarding school, he gave me a great interview for the school paper, along
with the original of one of his most famous drawings, which somebody swiped from my dormitory room in Lower Dunworth. (Be
warned, whoever you are: Interpol and the Friends of Dr. Millmoss
are on this case, big time, and expect a break any day now.)

I studied Peter Arno's stuff closely while I was growing up,
because I'd picked up the news somewhere that he was sophisticated. (I can't recall anyone at home using that word in conversation.) His men and women were inexorably stylish and stayed
out late drinking, but there was also something outré about them,
because they looked out of scale and were dazzlingly over-lighted.
They reminded you of the movies. His drawings appeared to be
about New York and Westchester and the Hamptons, but I think
only people from out of town ever believed that portrait. Arno's
jokes were racy, and his line was bolder than anyone else's—the
gleam of a tuxedo lapel, the slash of lipstick, the carnal tilt of a
sugar daddy's mustache—and he overdressed his grandes dames
and theatregoers and equestrians (and underdressed his showgirls
and bimbos) because it was so much fun for him to draw them that
way, in costume. My parents had dressed up in evening clothes
and gone to parties, too, back when they were still married—it
was a thrill to watch them taxiing off into the night—but in the
mornings they got up and went to work. Parties didn't go on all
the time, the way they did in Arno's world: I knew that much.
Arno felt free to play with us this way because he was sure about
his eye—he could draw a sophisticated robin—and certainty is the
heart of cool. Even his captions had dash—"Hey, Jack, which way
to Mecca?" and "Well, back to the old drawing board" and "Fill 'er
up!" and "Wake up, you mutt! We're getting married today"—and
brought back the work in a rush when you thought of them later. (I
must have spotted that last one in an early Arno album, for a snor-

ing man and a naked woman in bed together was altogether too racy for Ross, which meant that it didn't appear in his not always sophisticated magazine.)

Charles Addams was another bravura captioneer. His outlandish dramas were often served up with innocuous lines that clarified and darkened the situation, both at the same time: "It's the children, darling—back from camp" (each of them inside his or her own portable kennel), for instance, and "Oh, speak up, George! Stop mumbling!" Was I the only person, I wonder, to notice that George must have got himself out from inside that bulging python later on, only to be carried away, in another drawing, by a giant bird, whose burdened shadow wings past the wife—"George! George! Drop the keys!"—and across a beach as the creature departs overhead? I have been thinking about Addams's "Congratulations! It's a baby" for sixty years now, because my mother gave me the drawing—for Christmas, I think—while I was still in my teens. I have since handed it along to my own son, and he now tells me that it is out on loan to some gallery or other, with the label "From the collection

"Visiting hours are over, Mrs. Glenborn."

of John Henry Angell." In the drawing, a young nurse has just popped her head out of the maternity ward to give the happy news to the brand-new dad: an ancient, egg-shaped gent who has lifted one frail hand in surprise.

Cartoons in this magazine—most of them, at least—reward the noticer, and part of the pleasure for me with a George Price was always to go over it again, after that first dazzled look, and take in the mechanics: the framework of the hospital bed, under the sheet; the perfect empty glass on the table, with the perfect straw inside; Mrs. Glenhorn's chin and mole and hat; and the line of the middle fold on the back of the nurse's uniform, which ends, like all Price's lines, in a point. He worked in wire and steel, I sometimes like to think, and then drew the sculpture onto the page.

ADDAMS (TO GO BACK a step) is a good place to convene the gallery talk proposing that the best cartoons are captionless: brilliance of idea and skill of execution will carry the day, as with a Raphael or a Cézanne—or with thirty-six hundred–odd *New Yorker* covers. How about those unexplained Addams ski tracks that flow unconcernedly around and past the mid-slope pine? Or his similarly silent police lineup of sullen goldilocked little suspects arrayed under the kliegs as they are studied by three bears?

I take no stand here. Whatever works, whatever warms me, whatever makes me laugh is the drawing for me. Contemporary artists for the magazine take obdurate pride in writing their own captions, scorning the collaborative efforts of the past, when an editor or a writer—sometimes it was White, sometimes Gibbs or Peter De Vries—came up with the line that ran under a drawing. (I respect this moral stance, but I have to confess that I don't quite get it. Should there have been only one Gershwin? Would Richard Rodgers's songs sound better if he'd barred the door against Lorenz Hart?) Captions seem to come naturally with certain artists. Charles Saxon's suburbanites, as I recall, sometimes even turned up with ribbons of text underneath, adding to a murmurous satire. His wide-bottomed, no-longer-quite-young Fairfield County denizens, in Bermuda shorts and bankerish socks, were ridiculous but easy to love. They were sweet, and you laughed at that—but not for the reasons that made you prize an Addams. I never felt the need to work out a code or a theory of pleasure about any of this, I mean, or to weigh jokes on some seismic scale. By good fortune, I've been a consumer but never an editor of *New Yorker* art.

I know readers who are forever complaining about the art: it isn't as funny as it used to be, it's bourgeois, it's repetitive, it's childish, it isn't seriously funny. They want our art to be higher—a Steinberg or a Daumier every week, or nothing at all. A contributor friend of mine once announced that there should be no more cartoons in the magazine. "That time is over," she said firmly. I nodded sadly, pretending to agree, and remembered the moment when Woody Allen told me that he wouldn't be writing many more comic pieces for us. "Being funny isn't for grownups," he said. (He has relented a little, I notice, in his movies.) I think there will always be days when I don't trust in laughter, either, and weeks when I despair that we have succumbed here to the kind of humor that Philip Hamburger calls "post-funny," or that we're not funny at all. Then I open the next issue and find a Leo Cullum dog happily showing his dog wife the architect's model of their new doghouse, and I relax. It's always been this way. "There have been good weeks" was the best that E. B. White could offer in his introduction to the first *New Yorker* album, back in 1929.

The same cartoon situations keep coming up—dog jokes and psychiatrist jokes, witch recipes and board conferences, dinner parties and desert islands, golf and space aliens, and a lot more, over and over. Another skiing cartoon? Another skiing cartoon without a caption? What could be better than Frank Modell's turtlenecked downhiller, with his broken leg up on a hassock, who is being visited by his dog—a dog bringing a single slipper? Because Frank is lighthearted, he's made it clear that the dog is more upset about the accident than the dolt in the chair. The dog's gaze catches ours,

and we want to turn back the page and discover the moment all over again.

The flair and charm of these remarkable artists—dozens of them, down the years—lend a dash of style to us readers, in turn, as we grow familiar with their stuff. Almost without our noticing it, their tones and views can intersect with something of our own, and confer a momentary élan or a rubbed-off, lighter view of the familiar: perhaps only a child or a grand-child of ours sneaking a look at herself in the mirror—a little girl straight out of Steig. Sometimes when I'm out in New York, I'll watch a couple across the room talking, or see some parents and chil-dren together, and recognize a pattern there, an angular grace, that comes only from Robert Weber. Pure Booth, we think, catching sight of dogs and auto parts lying about outside a grungy road-side garage, or, perhaps later that same

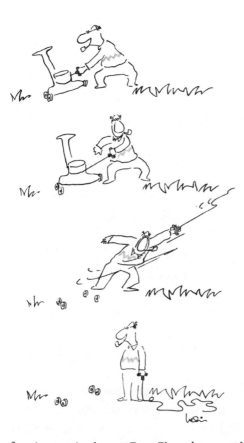

evening, at dinner with mid-Vermont friends, feel a furry Koren glow falling around us from the candlelight and the sweaters and the irony. This frilly woman walking toward me in the sunshine has a Victoria Roberts smirk, while a bunched-together, rushing pack of teen-agers in their blown-up windbreakers and enormous jeans has the dash and swirl of a Lee Lorenz drawing. Avenues and corners and mounted cops and sunsets can turn into Steinbergs without warning; dustballs and desserts and furniture wiggle to a Roz Chast beat; and the smallest moment, the most ordinary sort of enterprise, can surprise us with a flashback. Sometimes in August, cranking up my ancient Deere lawnmower, I'm tugging at Arnie Levin's flyaway model. If only!

I CAN'T REMEMBER THE last ten years of *New Yorker* cartoons, and perhaps not even the last ten weeks' worth, but the magazine's art and artists still surround me. Ever since I first came to work here, in 1956, the artists have been clustering in on Tuesday morning, carrying their latest drawings and roughs to show to the art editor, and cheering me up with their engaging gloomy smiles. Many have become friends of mine, and have then been roped into gifts or collaborations. Jim Stevenson's elegant watercolor of a batter turning away as he heads for the plate became the cover for my first baseball book (the painting hangs before me, here on my office wall), and Koren's animal nine has taken the field on a different diamond for the jacket of a book of casuals. (Ed may be the only artist who can draw a West Side monster.) The only baseball card I've had framed is Roz Chast's depiction of Dwayne Cudahee's 1934 season with the Akron Acers (he went hitless in two hundred and eighty-six at-bats), and, not far away, I can study Bruce McCall's baseball moonscape—the moon as a beat-up batting-practice fly ball. Saul Steinberg illustrated some of my baseball pieces, and so did David Levine; luckily for me, both were fans of the game. Back in the early fifties, Steinberg became so enamored of baseball that he took road trips with the Milwaukee Braves; when he had to follow them by television, he would put on a full Braves uniform and cap before he settled down in front of the set. Artists aren't like the rest of us.

The men and women in that Tuesday-morning artists' circle are devoting their lives to the daunting proposition that they can go on being fresh and funny, week after week, and that, in spite of rejections and changes in the magazine's style and price and size, *The New Yorker* isn't going to let them down. They know we can't do it without them. Almost everybody can write—or so it is claimed, by the thousands of submissions—and many of us can learn to edit, but only artists can draw. Theirs is the vernacular that keeps us young and lowdown and not too full of ourselves—and funny on the good weeks.

Onward and Upward with
the Arts, December, 1997

PAST MASTERS: MARK TWAIN / JOHN HERSEY / HENRI CARTIER-BRESSON

HUCKLEBERRY FINN

In my boyhood summers, we lived in a Dutch-fieldstone house a dozen yards from the western shore of the Hudson, and the river's damp sounds and smells, its wide white expanse of glassy or wind-mottled water, its brackish tides, its ceaseless movement, and its night lappings impinged on my young consciousness unawares. Twenty miles up from the Battery, I waded in the Hudson, swam in it, fished in it (for eels and tommycod and blue crabs), skipped stones on it, shot fireworks over it, and all day dozily studied its upstream and downstream traffic. Catboats, rowboats, and run-abouts appeared and went away, while, over in the eastern channel, river freighters and sluggish tugs with low processions of barges made passage with banner-streaming vessels from the great white fleet of the Hudson River Day Line. Way off, along the New York Central's water-level route, trains silently drew and redrew the straight line of the farther bank.

I must have been eleven or twelve when I first encountered "Huckleberry Finn," but from the moment Huck and Jim took to the river—*their* river, the Mississippi—I was overtaken with a thrilling proprietary excitement, because, of course, Mark Twain had it right: this was what a great wide-water, north–south stream was like, and here was how it felt to pass time on its banks. For the first time, literature had confirmed for me a patch of life that I recognized from my own experience.

In the book, Twain appears to give little attention to scenery, but his river-prospect interludes preserve the clarity and unhurried gazings of an empty-sky morning passed within the sound of moving water:

> A little smoke couldn't be noticed, now, so we would take some fish off of the lines, and cook up a hot breakfast. And afterwards we would watch the lonesomeness of the river, and kind of lazy along, and by and by lazy off to sleep. . . . Next you'd see a raft sliding by, away off yonder, and maybe a galoot on it chopping, because they're most always doing it on a raft, you'd see the ax flash, and come down—you don't hear nothing; you see that ax go up again, and by the time it's above the man's head, then you hear the *k'chunk!*—it had took all that time to come over the water.

The famous passage—it comes along early in Chapter 19—lies near the center of this most central American novel, and one returns to it each time with refreshed alertness. One might even look at that "sliding by" and then recall how often Twain uses the word or a variant—not just when he is writing about the river but when he is writing about Huck Finn himself. Huck by turns slides out of houses and bedrooms, slips off quiet, slides into a canoe, slips down a ladder, clears out away from his drunken father, and, with his companion, Jim, hurries again to the raft and lets her go a-sliding down the river. Each of these hero-outcasts holds secret hopes of finding a place for himself somewhere in proper, dry-land society,

but they are kept on the run by the grownups they encounter—
thieves and lynchers, rapscallions and skin-artists and murderers—
during their precipitous vertical odyssey. Almost without noticing,
they discover that the great sliding river itself is the only constant,
their one fixed home.

"Huckleberry Finn" invites rereading, but I find less sunshine
in it each time around. Its cruel and oafish backwater crowds, and
the itinerant grotesques who prey upon them, don't feel all that
funny or far away, and the bitter pains of Jim's condition, on which
Twain poured out his irony, are dated more in details than in sub-
stance. I notice, too, as I did not before, that Huck and Jim become
older in the book, partly as the result of their comical and horrific
experiences but really because they are also riding that other stream
whose insensible, one-way flow is felt perhaps even by children staring at distant sails and trains on a summer afternoon. In the end,
the two run out of river, and so does their story, which becomes less
when it must find a way to stop. Time has slid away, and we wish
ourselves upstream again, beginning the voyage.

Sidebar, June, 1995

HERSEY AND HISTORY

John Hersey's "Hiroshima," which famously constituted the entire
editorial contents of this magazine's issue of August 31, 1946, is a
work of sustained silence. Its appearance, just over a year after the
destruction of the Japanese city in the first atomic attack, offered
one of the first detailed accounts of the effects of nuclear warfare on
its survivors, in a prose so stripped of mannerism, sentimentality,
and even minimal emphasis as to place each reader alone within
scenes laid bare of all but pain. The piece tells the stories of six
people—two doctors, two women, a Protestant clergyman, and a

German Jesuit priest—as they experience the bomb, suffer injuries, and struggle for survival in the nightmarish landscape of ruin and death, and does so with classical restraint. Hersey never attempts to "humanize" these victims but instead allows them to keep their formal titles—Mrs. Nakamura, Dr. Fujii, Father Kleinsorge, and so on—throughout, thus clothing them once again in the privacy and individuality that the war and the bomb have blown away. This was not the way we in America were accustomed to thinking about Japanese citizens, whether seen as the hated enemy or the faceless dead, in the mid-nineteen-forties.

"Hiroshima" is a short piece, given its concerns, and was read everywhere, one may assume, at a single sitting. Its thirty-one thousand words suffice because they abstain from the smallest judgment or moral positioning, and leave the reader to deal with the consequences and the questions. Nothing in the work has been dramatized, but many individual scenes begin with a simple few words—"Early that day," "It began to rain," "Some time later"— that sound like stage directions. Indeed, the meticulous, restrained flow of Hersey's words, the slow conversations of his handful of characters, and the flattened, burnt-out scenery of the destroyed city contrive to shift the piece from contemporary war reporting to what feels like ancient tragedy. In the same way, the decision to run the piece intact in *The New Yorker*, with no other text (William Shawn, then the managing editor, conceived the idea and persuaded Harold Ross to go along with it), cleared its setting of familiar and reassuring distractions. What happened at Hiroshima is all that we are allowed to think about.

It is difficult, in this news-drenched age, to imagine how "Hiroshima" was received in its time. Newspapers everywhere devoted lead editorials to it and reprinted front-page excerpts, while the American Broadcasting Company had the piece read aloud (this was just before the television age), over national radio, across four

successive evenings. The article became a book, and the book has
sold more than three and a half million copies and remains in print
to this day. Its story became a part of our ceaseless thinking about
world wars and nuclear holocaust. Neither of these disasters has
come to pass in the past fifty years, and that long and unexpected
silence, one must conclude, found its beginning in the murmurous
eloquence of John Hersey's report.

Sidebar, July, 1995

DISARMED

Visiting the splendid "Henri Cartier-Bresson in America 1935–
1975" show at the Equitable (through November 2nd) brought
back for me some brief but still vivid moments spent with the
Magnum grand master forty years ago. He was not just the most
revered but the most enjoyed member of that celebrated entourage
of photographers—Robert Capa, Chim Seymour, and Elliott Erwitt
were some of the others—whose work was repeatedly featured in
Holiday, where I was a young editor, and whenever he turned up
at the office, a diminutive, monkish-looking gent, with smile and
Leica at the ready, he was received with complimentary disrespect.
"Hank!" cried our art director, Frank Zachary. "Hank Carter! Got
the snaps, Hank?"

It was Zachary's notion that the suave and cosmopolitan C.-B.,
a Parisian to the core, would respond happily to being treated like
an aspiring night-beat news photog with a big-circulation American daily, and even proposed to him that he should go everywhere
wearing a porkpie hat with a "Press" placard stuck in the hatband,
just like in the movies. "Oh, Franghnk!" Cartier-Bresson protested.
He was laughing. "'Got the snaps'—you are . . . you are exceptio-
nale!" Always, of course, he did have the snaps, and then some, and

when we took him out to lunch he would sometimes swiftly lift the Leica, barely pausing in midstride or midsentence, and catch another one—a passing dog or grande dame, a delivery boy across the street with his face at that instant lifted toward the sun—that the rest of us had never noticed.

His cameras were not in evidence on a day when Frank and I called on him and his wife, Eli, in their apartment on the Rue de Lisbonne, in June of 1956. I remember their warmth and charm but nothing else about the day except for a heavy, exotic-looking dagger with a curvy double edge that lay on top of a sideboard, its elaborately chased blade catching gleams of sunlight. When I approached for a closer look, Cartier-Bresson and his wife said, in one voice, "Be careful!"

Seeing my surprise, he explained that the knife was a Malayan kris, and that the dark sheen along its blade was probably poison. "I don't want it to cut you," he said.

"I wasn't going to touch it," I said. I felt like a reprimanded child.

"He means it will cut you if it wants to," Eli said. She herself was Balinese, strikingly so, and again I stopped in my tracks. She spread her hands in distress and said to her husband, "Can we tell Roger why it's out on the table like this?"

"Yes," Cartier-Bresson said gravely. "Normally, in the everyday, the kris rests in this drawer, here below, but now and then it asks to get out."

"It asks?" I asked.

"It knocks," he said, rapping a double rap with his knuckles on the sideboard. "And when it asks again we take it out and put it just here for a few days."

I don't think I laughed. I said nothing, and Cartier-Bresson, anxious to put me at my ease again, gestured apologetically and remarked that belief or superstition, call it what you wish, was everywhere. "After all," he murmured, "there are thousands or millions of Frenchmen walking around with a bit of butcher's string tied around their waist to ward off the *mal au foie,* the liver disease that we French keep as an obsession."

A suspicion occurred. "Henri," I said. "Forgive me, but do you have a piece of string tied around your waist?"

Smiling and shrugging, exuding an interested excitement that was close to pride, he unbuttoned the bottom two buttons of his shirt and revealed a snowy *ficelle* just inside his waistband, neatly double-tied. He looked like a rolled roast, a genius ready for the broiler.

"So far," he said carefully, "it has done its work."

Talk, November, 1996

THE LATE SHOW

An hour after sunset on a Dallas-to-LaGuardia flight last week, a mottled, blocky mass of gray slowly presented itself off the portside windows of our plane—a steeply vertical theatre of cloud rising at its top almost to our announced cruising level of thirty-three thousand feet and illuminating itself garishly from within with all the promise of a major out-of-town opening. "Overdramatic" was the first thought that came to me at my west-facing window, but as the plane moved closer I began to see that this was no ordinary midland midsummer night's thunderstorm. Most of the sunset's traces had drained from the sky by now, but this monster had brought its own light system. Nearly continuous flares and bloomings and fadings from inside its lumpy body suggested a north–south mass of perhaps forty miles, and the closer bolts—blinding-white tree trunks of lightning that threw out limbs and root systems and jagged tendrils and stemlike afterthoughts—revealed an almost sheer wall of storm facing us and falling precipitously away into the darkness. The front, still some miles to the west and mostly below us, was not an immediate concern, but its dimensions and statements did not permit us the customary half-lidded, sidelong glances of the airborne. "For those of you who missed the Fourth of July, there's quite a show down there, off to our left," the pilot told us, and when some people across the aisle got up and leaned closer for a look, the next crazed shot of light gave them the faces of night riders and clowns.

Our flight came four days and thousands of airline flights after the T.W.A. disaster at Moriches Bay, but I don't think that a single person on our smaller plane failed to connect that unimaginably stopped journey with our own trip and its unscheduled present sideshow. Now *this,* I thought, and I reminded myself how many other airliners were headed for New York or Chicago or Sioux Falls or Ottawa just then, and how long the odds were that anything amiss would happen to ours. I wanted safety in numbers and anonymity; I wanted this storm not to notice us. Then, still staring out of my plastic oblong, I saw that this phenomenal airspace had come with lesser mesas and peninsulas of storm stretching away up ahead, still parallel to our path but closer now, and putting out their own spritzes and fistfuls of lightning, and this time a line came to me from that old Broadway biblical play "The Green Pastures": "Gangway for de Lawd God Jehovah!" Under the foot of our cloud I glimpsed the faint yellow gleams of some Tennessee or Kentucky hamlet below, and I could almost feel the air suddenly becoming cooler down there, and the leaves beginning to stir, and some householders, peering up at the approaching familiar melodrama, getting up to move a flowerpot off the porch railing and to call in the cat or the kids.

Nothing happened on our flight. The storm, by now presenting a pinkish sheared-off anvil shape at its top, was pulled slowly offstage behind us; reading lights were snapped out; and our plane, now a tunnel of sleeping strangers, slid along on its homeward slot, comforting us now and then with a soft little jiggle. Because none of us could know what it is like to fall from the sky or be blown out of it, or to come apart into fragments, we could squirm lower in our seats, punch the dinky pillow and fold our arms, and, just before sleep, remind ourselves not to forget, not quite yet, the imperial beauty of that thunderstorm and the boring but generally ongoing solipsism of pure luck.

Unpublished, July, 1995

PAST MASTERS: DONALD BARTHELME

———

DON B.

Donald Barthelme died the other day, at the age of fifty-eight. His departure came much too soon for his readers and stricken friends to attach to him that sense of satisfaction and gratitude one extends almost reflexively to an author who has achieved a longer span, but the brilliance and the dimensions of his work would have honored several lifetimes. He was the author of four novels (one to be published next year), nine collections of stories, and a celebrated book for children. His contributions to this magazine extended across twenty-six years, and included dozens of unsigned Notes and Comment pieces, some film criticism, and a hundred and twenty-eight stories—these last of such a dazzling, special nature that each one was invariably spoken of, here and elsewhere, as "a Barthelme." The tag was almost essential, because a typical Barthelme story was simultaneously rich and elusive, evanescent and nutritious, profound and hilarious, brief and long-term, trifling and heartbreaking, daunting to some readers and to others a snap, a breeze, a draught of life. During his lifetime Donald Barthelme was variously summarized as an avant-gardist, a collagist, a minimalist, a Dadaist, an existentialist, and a postmodernist, but even a cursory rereading of his work leaves one with the certainty that none of these narrowings are of much use. Categories seemed to accumulate around him of their own accord (the phenomenon must have pleased him, for he loved lists), but a brief rundown of some common ingredients in his fiction only brings back his unique swirl of colors and contexts: songs, museums, headlines, orchestras, bishops and other clerics, jungles, babies, commercials, savants and philosophers, animals (gerbils, bears, porcupines, falling dogs), anomie, whiskey, fathers and grandfathers, explorers, passionate love, ghosts (zombies and others), musicians, filmmakers, recipes, painters, princes, affectations, engravings, domesticity, balloons, battalions, nothingness, politicians, Indians, grief, places (Paraguay, Korea, Copenhagen, Barcelona, Thailand), dreams, young women, architects, angels, and a panoply of names (Goethe, Edward Lear, Klee, Bluebeard, Cortés and Montezuma, Sindbad, Kierkegaard, President Eisenhower, Eugénie Grandet, Snow White, Captain Blood, the Holy Ghost, Perpetua, Daumier, the Phantom of the Opera, St. Augustine, St. Anthony, and Hokie Mokie the King of Jazz).

This explosion of reference, this bottomless etcetera, may account for his brevity—short stories and short novels—and for the beauty of his prose. His names and nouns were set down in a manner that magically carried memories and meanings and overtones, bringing them intact to the page, where they let loose (in the reader) a responding instinctive flood of recognition, irony, and sadness—too many emotions, in fact, to work very well within the formal chambers of a full novel. The Barthelme sentences, which seemed to employ references or omissions in the place of adjectives or metaphors, were sky blue—clear and fresh, and free of all previous weathers of writing. It was this instrument that allowed him to be offhand and complex and lighthearted and poignant all at the same time—often within the space of a line or two. In an early story, "Philadelphia," a man named Mr. Flax describes an imaginary tribe and culture in this fashion:

> The Wapituil are like us to an extraordinary degree. . . .
> They have a Fifth Avenue. . . . They have a Chock Full o' Nuts
> and a Chevrolet, one of each. They have a Museum of Modern
> Art and a telephone and a Martini, one of each. . . . They have
> everything that we have, but only one of each thing. . . . The
> sex life of a Wapituil consists of a single experience, which he
> thinks about for a long time.

Many readers had difficulty at first cottoning to writing like
this. They were put off by Barthelme's crosscutting and by his terrifying absence of explanation, and those who resisted him to the
end may have been people who were by nature unable to put their
full trust in humor. Barthelme was erudite and culturally rigorous,
but he was always terrifically funny as well, and when his despair-
ing characters and jagged scenes and sudden stops and starts had
you tumbling wildly, free-falling through a story, it was laughter
that kept you afloat and made you feel there would probably be a
safe landing. It was all right to laugh: sometimes (he seemed to be
saying) that was the only thing we should count on.

All this took some getting used to—readers who encountered
his long and ironically twisted "Snow White" in this magazine
in 1967 wrote us in great numbers to ask what had happened to
these people—but if you could give yourself to the tale (there was
no code, no set of symbols, no key) you were all right. One writer
here said last week, "Somehow, he taught us how to read him—it's
almost the most surprising thing about him—and what had felt
strange or surreal in his work came to seem absolutely natural and
inevitable. And there were times, particularly in the Nixon years,
when his stuff seemed more real—saner and much more coherent—
than anything else going on in the world."

Donald Barthelme was tall and quiet, with an air of natural
gravity to him—a *light* gravity, if that is possible. He had an Ahab

beard and wore Strindbergian eyeglasses; some people thought he looked more postmodernist than he wrote. He was entertaining and sad, and without pretension. He took himself seriously but presented himself quietly. (Anyone who happened to see it must still remember a television interview, years ago, in which Barthelme responded to a question about another contemporary literary figure with a brief sigh and then said, "Yes, I know him. His big books are always leaning against my little books on the shelf.") He was a great teacher, unfailingly generous and hopeful in his estimation of beginning writers. He was busy in intellectual and literary circles, here and in Europe. He was a romantic and a family man (as anyone who reads him can see), and an exceptionally gentle and affectionate father. Many people, of all ages, seemed to find a father in him, in fact, and they are missing him now in a painful and personal fashion. One woman on our staff, a writer, said, "When he was writing a lot, you had this sense that there was someone else sort of like you, living in your city, and saying things that meant something about your life. It was like having a companion in the world." And an older man, also a writer and contributor, said almost the same thing: "He always seemed to be writing about my trashiest thoughts and my night fears and my darkest secrets, but he understood them better than I did, and he seemed to find them sweeter and classier than I ever could. For a long time, I felt I was going to be all right as long as he was around and writing. Having him for a friend was the greatest compliment of my life."

Comment, August, 1989

LONG GONE

DIAL AGAIN

Verizon has applied the branding iron, and starting this week everybody in Manhattan must punch in a 1 and then a 212 (or a 646 or 917) in front of the old local number before talking to his or her office or bookie or life companion or dog-walker or newspaper-delivery service (where was our *Post* yesterday?). It's not such a big deal—I already knew I was a 212—but eleven numbers instead of seven are now required to bring about a conversation, which means a further lowering of the gray digit cloud that hangs over each of us, Pig Pen–like, from the moment we get up in the morning to the time we brush our teeth at night. The added numbers also signal the end of my hopes that the phone company might someday see the error of its integer infatuation and turn back to the exchange letters and (before that) the sprightly full exchange names that once identified us. I've lived at the same Manhattan address for thirty years and in that span have gone from a LEhigh 4 prefix to LE 4 to 534 and now to 1-212-534, which is the wrong direction. Yes, there are zillions more number variations now available than what can be wrung out of those puny alphabet groups jammed onto your Touch-Tone, but let's try harder. Why not some fresh exchanges instead? Why not WEevil 3? What about OSiris 4? What's wrong with LUst 7, BOwwow 9, or LInoleum 6? The number I know best, next to my own, belongs to our friends Allan and Marie, who have converted their drab, Upper West Side 496–5844 into the mnemonic GYM LUGG.

I'm an old New York guy, and can recall the day in 1930 when our ATwater 8435 took an extra digit and became ATwater 9-8435. Growing up, I began to apprehend that Manhattan telephone exchanges, which were geographically assigned, were a guide map and social register to my delightful city. West Side school friends of mine could be reached at the MOnument or CAthedral or RIverside exchange. My father worked at the WHitehall exchange, down near Wall Street, and my mother at the mid–West Forties' BRyant 9. BUtterfield 8 was just south of us on the Upper East Side, with TRafalgar, REgent, and RHinelander not far away. When my parents were divorced and my mother moved to East Eighth Street, she became a SPring 7, and neighbors and stores and movie theatres in that neighborhood had lively ALgonquin, CHelsea, and WAtkins handles. If you called up one of the Times Square movie theatres, to find the next showtime for "Cimarron" or "Rasputin and the Empress," the exchange was probably LOngacre. In my early teens, I was in love with a girl named Rosie, who lived a dozen blocks away, and we passed endless, almost wordless half hours together on the phone, ATwater and ENdicott breathing as one, until the inexorable "Oop, my dad—bye."

Folks all over New York (and all over the country) have similar names and allusions deep inside them, and once sensed the social significance of a nice exchange number. Bruce, a colleague of mine, grew up in the Grand Concourse area of the Bronx, with a home WEllington 5 exchange that wasn't as tony, he says, as BAinbridge, over near Mosholu Parkway. My wife, a Queens girl, understood that her own HAvermeyer 8 exchange was better—"but only a little better"—than her grandmother's NEwtown 9. It's my theory that, back in the telephonic Eocene, New York Tel wanted to comfort its better patrons with exchange names that suggested brokerage firms or Waspy lawyers, and came up with WIckersham, VAnderbilt, BOgardus, BArclay, and BUtterfield. RHinelander looks snooty, too, but is ethno-geographical if you think about it, since most of its customers lived in the Germanic, East Eighty-sixth Street area of Yorkville. Later Manhattan exchanges like OXford and my own LEhigh, which were tacked on in the fifties, lacked the lime-flower-tea cachet. My friend Tad remembers moving into Manhattan from the suburbs a little after this and being issued a new YUkon number. "That's when I knew I was an outsider in the big city," he said. "I was hanging on by my fingernails."

Two old tunes about Manhattan telephone exchanges: 1. Glenn Miller's "PEnnsylvania 6-5000," which was the phone number of the Pennsylvania Hotel, where Miller (and Benny Goodman, too) often played the Madhattan Room. 2. Fleecie Moore's "Caledonia"—a girl named for the exchange, as in "CaleDOHNNyah, whatmakes-yourbigheadsohard?"

Back in the time of John O'Hara's 1935 novel "BUtterfield 8"—which is to be called "1-212-288" in future editions—people never heard a recorded message when they made a call. If they needed help, they got to talk to an operator. On page 38, a man is trying to reach a New York girl he hasn't seen in years. "Will you try that number again, please?" he says. "It's Stuyvesant, operator. Are you dialling S,T,U? . . . Well, I thought perhaps you were dialling S,T,Y." But nobody's home.

Talk, February, 2003

THE CRIME OF OUR LIFE

Burglaries and street robberies in New York City have declined by an astounding eighty per cent since 1990, and even lifelong Manhattanites like me have almost forgotten the mixture of anxiety and scary anecdote we all shared back in the seventies and eighties, whatever our address. Leaving a neighborhood bar or coming home from a late movie, you scanned the shadowy sidewalk up ahead and slipped out into the empty car lane if you saw anyone approaching. Street gutters glistened with smashed window glass, and, locking up your VW in a fresh parking space, you left a pleading note on the dashboard: "No drugs, no radio, no nothing." Neighborhood mayhem back then terrified and shamed us all, and gave out-of-towners another reason to hate New York; if you were off visiting an aunt in Topeka or Missoula and told a neighbor where you came from, you'd get a two-beat pause and then the unvarying "Right in it?" Crime had become another garish New York inconvenience: something else to put up with and try to manage with a bit of cool.

Stories abounded. My colleague Philip Hamburger, an instant before his second or perhaps third street mugging, heard the perp voice behind him murmur, "Sorry, Mister, but you're going down." Jay, a West Village filmmaker, told me that he was fed up with crime and had armed himself against muggers with extensive karate lessons—and won himself a trip to the E.R. at St. Vincent's when his chance came up, on Horatio Street, shortly thereafter. An upstairs neighbor in our East Nineties walkup had a better defensive plan: the Insta-Scream. When I heard familiar high-pitched screechings from our street-level vestibule one night, I said, "Oop, that must be Kevin again," and buzzed him safely in.

A bit before this, perhaps back in the late fifties, Gerald Murphy, the iconic painter and style-setter, heard stories like this and prepared himself (he was in his upper seventies by then) by search-

ing out an ancient but stylish little sword-umbrella left to him
years before by his father, the owner of the Fifth Avenue leather
shop Mark Cross. Coming home via Central Park late one spring
afternoon, Gerald was confronted by five or six lurking teen-agers,
who asked him for a light. Unclicking the blade, he cried, "A light!
A light—I'll give you a light!," and swished it about in the manner of Douglas Fairbanks. The kids, unaware of any gleams of steel
in the twilight, laughed wildly, then closed in, until the tip of the
blade pinked one of them on the arm. "Yow—a fuckin' sword!" he
cried, and they vanished like squirrels over an embankment.

Carol and I somehow missed the early flooding waves of
apartment-house break-ins, and we felt almost a sense of belonging
the evening we came up the stairs and saw our removed apartment
front door neatly propped against an adjacent wall. A bit later,
while we were counting our losses, Carol emerged from her closet
with a favorite blue dress over her arm. "And what was wrong with
this, I'd like to know," she said indignantly.

Along about this time, our friends Bobbie and Spencer Klaw
were at home one Saturday night in their modest brownstone on
Charlton Street with three of their four daughters and Bob Schultz,
a young son-in-law, when they heard frantic sustained barking aris-
ing from the basement just below, from Jessie, a Lab puppy shut
away there for house-training. Spencer, rushing to the cellar stairs,
encountered a slight man carrying a knife, with a bandanna across
his face. "Take it easy," he said. "I need a hundred dollars."

Spence, somehow mistaking this insane housebreaking for a
prank, said, "I don't know who you are, but this is really in bad
taste." He snatched off the bandanna, revealing a stranger: an addict
in need of a hundred bucks.

There was some jittery wallet- and pocketbook-scrabbling, but
the home team could only come up with about sixty-five, combined. "There's gotta be more, so show me," the man said, nod-

ding toward Bobbie. She and the crook went up the narrow stairs together, toward the bedrooms, with the man calling back, "I got the lady, so don't call the cops or nothing."

Left alone, the living-room Klaws consulted in whispers, telling themselves that they had a big advantage in numbers. "Look, Spence," Bob Schultz said, "if I stand over beside this lamp you can say something to get his attention and I'll conk him from behind—O.K.?"

Positions were taken. Bobbie and the man clumped back down. There was a terrifying scuffle, then a frozen tableau but no bloodshed. In final negotiations, the man grabbed Spencer's watch and his empty wallet but declined proffers of the girls' piggy banks or Becky's flute. "Are you sure?" Bobbie said. "It's a really nice one." A minute later, he'd put away his knife and slipped out the door.

Oh, yes—the lamp. Telling me about it a week or so later, Spencer said, "Roger, if you're ever going to hit somebody over the head with a table lamp, remember to unplug it first."

Post, June, 2013

PAST MASTERS: VLADIMIR NABOKOV

LO LOVE, HIGH ROMANCE

Poised and trim in midshelf among its distinguished, self-assured, and sometimes overweight family of Nabokovs, "Lolita" has kept its paradoxical allure even in middle age, perpetually inviting us for a return visit. With a new movie version about to open in England and France, and waiting in the wings for an American distributor— Jeremy Irons has taken on the Humbert role, which was played with such classic understatement by James Mason in the 1962 film by Stanley Kubrick—there will never be a better moment to go back to the elegant, uneasily beautiful novel itself and ask ourselves again what the author could have had in mind. If we feel cautious about a reunion, it cannot be from doubt about the merits of this horrific comic masterpiece, or even from an urge to preserve those splashings of pleasure and surprise that came with an unforgotten first reading. Rather, there may be an unwillingness to subject our numbed contemporary responses to these once notorious doings. It would be an almost incommensurable loss if the tale had turned docile because its famous and deplorable theme—the double seduction of twelve-year-old Dolores, or Lolita, Haze, subteen incarnate, by her suave and pederastic European stepfather, Humbert Humbert, and (it turns out) of him by her, Hum by Lo—now felt only like another sedative shocker or case history on the talk-show circuit.

We look on these matters differently now, to put it mildly. Monster child molesters, just sentenced or about to be released from custody, are the subject of mall demonstrations and gloomy op-ed musings, while book reviews invite us to pay attention to the latest true-life confession, sometimes given the soft backlighting of fiction, about somebody's charmingly concupiscent dad or the restored memories of another miserably suppressed and fumbled-over childhood. It's not much of a stretch to envision Humbert and Lolita, each in Reeboks, sitting side by side onstage at "The Jenny Jones Show" and proudly staring out at us from the screen (he is wearing a Chicago Bulls jersey) while the giveaway headlines appear in turn beneath them in the close-ups: "Has sex with his late wife's kiddie daughter" and "He doesn't know she's been doing it with her drama teacher." In no time, the stage will be stuffed with other, almost identical couples, each proclaiming a similar creepy proclivity and prepared to shout back at the tauntings of the titillated but never quite shocked studio audience.

Conspicuous by rumor long before it saw print, "Lolita," Vladimir Nabokov's twelfth novel, was turned down, on content, by four American publishers before its initial publication, in 1955, by the Olympia Press, in Paris. When Putnam brought it out here, in August, 1958, it already bore a postscript by the author, commenting with brisk pleasure on the disappointment of some readers who had become bored when its erotic early scenes were not continued or amplified in the tale, and on the letdown of others who found "no moral in tow." Critical response in this country was, well, *tense,* ranging from brave lit crit (Harvard's Harry Levin saw the book as "a symbol of the aging European intellectual coming to America, falling in love with it but finding it, sadly, a little immature") to sounds of vein-swelling outrage (the *Times'* Orville Prescott, in a

famous venting, called it repulsive, and "dull, dull, dull in a preten-
tious, florid and archly fatuous fashion"—a notice, of course, that
may have served as starter's pistol for the book's bolt to the front of
the best-seller lists, where it stayed for six months).

Other readers' reactions back then, including my own, reflected
a struggle between a private, perhaps unconscious anguish over the
story's sexual complexity and a dazzled admiration for its satiric
brilliance and literary weight. Katharine White, Nabokov's longtime editor at *The New Yorker,* told him in a letter that, as one with
five potential nymphets in the family, including "a golden-skinned,
thin-armed nine-year-old," she had been made "thoroughly miserable" by the book, in spite of her recognition of its virtuosity.
Apparently, no consideration was given to publishing "Lolita" in
the magazine, in whole or in part, and Nabokov had been specific
in his instructions to White that the typescript he had sent her
not be shown to William Shawn, the editor. A reflexive protection
of Shawn's supposedly delicate feelings—this time by an author,
of all people—was almost customary practice, but this example
appears peculiar from a distance, since it was *The New Yorker*'s own
thoughtful and unstintingly appreciative review of the book, com-
missioned by Shawn and written by the late Donald Malcolm (and
published in November, 1958), that Nabokov declared to be his
own favorite. Nothing about "Lolita," then or now, is free of irony.

Responding to the anxious "Why did Nabokov *do* it?" question
of that day, Malcolm proposed that "the artistic (as against the clinical) interest of the novel is all the justification its story requires,"
and the book, even when it is read for a second or third time, still
refreshes and startles with its inundating flow of high invention:
Humbert, the cosmopolitan pervert and logomath, self-presented,
with personal history, first marriage, and fatal predilection attached;
"nymphet" defined and personified (what other new word and anar-
chic concept has slithered as swiftly into the language?); the sepa-

rate deaths of Humbert and Lolita announced, disconcertingly, in the italics of a foreword; a murderee, the evanescent Quilty, identified as if by accident; and so on. Humbert, ensconced chez Haze in small-town America, groans and quivers at each gesture of his inamorata, the unremarkable pubescent Dolores, for he has incarnated in her an avid lost predecessor from his childhood. Almost as an aside, he marries the child's widowed mother, the over-available Charlotte (it is a means of holding on to his ghastly perch), and, after barely averting a clumsy uxoricide, is miraculously set free— the rest of the story leaps into view at the same instant, Mom and the whole social order done in at the same stroke—by a tiny street accident. Toying with us, the author-plotter gives four careful pages to planning the almost perfect drowning of Charlotte before changing his mind ("The fatal gesture passed like the tail of a falling star across the blackness of the contemplated crime"), and then offs her, by passing Packard, in a paragraph. These first hundred-odd pages of "Lolita" are a soap and a half.

If the infamous erotic passage (Humbert robed and aflame in purple silk dressing gown, with the sunburned girleen, all apple and indolence, half lying upon him on a shared davenport) has lost any of its reptilian allure, it is because of its own celebrity: "There she lolled in the right-hand corner, almost asprawl, Lola the bobby-soxer, devouring her immemorial fruit, singing through its juice, losing her slipper, rubbing the heel of her slipperless foot in its sloppy anklet, against the pile of old magazines heaped on my left on the sofa—and every movement she made, every shuffle and ripple, helped me to conceal and to improve the secret system of tactile correspondence between beast and beauty—between my gagged, bursting beast and the beauty of her dimpled body in its innocent cotton frock."

Nabokov's first and best joke was this tactical coup of placing himself within the first person of Humbert, from which vantage he is free to boast and confess, interrupt and explain, to lecture, to double back, to evoke, to pant and bemoan, and, generally, to set loose an ironic playfulness that deepens and disarms horror. In "The Magician," an earlier, never published short-story version of the same basic situation, Nabokov clung to the third person and did not arrive at the debauching of the child until the final pages, after which his pre-Humbertian protagonist, called Arthur, threw himself under the wheels of a truck. Missing was the lyrical exuberance, the incautious "I," that sets the novel free in its very first lines: "Lolita, light of my life, fire of my loins. My sin, my soul. Lo-lee-ta: the tip of the tongue taking a trip of three steps down the palate to tap, at three, on the teeth. Lo. Lee. Ta."

Early readers who were scandalized by Humbert's furtive Sunday-morning spasm must have been baffled by the author-seducer's advance invitation to "participate" in the drama and to "see for themselves how careful, how chaste, the whole wine-sweet event is if viewed with . . . 'impartial sympathy.' " He has us there; even today, the paradox defies us, breathtaking and awful even as we watch it coming and understand how it has been brought about. How can we loathe this creature while his keeper stands there smiling beside him, or within him, sardonically in charge? How can we dismiss the one or hope to go on without the other?

Games are central to the novel, but I think we are a little more at ease with Nabokov's prodigious brightness today, and, now that a couple of generations of grad-school section men have had at the work, perhaps more free simply to enjoy whichever figures and cryptic messages swim up to us from within the patterned and enigmatical text. We no longer feel the need to test ourselves or top each other, I mean, and can settle for a cheerful pass-fail. For me, the author's joyfulness often matters more than his oracular gifts. Although I was tickled to spot the villain's name hiding within the murmuration of *"comme le lac est beau car faut qu'il t'y mène,"* and was startled when the recurrent minor character Vivian Dark-bloom, this time glimpsed as "the bare shoulders of a hawk-like, black-haired, strikingly tall woman," became the author himself, anagrammatized and in drag, I took almost more pleasure in some direct hits: the brusque, two-word expunging of Humbert's mother within a parenthesis "(picnic, lightning)"; or "a row of parked cars, like pigs at a trough"; or a Nabokovian hydrant—"a hideous thing, really . . . extending the red stumps of its arms to be varnished by the rain which like stylized blood dripped upon its argent chains."

Most of the ironic riffs have kept their zing—stepdad Humbert, reading up on the difficult teen years in a book called "Know Your Own Daughter," or the unforgettably awful Miss Pratt, a school principal, discussing the sexual-maturing process with the appalled (appalled by jargon) Hum. But the author's celebrated connoisseur-ish observations of the American roadside encampments where the guilty couple pause or sleep over during their travels, with "the would-be enticements of their repetitious names—all those Sun-set Motels, U-Beam Cottages, Hillcrest Courts, Pine View Courts, Mountain View Courts, Skyline Courts" (what a gourmandish, Continental relish Nabokov took in their listing and naming), feel dated and sadly sweetened today. Had we been as medianed, I-95'd, and Best Westernized back then as we are now, where would our weird lovers and their master have found their rest?

ITS APEX OF IRONY traversed at the instant when the captive child, whispering in the debaucher's ear, lets him know that she has been there and done that ("For quite a while my mind could not separate into words the hot thunder of her whisper, and she laughed, and brushed the hair off her face, and tried again, and gradually the odd sense of living in a brand new, mad new dream world, where everything was permissible, came over me as I realized what she was suggesting"), "Lolita" now shifts beneath our feet and becomes a different story altogether. Humbert, given his way, becomes obsessed not with passion but with the anxiety of the mundane. During their year of travels, a coast-to-coast-and-back, twenty-seven-thousand-mile hegira of burgers and wilderness, "cottage-cheese-crested salads" and backwater burgs, he must protect their drab secret by enlisting Lo as a co-conspirator and, in addition, must see to it that his depraved darling is fed and entertained and kept in passable temper—kept as companion as well as paramour—and, within limits, also permitted to be herself, act her age. Not surprisingly, he finds her brattish and exasperating, "a disgustingly conventional little girl," subject to "fits of disorganized boredom, intense and vehement griping, her sprawling, droopy, dopey-eyed style, and what is called goofing off." In no time, she turns idly whorish, too, enhancing her allowance by the blackmail of withheld sexual favors. "There is nothing more atrociously cruel than an adored child," Humbert sighs. Embarrassed, he finds it necessary to apologize to the reader for his unexpected fall from pure lust, and insists that "in the possession and thralldom of a nymphet the enchanted traveler stands, as it were, *beyond happiness*."

More is going on here than dark comedy or a farcical switching of sympathies, for Humbert has been visited not just with a hellish particularity but with the deeper affliction of recognizing truth. Late at night, feigning sleep, he hears Lolita weeping in the dark, and must admit as well that "it had become gradually clear to my conventional Lolita during our singular and bestial cohabitation that even the most miserable of family lives was better than the parody of incest, which, in the long run, was the best I could offer the waif." Lionel Trilling wrote, "Less and less is it a *situation* that we see [in "Lolita"]; what we become aware of is people. Humbert is perfectly willing to say that he is a monster; we find ourselves less and less eager to agree with him."

Nabokov's elusiveness, it dawns on us, is not just playful. Forever changing sides and withholding judgment, he has contrived to
forestall both our outrage at his nasty hero and our contemptuous
dismissal of his trivial, complicit Juliet. His irony is never patronizing or angry, and for this alone he appears—what shall we call
it?—premodern in his patient seriousness and relentless search for
another level. Almost ruefully, we sense that by reserving some
fragment of sympathy for readers who saw their own daughters or
granddaughters or friends' daughters personified in Dolores and
still wanted them innocent, we have insisted on a type, while deny-
ing evidence of the possible; there is the thrill of adventure in this
shift within ourselves, however oddly and painfully it has come
to pass. Nobody was ever seduced by a book, Jimmy Walker is
believed to have said, but that was before Lo.

For me, what happens midstream in "Lolita"—just before her
elopement with the evil and offstage Quilty—is an even more
indelible business than the deepening madness of the later pages,
with that recapitulative, spellbound return tour by Humbert of
the haunted motels and hamlets he had frequented with Lo, and
the dreamlike assassination of Quilty, visible at last and intolerably
loquacious even as he is being shot down and repunctured during
his operatic end. What I go back to is a passage where Dolores, a
bit older now, is playing tennis, Hum-watched with such intensity
that nothing else matters: "My Lolita had a way of raising her bent
left knee at the ample and springy start of the service cycle when
there would develop and hang in the sun for a second a vital web
of balance between toed foot, pristine armpit, burnished arms and
far back-flung racket, as she smiled up with gleaming teeth at the
small globe suspended." On and on he goes for a page, then another
page, of on-court Lo ("her nimble, vivid, white-shod feet"; "the
polished gem of her dropshot"), an absurd sportswriter who even
envisions her at Wimbledon one day, along with "her gray, humble,

hushed husband-coach, old Humbert." Almost before he says it, we
know what has happened. "Did I ever mention that her bare arm
bore the 8 of vaccination? That I loved her hopelessly? That she was
only fourteen?" The moment is sealed with a Nabokovian flourish:
"An inquisitive butterfly passed, dipping, between us."

No one can be more reluctant than I to search out a weightier, less playful substratum in a work of sustained comic pleasure,
but we are in the proprietor's hands here, and there appears to be
little doubt about his intentions. For all its glittering distractions
and diversions, this is a love story, after all—an unexpected grand
romance, with a poignance and conviction that match anything in
our old box of American valentines: "A Farewell to Arms," "The Age
of Innocence," "Ethan Frome," "The Scarlet Letter," "Sister Carrie,"
"The Great Gatsby," and more. Eloquent Humbert is alone at the
end, and all his joys have become heartbreaking and ridiculous. A
persistent sadness infects what has gone before and what will come
next. The given condition of "Lolita," one unexpectedly recalls, is
that we have been permitted to read this story only because both
lovers are dead: the child Dolores is to die of her child, die while
giving birth, and Humbert will succumb to coronary thrombosis,
a broken heart.

Another three years must go by, late in the book, before Humbert, still on the trail of Quilty, finds his lost Dolores—Dolly Schil-
ler now, pregnant and married to a luckless young mechanic. No
matter: "There she was with her ruined looks and her adult, rope-
veined narrow hands and her gooseflesh white arms, and her shal-
low ears, and her unkempt armpits. . . . I looked at her and looked
at her, and knew as dearly as I know I am to die, that I loved her
more than anything I had ever seen or imagined on earth, or hoped
for anywhere else." And: "Lolita, pale and polluted, and big with
another's child, but still gray-eyed, still sooty-lashed, still auburn

and almond, still Carmencita, still mine; *Changeons de vie, ma Carmen, allons vivre quelque part où nous ne serons jamais séparés;* Ohio?"

He offers her money, four thousand dollars, for her missed trousseau, and unhesitatingly asks her to leave with him—leave on the spot, come as she is and live happily ever after. She can't believe the money and she can't believe *him.* "No," she says, turning him down. "No, honey, no." It is her first endearment—almost the first time, come to think of it, that she has noticed him at all—and perhaps the first moment that we see him clear. This is the Humbert we once recoiled from while he masturbated over a purloined sock belonging to the child Lo, but we can forgive him now, perhaps even tearily, because we recognize that it is not obsession but delusion that has brought him down—the oldest delusion in the world but one we have all suffered from at one time or another, and, with any luck, may fall victim to again any day now.

Books, August, 1997

GREETINGS, FRIENDS!

Frank Sullivan was the inventor of *The New Yorker*'s delightful "Greetings, Friends!" Christmas card in 1932, and sustained it with but a single interruption for the next forty-one years. I was his editor in the late stretch in this epochal run, and, with some hesitation and much screeching of gears took it over in 1976, after his departure. Ian Frazier succeeded me in 2012 and continues to bring the sweet old chestnut vividly back to life each December.

Early on, I described my "Greetings" within its lines as "this dogged caterwaul," and said it again the following year, when it became "a catatonic doggerel." Knocking off fifty-six rhymed couplets that playfully and sometimes gracefully hail several dozens of famous to anonymous statesmen and jockeys and ballerinas, plus a few slipped-in neighbors and friends' babies, turned out to be the toughest beat I'd ever encountered, and by far the most fun. A sample couplet perhaps shows why: "Come, Will Morris; come, Maury Wills: / Make with the tonsils for Beverly Sills." A rhyme of Frank Sullivan's from that 1932 first edition better sums up the whole enterprise: "I greet you all, *mes petits choux:* / I greet the whole goddam *Who's Who.*"

My purpose in writing "Greetings" was purely to entertain, and my working method largely an effort to avoid panic. Initial attempts, beginning each year in late summer or early autumn, produced frantic lists of potential greetees jotted down while my prose-ridden brain tried once again to think in meter and rhyme. (Carol, hearing my finger tapping on the mattress in the dark, sometimes muttered, "You're counting beats again.") Most of the names in my slovenly worksheets never made it into the poem, and some that actually saw print got there—sorry!—only because of a rhyme. Head-of-the-line or mid-line names made it on merit.

Selecting names that mixed and matched, and echoed, ideally, with only a vague celebrity, was lonely work, and I unashamedly called on friends and colleagues to supplement my own top-of-the-head rosters of rappers, philosophers, coaches, divines, Olympians, foreign ministers, racehorses, chefs, fashionistas, and the like. The verse needed to be Christmassy but not sappy, and little bursts of lines and the occasional neat pairing ("With libretti, *con amore,* / For Tipper Gore and skipper Torre") usually turned up just before deadline, and made me laugh, too.

Here are a pleading in-house letter requesting names; a couple of my childlike worksheets; and finished verses of mine from 1998 and 2009.

2015

TO: STAFF
FROM: ANGELL
SUBJECT: CHRISTMAS NAMES/RHYMES

Greetings, Friends and Colleagues!

I need help from each of you with suggested names for our annual Christmas verse. Please consult attached recent samples (there wasn't a verse last year: I blew it), which will give an idea of the kind of people I like to mention. You can include some very obvious celebs—please do—but it's the mid-level name that works best: someone the reader will remember, too, if reminded. But we can have interesting or lively others, as well, from any walk of life or line of work. A perky or unusual name doesn't hurt, but that's not the first requirement. Minority names are a must.

Please send me names of artists, rockers, lesser-known athletes, politicians, documentary filmmakers, dancers, cyberbiggies, bankers, TV talk-show hosts and sit-com or series actors, senators and reps. and lobbyists, sculptors, Olympians, White House types, explorers, Nobelists, jazz or country performers, environmentalists, poets (I love poets), etc., etc., etc. I particularly appreciate women's names, and I like different age groups: the remembered old actor or statesman, and the teen-aged star (Tony Randall/Serena Williams). Foreigners, too, please—premiers, marathoners, political heroes, film directors, conductors, whatever. No bad guys or notorious victims or losers, please: no Jerry Springer; no Tripps, Newts, or Starrs. Instead, give me names you'd like to see in there. Don't be shy and don't worry about being obvious. If every list I get begins with Jesse Ventura, I'll be happy.

I also much appreciate rhymed names, in pairs or more, or even full couplets (I'm shameless) and also names that rhyme with Yuley verbs or adjectives. One way that seems to work is to compare your list with those of other pals here, and then jot down the new names that will surface right away. This is fun, I mean, or should be. And a big P.S.: Assume that I won't know the names you know by heart, so please attach a tag that identifies them.

I need this stuff soon. E-mail is O.K. Many thanks: thanks to you all. None of you will get any credit for this, except in my heart.

Undated

LATE A-LIST

- Rory Stewart
  Simon Jones   and meet
  David Wright
  Haskeem Thabeet
  Peter Sellars
  Nico Muhly
           yours truly
  Bjork and Bo

- CAPTAIN SULLY
  Colson Whitehead
  JAY-Z   Nico Colson
- Frank Bruni
  Katherine Bigelow   not back
  Robert Gates
  Danica Patrick
  Freeman Dyson

- Michael Wie
- Ang Lee
  Robert Gibbs
- Sotomayor   "justice"
                  upon

me nuts   Casey Keith + Ron
networks Robert Gates
          Leon Botstein
          Ronzo Piano
          Peter Orszag
- CHLOE SEVIGNY   poopy beat   wait sorry
  Steven Chu

Ethan Canin
Kurus Vonnegut
Stella McCartney
        nso
  choose those cruz
  Penelope

Champagne Whitesceano
          Eric Holder
  we've chesapeake
          grocery coller
  Sonia Sotomayor

  Reazo Piano
  Janet Napolitano

Faded classmates now in Pecos,

Girlfriends gone to Turks and Caicos;

Valued readers (sometimes dozing),

Tennis partners (or opposing);

Colleagues ~~either~~ hailed *upon* the stairway

Gone, alas, to grave or fairway .

I hail you each, dears, tho' in absentia

And rue the rhymes I never sent ya .

~~Kith from Cancun, friends from Denver~~

I see you, dears, tho' now less clearly

And hug you *each* ~~here~~ almost sincerely

..

nice?

better

it's OK but

~~I see you, dears, tho' now less clearly~~

~~And love you each ...~~

GREETINGS, FRIENDS!

Dear hearts and friends, huzzah, well met,
Regathered from the Internet;
God bless you each wherever reachable,
And keep you hale and unimpeachable.
Pals, note this page, this poet's cottage,
Freshly wreathed with major wattage;
Blazing waits in neon raiment
Grace our rooftop infotainment;
Plus yon Magi, in depiction,
Testing Con Ed's pow'rs of fiction,
Draining volts from here to Yonkers,
Driving all the neighbors bonkers—
Well, never mind: for anodyne
We'll let our softer thoughts incline
Toward Sen. John Glenn, the senior flier,
Judi Dench, and Danny Meyer,
Not forgetting folks to thank
Like Paul O'Neill and Barney Frank.
Or to append a hug or two
For Hedda Sterne and Harry Wu.
Or clap the shoulder, man to man,
Of Daniel Patrick Moynihan.
I wish a most agreeable Yule
To Wyclef Jean, Fintan O'Toole,
Kofi Annan, Anne-Sophie Mutter,

Tony Judt, and Justice Souter;
Nor ask less by a scintilla
For Prince Chas. and his Camilla,
Cameron Diaz, Peter Gomes,
Peter Gammons, and Puffy Combs.
Now gather, gang, and sound a paean—
Fans of life or fans Wrigleyan,
Butcher, baker, cook, or grosa—
Happy Christmas, Sammy Sosa!
Say, David Wells and Two Fat Ladies,
Step aboard my stretch Mercedes
And we'll go mail by Special Handling
Warm thoughts to Seal and Garry Shandling;
And, playing Santa, stuff the socks
Of Chuck Schumer and Michael J. Fox;
And drop off puppies, by comparison,
Chez Darryl Straw and Daisy Garrison.
Renée Fleming! Adam Clymer!
Cheers from this endemic rhymer.
Ho, Sam Raimi, Samuel Ramey;
Yo, John Irving—you, too, Amy!
Bon Noël, Zinedine Zidane,
Pascale van Kipnis, Wu-Tang Clan;
What say, José Saramago;
You Bulls still idle in Chicago:
We hail you all and wish you well
In this reissue of Nowell.
Now, Sister Wendy, come with me
And we'll go sit on Santa's knee,
Joining in a jolly dandle
With Frieda Hughes and Tony Randall,
While Venus Williams finds a lap

Between Mark Green and Gordon Clapp,
Deepening this steamy drama
With Ginger Spice, Simon Schama,
Tori Amos, Cammi Granato,
And, yes, I guess, ol' Al D'Amato.
Ye feathered seraphim, deploy
Fit songs for Arundhati Roy,
And hit selections from on high
For Frances Bean and Evan Bayh,
Plus strains of Bach or Boccherini
For Frank McCourt and Clare Rossini.
Boys choirs, come on!—we count on you,
And Robin Cook and Bob Giroux,
With libretti con amore
For Tipper Gore and skipper Torre,
Chamique Holdsclaw, Dominique Swain,
Sharon Olds, and Shania Twain.
Come New Year's, dears, we'll all be chillin'
With Sharon Stone and Jakob Dylan:
With smiling faces 'round the table
Let's slurp up all the Mumm's we're able,
Growing inly far less nerdy
(More like Vinny Testaverde);
Then gath'ring near the gleaming tree
We'll search out *intime* company
Like Lauren Holly, Ian McKellen,
Iggy Pop, and Polly Mellen.
As midnight bongs, we'll boogie down
With Tony Blair and Tina Brown;
Jeff Van Gundy, Webster Slaughter,
Chelsea Clinton (well-known daughter);
P. D. James, J. D. McClatchy,

David Salle; Itchy, Scratchy;
The Bros. Bush, the babies Hanson;
Adam Moss, and Marilyn Manson!

Our muse is stuck; more luck next time
To those with names we couldn't rhyme.
Felicitations, everyone,
This woeful year is nearly done;
Pray this gentle season lend a
Sense of calm to your agenda,
And may our inmost selves aspire
To higher things, like Mark McGwire!

December, 1998

GREETINGS, FRIENDS!

Good neighbors, hi—but O.M.G.,
The time's at hand again, I see,
To cobble up these Christmas lieder,
Fit for friend or distant reader.
Our deadline's near, so off we go,
Ignoring tweets and vertigo,
Counting beats and storing linage,
Melding Keats and major signage:
Names and rhymes and scenes of winter,
Parties, Magi—hit the printer!
God Jul, old friends, let gladness reign

O'er Sean Penn, then Dennis Lehane;
And season's joy sift slowly down
On Agyness Deyn and Tina Brown,
Jay-Z, Kobe, Simon Schama,
But first of all on Prez Obama:
Hail to the chief, our frequent flier!
Wassail from this creaky crier—
The same, along with love and kisses,
To Michelle and two First Misses.
Yo, Clive Owen! Yay, Jane Brody!
Happy days, Diablo Cody!
V. S. Naipaul, Rafa Nadal,
We hug you one and each, et al.;
Rory Stewart, Nico Muhly,
We admire you more than duly.
Let's carve a niche within these lines
For Mary Karr and Razor Shines,
And scope out Yuley tropes to match
Lady Gaga and Orrin Hatch.
Now choirs of angels wait upon
The Mets' own Gary, Keith, and Ron;
And lay a lissome roundelay
On Peter Gelb and Tyson Gay,
Yuja Wang, Stephenie Meyer,
Michelle Wie, and Pico Iyer.
By bike or sleigh or Segway borne,
We'll tour the 'hood this Christmas morn
And, lightly latte'd, press a call
To wake up Maggie Gyllenhaal.
With Tom DeLay we'll drop a gift
Chez Taylor Branch and Taylor Swift,
And say hello, as is our habit,

To Tim Tebow and Milton Babbitt;
We'll hang these greens beside the doors
Of Wyclef Jean and Michael Kors,
Then bunch up hay and pachysandra
As lunch for Rachel Alexandra.
Then it's on to glögg with Robert Pinsky,
Sarah Smith, Mika Brzezinski,
And hotties ever on the scene
Like Susan Rive and Billy Beane.
Bring bijoux, Santa, if you can
For Mary D. and Steely Dan,
And pleasant toys or duds as well
To buoy Zooey Deschanel,
And action games to seize Prince Andrew,
Paolo Szot, and Mary Landrieu,
Adding stops along your circuit
To please the likes of Brian Urquhart,
Wanda Sykes, William H. Macy,
Robert Gates, and Lorraine Gracey.
This New Year's, dears, to beat the blues,
We've booked a tiny guilt-free cruise:
In distant parts like cool St. Bart's
We'll bare our bods and warm our hearts;
At Zürs or Vail we'll slip downtrail
Betwixt Drew Brees and Milky Quayle;
With Susan Boyle, the startled diva,
We'll tan at Sanibel Captiva,
Or linger in Himal'yan shadow
With Sergey Brin and Rachel Maddow;
Or, saving bucks, just grab a chair
Downstairs from here, in drab Times Square.
But sooner, friends, and by your leave

THIS OLD MAN   101

You'll find us home this Christmas Eve,
While kids and neighbors raise the fir
And pleasing meetings reoccur.
Look, there's Frank and Carla Bruni,
Joe Girardi (not in uni),
With Ethan Canin, midst the crush,
Beside Claire Danes and Geoffrey Rush.
Chamique Holdsclaw! Eric Holder!
Here's some Mumm's that's growing colder,
And now there's dancing—come and choose
Bo or Björk, Penélope Cruz,
Anna Paquin, Renzo Piano,
Or Janet Napolitano:
We'll glide about till dawn comes by,
With Johnny Depp, Anita Desai,
Donald Hall, Beverly D'Anne, and
The Dalton Teachers Marching Band!

This rhyme's run dry, our end is near;
We'll see you guys same time next year,
With these weary thoughts refitted
And names of friends so far omitted.
A happy new year, if you can,
And if not, then just stick to the plan;
Christmas lifts us by design,
And peace on earth's the bottom line.

December, 2009

ICE CREAM AND ASHES

Summer movies aren't about summer and they don't have to open during the summer movie-theatre doldrums. For me, they're the movies that come up in conversation at night with friends on the porch or during a long drive, or even late in bed when somebody says, "What was the name of that movie where the cow falls down a well and everybody's looking for that famous old Irish tenor who's disappeared and—wait a minute, it's, it's—" And you say, "Oh, my God, yes, it was—I know this—it was Ned Beatty!" And the first person says, "Yeah, got it now—Ned Beatty, can you believe? In 'Hear My Song.' I think it was English or maybe Irish but, you know, not Irish. Great movie, remember?"

Summer movies aren't classics and don't always make money, but they make friends. Some of them are counter-classics, like "Remember the Night," the 1940 Barbara Stanwyck–Fred Mac-Murray thing that isn't "Double Indemnity." This time, Fred is a young New York prosecutor who's about to send Barbara away for a jewelry-store shoplifting rap when the trial goes into Christmas recess. Barbara has no place to stay for the holiday, and so Fred, what else, takes her along to his Indiana home, where Mom (Beu-lah Bondi) and the tree and popcorn and songs around the piano and love and tears are waiting; the script is by Preston Sturges, so not to worry. Other summer movies—I'm thinking of "Tremors," that 1990 Kevin Bacon-vs.-underground-monster-worms battle—start off small and end up in multiple sequels and play all year round on back-channel TV. "Trees Lounge," by contrast, opened and disappeared in a nanosecond in 1996, leaving only a handful of fanly conservators to recall Steve Buscemi (who wrote and directed it as well) as a shaky alcoholic slowly driving an ice-cream truck around Valley Stream, Long Island, and making out with the junior-teen Chloë Sevigny.

Another summer movie that sneaks into mind—one of its devotees was the late Saul Steinberg—is pre-suburban by about eighty thousand years. Without access to Con Ed, members of the Ulam tribe have to carry their light and power around with them in a small basket containing smoldering coals. When a careless elder Ulam slips while crossing a swamp and drowns the spark, there's a crisis. Three strong pithecan homeys are dispatched to find and grab off a fresh ember or burning branch from their nearest heat-keeping neighbors, hundreds or perhaps thousands of miles away, who will mash them with a boulder or have them for lunch if they fail. This, in a gourd-shell, is the story line of "Quest for Fire," a captivating 1981 French-Canadian caveman movie, which was recently retrieved via Netflix and, by popular demand, played two nights in a row at my place. No subtitles are offered, since the film's language, created by Anthony Burgess, comes largely in grunts, but different grunts, depending on tribe. The actors' primitive lopings and body language and their styles in rock warfare were choreographed by the celebrity ethnologist Desmond Morris. This exhausts the film's list of stars. Our heroine, Ika (the lithe Rae Dawn Chong), is talkative in a high-pitched-screamy sort of way, coming as she does from the more advanced Ivaka, and she dresses fetchingly in ashes and little—well, actually, nothing—else. Ika knows stuff, like how to make fire with a palm-whirred stick, and—scandalizing the Ulams—frontal sex.

Being non-ironic, "Quest for Fire" will never remind you of those persistent Geico caveman commercials, but it takes on any built-in resistance to Neanderthal entertainment with suavity—my

own disappearing about thirty minutes along, when our three fire
hunters are treed by sabre-toothed lions in a bending, inadequate
sapling. There's a falling-nut joke a little later, though the director,
Jean-Jacques Annaud, isn't after laughs but emotions: long, sweeping shots of thickly vacant landscapes, dotted at one corner by a
minute campfire (the movie was shot in Canada and Scotland and
Kenya); an unexpectedly charming herd of woolly mammoths; and
the prognathous Ron Perlman picking at a bone as he awaits the
dawn of cogitation. There are wolves and bears but no dinosaurs,
and Annaud has you holding your breath when the hairy Naoh
(Everett McGill) nervously throws a stick at a low, menacing appa-
rition he's not seen before: a hut. "Quest for Fire," it turned out, was
never quite a box-office hit, and it wasn't solemn or cheesy enough
for a cult. Catching it again, you remember the terrific music (by
Philippe Sarde) and the kick, back then, of finding friends of yours
who had also just come upon this strange little flick for the first
time and were dying to talk.

                                              Sidebar, June, 2007

TWO EMMAS

Late on February nights when my circling mind returns to our
summer cottage in Maine, it often fastens on the books stuffed
into two narrow but tall bookshelves that face each other there on
opposite sides of our ill-lit living room. Paperbacks for the most
part, they are survivors of a rigorous multi-summer select-and-
toss procedure, which is to say that every one has been read or
reread and then put back up there again for the second or third or
fourth time, perhaps to be read again someday. "Good Behaviour,"
"Endurance," "Framley Parsonage," "Get Shorty," "Daisy Miller,"
"Dracula," "BUtterfield 8," "Goodbye to All That," "Why Did I

Ever," "Oblomov," "The Heart of the Matter," "Sailing Days on the Penobscot," "The Moonstone," "Possession," "Morte d'Urban," "Quartet," "Emma" . . . there are many dozens more. I know these beauties so well that I can see the shelf and almost the slot where each one belongs. Our "Emma" is a slim little hardback, in the old pinkish-red Everyman's Library edition. Three or four of the scattered Evelyn Waughs come in that crimson hardback edition, but "Scoop" was briefly left out in a shower one afternoon—I think by a daughter—and is thus thicker and paler than the others. Other fat books—"Martin Chuzzlewit," "Orley Farm," "The Forsyte Saga," and the like—are in paperback, and wait to get taken down during one of those tedious weeks of Down East fog.

It's a kick for me to think of these arrayed words and sentences and pages sitting in the dark at about nine degrees, with the wind battering at the closed-up shutters and our old house groaning and creaking in the night, and our library waiting there for us to come back again in summer. Then Carol and I and maybe a visiting niece will be sitting on our porch reading, and now and then raising our gaze to the glittering adjacent bay.

There's a sweet dab of guilt attached to rereading. Yes, we really should be into something new, for we need to know all about credit-default swaps and Darwin and steroids and the rest, but not just now, please. My first vacation book this year will be like my first swim, a venture into assured bliss. This summer, I mean, I could be starting with Margaret Drabble's "The Garrick Year," a 1964 novel preserved in a bendy, yellowing old paperback so popular at our place that it resembles a leftover picnic sandwich. It's a short, romantic novel about actors and the theatre and marriage and sex and babies, written when Drabble was twenty-four years old—it's her second novel—and married to an actor, Clive Swift, and both were members of the Royal Shakespeare Company. End of bibliography: this book belongs to Drabble's heroine, Emma Evans, who is married to the dashing, muscular Welsh leading man David Evans, and the mother of their very young children, Flora and Joseph. At the book's beginning, she is bitterly unwilling for him to take them all off, along with their French nanny, from London to Hereford for a festival season of repertory. She loses that battle but little else. Emma, the daughter of a theologian, is tall—taller than David—and sometimes works as a model, and she is extremely, extravagantly intelligent. The book is told in the first person, *her* first person, which means that there are many unsparingly critical and deliciously bitter views of the vanity of actors and the babyish needs of actors' lives and, in many cases, their stupidity. David is not stupid but deeply entranced with himself; their squabbles, while entertainingly harsh and vigorous, are never hostile. They're both still young, though ground down, as she puts it, and it's nearly in relief that Emma begins an almost terminally delayed—they never have any time for each other—love affair with David's boss and director, the successful and attractively grownup Wyndham Farrar.

But never mind all this. What we're here for and why we want to stay in "The Garrick Year" is Emma's eccentric smarts and her egotism and punishing self-assessments. Speaking at one point of two-year-old Flora, she says, "I take her too seriously, my daughter, as I take all others." She finds the tension between herself and Wyndham dismayingly adolescent—"I was shut up once more in an artificial world of waiting"—whereas he and we are rediscovering the terrific sexual power of brains. "You have your attractions, too," he says to her. "The attraction of the difficult."

There are three convincing surprises in the late going (Flora turning on the gas while at play is one of them), but it's the short, flashing bursts of conversation that rush us along. Things keep happening, with people like this around, but never easily or without sadness or letdown. On the plus side also, nobody says, "I love you." Margaret Drabble moved on to write deeper and more accomplished novels after this, but not one of them is quite so alive.

Sidebar, June, 2009

SIX FAREWELLS

BOB FELLER

I watched Bob Feller pitch plenty of times in my youth—there were only eight teams in each league then, and the same visitors turned up again at Yankee Stadium with something like the frequency of a persistent aunt at home. His Cleveland Indians were major rivals of the Yankees in my boyhood and early teens, and the Red Sox nowhere in sight. He'd glare in at the batter over his upraised left shoulder, kick his front leg straight across, and clump down in late delivery and at the same instant, it seemed, the catcher was straightening up with the ball in his mitt again. He threw hard from first to last, and visibly grew old on the mound (he pitched for eighteen seasons, with time out for service in the Navy in the Second World War), even while his fastball kept its shine and zing. He was dour in retirement, and—in my recollection, at least—ungenerous about the feats and fortunes of his star successors.

Feller died yesterday, at ninety-two, but the dream about him, which we all held and shared at one time, had predeceased him by decades. In August, 1936, he came off his father's farm in Van Meter, Iowa, at the age of seventeen and struck out fifteen St. Louis Browns batters in his very first start for the Indians. Three weeks later, he struck out seventeen Philadelphia Athletics, tying an all-time record set by Dizzy Dean. But for many of us the records were secondary to his journey. Fans then, young or old, had little knowledge of the enormous difficulties of baseball at its topmost level, and believed that the heroes on their favorite teams—midsized heroes, by today's measurements—were pretty much like their fathers or older brothers. With a dab of luck, you thought, that could be me someday. Then, just as you were getting ready to throw the fantasy away, Feller arrived and made it come true, not just for a Manhattan schoolboy but for countless young rural Americans already stuck on the farm or down in the mines who envisaged baseball as their path of escape. In the nineteen-seventies and eighties, I heard dozens of players and coaches and managers talk about this—Jim Kaat, the dominating Michigan-born, farm-bred pitcher, and a later Yankee broadcaster, comes to mind—and they all mentioned Bullet Bob Feller, who never played a day in the minors.

That time is gone or malled-over, and the dream perhaps lives on only in Ecuador or Hokkaido. We know everything about baseball now—and probably more stats than the players themselves—but none of it is about us. One of those stats concerns the Opening Day no-hitter that Feller threw against the Chicago White Sox, in 1940, an unmatched feat that I always used to bring up in the form of a terrific stumper: "Name the only major-league game in which the players on one side all ended up with the same averages they'd begun with."

The average is .000, and your average nine-year-old now knows the answer before you've finished asking. Thanks anyway, Bob.

Post, December, 2010

DUKE SNIDER

Duke Snider, the old Dodger hero, died yesterday, and I still feel that I owe him. I saw him play plenty of times, but carry only a fragmented memory of him in action: rounded shoulders, and that thick face tilting while the finish of his big, left-side stroke starts him up the baseline, his gaze fixed on the rising (and often departing) ball. A first-class center fielder, who eagerly closed the angle on line drives. Great arm. Good guy, terrific smile. Hall of Famer. Something smug in me used to relish him, even while I rooted against him. Growing up in Manhattan, I was a Giants fan first of all, a huge Yankees booster in the other league, and caught the Dodgers pretty much only when they played at the Polo Grounds. Which is to say a Willie Mays fan first and always; an awestruck admirer of Mickey Mantle when he succeeded Joe DiMaggio in center for the Yankees, in 1952, and aware of Snider, of course, over there in Ebbets Field: the third-best, or—since he overlapped Joe D.'s tenure by three seasons—maybe the fourth-best fabulous center-field slugger in town but a guaranteed superstar as well. If Snider was great, how much better did that make my guys? I met the Duke once or twice, long after he'd left the game—he was gone before I started writing about baseball—and wanted to apologize for patronizing him in my fan's heart. He didn't mind; he was a self-punisher, not a self-aggrandizer, and I don't think he worried about status.

Younger fans than I, even those in their seventies, may not have grasped how assured and intimate the neighborhood of winning baseball seemed to anyone living here in the city in the nineteen-fifties. The Yankees beat the Dodgers in the World Series in 1949, and played them three more times in the Series over the next nine years, losing only in 1955; they also grabbed championships from the Phillies, the Giants, and the Milwaukee Braves, while losing to the same Braves in 1957. Unaccountably, they hadn't made the World Series in 1954, but the Giants did, and swept the Indians. To put all this another way, sixteen of the twenty World Series participants from 1949 to 1958 were New York teams, as were nine of the ten champions. We took all this by course, and absorbed it by radio, picking up the late-afternoon scores from the newsstand guy's little set while we plunked down a nickel to look at the early innings in their tiny boxes on the front page of the World Telly; a taxi radio on the corner filled us in for another half inning. Probably the Duke had just done something big. Ah, the Duke—how cool that sounded, if we'd known "cool" back then—but, hey, the Yanks would win again, put your money on it.

This was the Golden Age of New York baseball—and so rich was the glow that you almost didn't have to go to the games to feel it around you. Duke Snider's fourth and final World Series—he batted .200 and hit the last of his eleven Series home runs—came in 1959, when his Los Angeles Dodgers beat the Chicago White Sox in six. Willie and my Giants had skipped town, too, for lack of attention, leaving us only with the Mick and that dopey song. So long, Duke.

Post, February, 2011

BOB SHEPPARD

Bob Sheppard, the peerless Yankee public-address announcer, who died yesterday, at the age of ninety-nine, laid his perfect syllables on more than five decades of Yankee lineups, from Joe DiMaggio to Robinson Cano, before being sidelined by illness in 2007. Right to the end, he expected to come back to work almost any day, but he never quite did. He will always be connected with the old Yankee Stadium, from where his voice now eerily comes back to mind more clearly than the looks and shadows of the place itself. A tall, spare, elegant gent—a vertical line of perfect prose—he remained exactly the same, even while the palace around him was losing its profile and waistline, despite rehabs, and eventually had to be wheeled away. Baseball never changes is what we used to think, and Bob Sheppard almost made you believe it.

We visited him at his old stand a few years ago, and on another occasion took time to notice the swift, precise path he took home after the last out:

> Up in the pressbox, every night ends the same way. Herb Steier, a retired *Times* sports copy editor, comes to every game and sits motionless in the third row, his hands in front of him on the long table. He doesn't keep score but watches the action intently, with bright, dark eyes. When the ninth inning comes, he gets up and stands by the railing behind the last row of writers, near the exit, and after the potential final batter of the game has been announced, Bob Sheppard, the ancient and elegant Hall of Fame announcer, comes out of his booth and stands next to him, with a book under his arm. (He reads novels or works of history between announcements.) Eddie Layton, the Stadium organist, is there, too, wearing a little skipper's cap. Eddie has a private yacht—well, it's a mini-tug, called *Impulse*—that he keeps on the Hudson, up near Tarrytown. He gets a limo ride to the Stadium most days from his apartment in Queens—it's in his contract—and a nice lift home with Bob Sheppard and Herb Steier at night. Eddie and Bob Sheppard make a bet on every single Yankees game—the time of the game, the total number of base runners, number of pitches by bullpen pitchers, whatever—but won't tell you which one of them is ahead. The stakes are steady: a penny a game.

Steier is Sheppard's neighbor, out in Baldwin, Long Island, and he drives him to work every day and home again at its end; they're old friends. Sheppard, a stylish fellow, is wearing an Argyle sweater and espadrilles tonight. This is his fiftieth year on the job at Yankee Stadium, and once in a while I ask him to enunciate a player's name for me, just for the thrill of it. " 'Shi-ge-to-shi Ha-se-ga-wa,' " he'll respond, ringing the vowels. It sounds like an airport.

The instant the last batter strikes out or pops up or grounds out Sheppard and Steier and Layton do an about-face and depart at a slow sprint. Out the door they go and turn right in the level corridor, still running. A few kids out there are already rocketing down the tilted runways. "Start spreadin' the noooss . . . " comes blaring out from everywhere (the Yanks have won again), but Bob and Herb and Eddie have turned right again, into the quiet elevator lobby, where the nearer car awaits them, its door open. Down they go and out at street level, still at a careful run. Herb's car, a beige 1995 Maxima, is in its regular slot in the team parking lot, just across the alley—the second car on the right. They're in, they're out, a left turn up the street, where they grab a right, jumping onto the Deegan, heading home. The cops there have the eastbound traffic stopped dead, waiting for Bob Sheppard: no one else in New York is allowed to make this turn. Two minutes, maybe two-twenty, after the game has ended and they're gone, home free, the first of fifty thousand out of the building, every night.

In 1982, Sheppard took a short vacation trip to New England while the Yankees were away on a road swing, and while in Boston paid a visit to Fenway Park, where his local counterpart, the Red Sox's announcer Sherm Feller, persuaded him to take the micro-

phone for a courtesy inning. By wonderful coincidence, his first batter was Reggie Jackson, now playing for the California Angels after
his five notable years in the Bronx.

"Now batt-ing," Sheppard intoned, "numb-er for-ty-fourr,
Regg-ie Jack-sson, for-ty-four."

Reggie, standing in, dropped his bat and looked straight up to
heaven.

Post, July, 2010

EDITH OLIVER

Edith Oliver was the almost perpetual Books editor of The New Yorker
as well as its Off Broadway drama critic.

I'm sad but also eager to say a few words about our colleague
Edith, who was such a pal to us all. Almost every day at our old
offices on the uptown side of Forty-third Street I'd find an excuse to
drop in on her, in her niche next to the stairs—to pass on a joke (I
can still hear that smoky laugh), or talk about a book or a movie,
or invite her into a shared groan over some bottomless paragraph
or pious Comment piece that had somehow found its way into the
comic weekly.

"Yes!" she would cry hoarsely, stabbing out her cigarette.
"Godawful. The worst ever. Bill Shawn has a lot to answer for this
week, baby. I give up."

The pattern was always the same: enthusiasm or outrage flung
out in introductory one- or two-word chunks, then a three- or four-
word development, and then the swift concluding flurry of annoy-
ance, agreement, shared glee.

She was a born enthusiast, even in her discontents, and she was
delightfully complicit. Whatever you and she were ripping up or

raving over, she made you feel that the two of you were in on it together, like kids in a tree-house—pals for life or at least for these two minutes. I always went back upstairs to my office feeling better, and often with some outrageous compliment still burning my ears. Often when a piece or a story or a book or even a play had come up with us, she would say, "*You* should have written it. It would have been better." This is the kind of stuff we have wanted to hear from our parents, of course, but Edith saw no reason to hold it back, and then she would laugh with you at such blather. "You're the best ever," she would tack on. "You know it."

She was sharp and quick and passionate in her judgments, but also profoundly loyal, which allowed her to say deadly things about people she knew without seeming to betray them. "The worst liar in the history of the world!" was her sentence one day on a man we deeply admired and respected, but she had taught me by then not to be shocked by candor. Edith knew how complicated and godawful we all are, and didn't mind a little savaging when it was called for. This freed her from small talk, and made you treasure her as a friend, even in absentia. Whenever you let her down with something dumb or careless you'd said or done or written, you knew she would soon be groaning or shuddering about it with somebody else, another friend—but that she still cared about you as much as before. I don't know any greater compliment.

Theatre friends of Edith's at this gathering will be talking about her as a critic, and I would only offer that here, too, she was a true pal. She never allowed the weight of her expertise or the privilege of her post or the passing insult to her intelligence to creep into her reviews. She never allowed herself to sound like a critic, that is. She was somebody you knew who cared about the theatre, and here was what she had seen and liked this week—or, too bad, didn't much like this time, except for the professional lighting and extremely useful set design. She always sounded like herself. She was loyal to the theatre but not in awe of it or pissed off by it: what more could one ask?

She was more loyal than the Boy Scouts and Lassie and Nathan Hale rolled into one. She was loyal to E. M. Forster and Cole Porter and Bob and Ray and Victor Pritchett and Lanford Wilson and Bill Shawn and her family and Fred and Ginger and to everybody here, her pals.

If it would bring her back, I'd take up smoking again, in a minute.

Tribute, Summer, 1998

MICHAEL MULDAVIN

Mike's arrival at Pomfret School in the fall of 1936, where he joined our junior class—there were about twenty of us—seems mysterious, almost magical, even now. Pomfret was a small place, and insular. There were about a hundred and twenty boys, in all, scattered over five terms—I mean *years*. In class, we were narrower: Long Island Republican and Episcopalian, with a scattering of Catholics and Democrats, and headed mostly for Yale. There was one Jewish kid; no African Americans, no girls. I was a New York City boy who'd grown up in an intellectual, divorced household, where my father— soon to become the National Chairman of the A.C.L.U.—let me speak my mind at all times. When Mike arrived I was already used to being a semi-outcast at Pomfret, but then suddenly here was Michael Semyon Muldavin, a suave, multilingual leftist with immense charm, spikey tan hair, a great laugh, an exotic faraway address, and a charming, gentle manner that ingratiated him with everyone—the old boys, the faculty, the faculty wives, even the football players. He saved my bacon. He knew a million times more than I did about the T.V.A., the Scottsboro Boys, the Comintern, Rexford Guy Tugwell, the Brownshirts, the Soong Sisters, Leon Blum, Sergei Eisenstein, Leon Trotsky, Diego Rivera, La Pasionaria, and the American Fruit Company, but he could talk about them—in history class or while watching an Achaeans vs. Ionians league hockey game, or late at night in a dorm—in a quiet way that held everyone's attention. Soon he and I were outcasts together, but that estate had become more respectable, almost desirable, and other smart kids began to edge our way. In our senior year, where Mike became one of the great assets of the Class of 1938, he sang in the glee club, appeared in the French Dramatic Club plays, and helped found a new debating society, the ProCon, where he was named best debater and also—it wasn't a known category—*kindest* debater. I remember him concluding an incisive and complex little talk he gave to the entire school one morning on some subject—it's long since gone—because he concluded it with a smile and slight bow, and said, "Thank you." Thank you for *what*? No one had said this before—not even one of our teachers. Why, thank you for listening, of course. Thank you for thinking about this with me. A bit of civilization, a touch of class, had descended on us.

The next year Mike and I were happy as freshman roommates at Harvard, in a top-floor double of Straus Hall. We had a bicycle built for two and scooted around Boston and Cambridge, under the trees. We biked downtown for movies or dinner, then biked home. I think he sat in front but maybe we switched around. We were both in the Student Union—he full-bore, I more idly. He was part of the Communist Left, then contesting for control of the Union—and a difficult position because of the onrushing war in Europe and the coming Stalinist entente with Hitler. Often when I'd come back to our room late from Widener there would be four or five serious S.U. guys there talking. They'd drop their voices when I came in and look at me in baleful fashion. Sometimes I put my arm across my face like a cloak, which deepened their mistrust, but it cracked Mike up.

We talked endlessly, in our room and at classes and meals. I wasn't bad in political debate but he was better. Once, at breakfast, I remember crying, "You just shifted your grounds!" And Mike said, "You noticed!" And we laughed again.

That spring we got involved in a union strike against a local Cambridge taxi company, and some ugly-looking guys—members of the union's "Education Committee"—used our phone to send scab drivers to distant addresses, where they got beaten up or had their tires slashed. Or so I was told. Soon, in any case, the strike was won but we had no phone. Mike had been the one supposedly in charge of handling our joint phone bill but late in the year our service was terminated for lack of payment. I protested and Mike said, "Don't worry. I know how to handle this sort of thing." He came back that day with a stamped, signed slip of paper from the Bell Telephone Company showing that our accumulated four-month bill of about seventy bucks had been settled in full for fifty-five.

"Wow!" I said.

"Never give in to the cartels," Mike said gravely.

"And the phone's been turned back on?" I said.

"Well, you can't have everything," he said, spreading his hands. "This is a victory."

He left college after our sophomore year, and dropped out of sight. I heard from him next at Hickam Field, in Honolulu, in 1944, where he called me up at the G.I. magazine where I was an editor, and proposed dinner. "I'll come by and pick you up," he said. "And by the way, what are you—what rank?"

"I'm a sergeant," I said. "And you?"

"I'm a captain."

"In what?" I said.

"I'm in Intelligence," he said. "Intelligence, *of course.*" He couldn't resist this.

"God *damn,* Mike!" I cried. He'd won again.

I HARDLY SAW HIM at all, down the years. Once in a while he'd call again, out of the blue, and we'd have a talk or a meal together—a year ago it was at the Century Club, in New York, with his son, Joshua, a Sarah Lawrence professor, in whom he took such great pleasure and pride. He seemed exactly the same to me. He'd always just arrived from someplace and was headed off tomorrow for some other coast or country or province. He talked as if I knew what he'd been doing in all these faraway places around the world, among people in desperate need. He always said "We" or "Us"—and then he'd add, "You know." I *didn't* know, and no wonder. In addition to acquiring a Harvard law degree, he'd become a clinical professor of medicine at the University of California, a medical economist, and a pioneer investment trader in China, Vietnam, and elsewhere. What I felt, then and now, was that all these concerns, all this rushing about, had assuredly been for us, for us all, and that he represented me as he did from the day he first arrived at Pomfret, with class and civilized hope. He did us honor.

Tribute, February, 2006

ANNA HAMBURGER

Anna Hamburger was the place your gaze stopped when you'd just come into a crowded East Side living room, dropped in at a friend's Village gallery opening, arrived at a neighbor's walkup for Christmas cheer, or looked past the surrounding strangers at the theatre

and discovered her, there across the narrow theatre lobby, at inter-
mission. Good, you thought, everything's all right now. You looked
again, as you moved toward her, waiting for her to spot you as you
got closer, and for that breathtaking welcoming smile—her huge,
heavy-lidded eyes opening wide—and for her to say your name in
greeting ("Raw-juh!" in a woodwind contralto) and put up her face
toward yours. Anna, who died last week, at the age of ninety, was
the wife of my long-term friend and colleague Philip Hamburger,
and wherever she went, he came, too. She'd had a long, happy marriage (and two children) with her first husband, the writer Norman Matson, and then this second brilliant go-round. She had ten
grandchildren and fourteen great-grands.

Phil and Anna were a couple in the gin-and-tonic, Héloïse-
and-Abélard sense. You rarely thought of them as anything but
two—he in his dark suit, with his curved little smile; she close at
hand, with pale lipstick and extraordinary hair. They belonged to
an aristocracy of energetic attendance and intense critical response.
"Have you read . . . ? Did you hear . . . ? Wasn't that . . . ?" And if
you'd read the book, by chance, or been at the concert, or happened
upon this particular op-ed disaster—or even if you'd somehow
missed it—you were swept aboard, listening and laughing with
this avid couple at this suddenly significant moment.

Anna grew up in Greenwich in the nineteen-twenties. Her
father, the Socialist labor reformer William English Walling, was
a contributor to the original *Masses,* and she never lost the conviction that the good guys would triumph in the end. After voters
had given Richard Nixon another term, or Fritz Mondale or Mario
Cuomo had come to grief, she and Phil would be on the phone
the next morning or have you over to dinner the next week. "How
could they?" she exclaimed, spreading her hands wide. "It's unbe-
*lee*vable!" Optimistic but never naïve, she was tough and comforting at the same time. "She knew exactly what people were like and

didn't let it bother her," one friend said of Anna the other day. "She took care of you," said another. In a community of the gifted, she practiced intimacy as if it were an art form, and became another New York genius.

Talk, December, 2002

PAST MASTERS: V. S. PRITCHETT

MARCHING LIFE

Always alert to oddity and happenstance, V. S. Pritchett, who died last March, at the age of ninety-six, often mentioned the linked, double ticking of his own life and the clock of the century, but he must have sensed also that this shared distance of time had become a distraction, almost a disservice, to him near the end. The same proviso applies to the massive accumulation of his writings—fifteen collections of stories, nine works of criticism, three biographies, five novels, seven travel books, and two classic works of autobiography—which led to the near-universal bestowal of the title First Man of Letters upon him, once he had reached his mid-seventies. The honorific never quite fitted. Pritchett was aged at the end, to be sure, but not ancient. He was non-monumental. He was not literary—not in many senses of the word, at least. He was not a stylist, for instance, and he liked to point out that he had been a hack long before he became a critic. Even his knightly robes kept slipping askew. The moment that he and his wife, Dorothy, got back to their house from Buckingham Palace, in 1975, where the Queen had dubbed him Sir Victor, they called up their friends to tell them what tune the Guards regimental band had played as he approached the kneeling bench: Frank Sinatra's "My Way." They were shouting with laughter.

Pritchett will be remembered by everyone who knew him for his curiosity—a tourist's eagerness that had left its stamp upon his expressive face and was never far removed from his writing. His eyes, always alert, and his mouth, which often showed a skewed half smile, seemed ready on the instant to flower into delight but could change just as quickly to a thoughtful, deeply inward look of consideration, with his domed head and large jaw somehow forming an apparatus for either procedure. A short, strong-looking man, with thick shoulders and an uptilted gaze, he appeared at times to be standing behind an invisible pub counter, or perhaps about to oversee the unloading of a shipment of crocuses or greyhounds. There was a strain of workaday London practicality about him, and the surprise was that this avidity should be directed toward books and stories and ideas, instead of the tradesman's ledger. His cheerfulness—friends and relatives and other writers (writers in particular) could be seen standing near him whenever the chance came along, as if they were warming themselves at an old-fashioned coke-burning fireplace—no doubt derived from a resiliency developed during an unpeaceful childhood, but later on it bore an unmistakable air of relief: the look of a writer who has found a way to keep at it, to write all the time, and thus not to miss any part of himself in the end. He had freed himself of the occupational self-pity that makes so many writers so much less fun to meet than one expects.

I was an editor of his for almost fifty years, starting at *Holiday*, for which he wrote vigorous, impeccable travel essays, and continuing, over a longer period, with his stories for *The New Yorker*, and we wrote each other ceaselessly back and forth, and talked about everything—well, maybe not his neckties. In time, I came to understand that the amiable attention he gave to even the smallest

suggested cut or rephrasing in his text was not a sign of polite-
ness or modesty but came from the intense, almost sensual pleasure he took in every part of the writing business. He is the only
writer I have known who would thank you for a rejection; he would
be disappointed when it happened, to be sure, but eager to learn
what had seemed to go wrong, and then you could hear in his
murmuring, diminishing tones over the telephone the processes of
revision already at work in his mind. "The Fig Tree," one of his
most celebrated and satisfying longer stories (it runs well over ten
thousand words), was sent back twice in its early form. In the first
revision, Pritchett had followed some suggestion of mine about a
different direction for the ending—a notion that clearly made matters worse. He thanked me once again and went back to work.
The third version, which came in almost a year after the first, was
a major restructuring, front to back, and required nothing from
this end except gratitude: he had got it right, and there was almost
more pleasure in that than there would have been in a perfect first
manuscript—of which he was also capable, of course. Writing is
hard work, and Pritchett was a practitioner who didn't resent its
ditch-digging days. "I am really just a daily journalist," he said
once. "I sit down every day to do it, because I have to do it, and now
I know how to do it. [I] actually do enjoy the act of writing, and it
is that which means the most to me."

Pritchett's fame, whatever its eventual dimensions, will probably rest upon his two-volume autobiography, "A Cab at the Door"
and "Midnight Oil" (published in 1968 and 1971, respectively),
and upon the "Complete Collected Stories" (1990), a handsome,
corner-of-the-bookcase volume of eighty-two stories, which, taken
together, present a mixture of weight and shimmering human
complication, and a unifying Chekhovian continuity. Readers may
also avail themselves of "The Pritchett Century," a new anthology,
selected by his son Oliver, who is a *Sunday Telegraph* columnist,

which combines excerpts from the autobiography; thirteen stories; parts of the novels "Dead Man Leading" and "Mr. Beluncle"; selections from Pritchett's biographies of Turgenev and Chekhov; eight samples of travel writing; twenty-one critical essays; and a posthumous appreciation, by John Bayley, that was first published in the *London Review of Books*. Any presumed anticlimax here is inappropriate, for the absorbing, well-written, and joyful obituaries that followed Sir Victor's death would make a lively little anthology all on their own.

I think the obit writers took their tone from "A Cab at the Door," Pritchett's detailed account of his semi-impoverished, bounced-about Edwardian childhood, and the means for survival he devised while he was in the toils of a dramatizing, self-destructive floorwalker-and-salesman father, whose repeated scruffy business failures and the family's furtive decampings explain the book's title; a derisive, emotional mother ("her greenish grey and fretful eyes quick and full of lies," as he puts it); and a family regimen built upon eccentricity and worry. I remember Pritchett, at dinner one night, telling us that no one had been invited to a meal at his house when he was a boy; and that if someone rang the doorbell unexpectedly at mealtime his mother would keep the visitor waiting outside until every crumb and vestige of the meal had been hurriedly swept off the table. "There was something shameful or sexual about being caught eating," he said. "I never understood it."

Young Victor made his escape not by the common route of scholastic achievement but through a precocious self-immersion in reading. The "Children's Encyclopedia," a collected "International Library of Famous Literature," and the complete Shakespeare, Dickens, Ruskin, Marcus Aurelius, Hardy, Cervantes, Thackeray, Wells, Coleridge, Marie Corelli—all flowed into him, on the quiet, when he was at an early age, and fixed him for life. "That I understood very little of what I read did not matter to me. I was caught by the passion for print as an alcoholic is caught by the bottle," he wrote. "In prose, I found the common experience and the solid worlds where judgements were made and in which one could firmly tread."

Apprenticed to a Bermondsey leathermonger at fifteen (there wasn't enough money to keep him in school), he read and took writer's notes on the sly, and at twenty, having finessed upper school and university altogether, found himself on his own in Paris. Within five years, he had become an itinerant journalist—on the Continent, in Ireland, in Appalachia—and a full-time student at the U. of V.S.P. While still in his twenties, he became a contributor to the *New Statesman* (he served as its literary editor later on), and began writing novels, short stories, and foreign pieces at the same time. His first travel book, "Marching Spain," recounts his solo journey, at twenty-six, across that country by foot (and without Spanish). There is a sturdy, incautious energy to a life conducted on these terms—a state of mind from an earlier time, but with more Fielding than Dickens in its nature—and his enormous lifelong reading, as well as his critical writings, seems to have come from the same place. "My purpose has always been the same: to *explore* the writers and their intentions," he wrote in "Lasting Impressions." He went on with this procedure in "Midnight Oil": "I have always thought of myself—and therefore of my subjects—as being 'in life,' indeed books have always seemed to be a form of life, and not a distraction from it." Instead of being awed or made uneasy by the great authors of the past, or giving way to anxiety about his better-placed, more assured contemporaries, he remained curious and generous, and gave his considering, sightseer's mind full rein. I like to think of him as someone who went through his century on foot, gaining by attentiveness whatever he had lost by passing up its speed and lightning arrivals, and I recall suddenly seeing this view of him come to life in a passage from one of his later stories, "On the Edge of the Cliff": "From low cliff to high cliff, over the cropped turf,

which was like a carpet where the millions of sea pinks and dai-
sies were scattered, mile after mile in their colonies, the old man
led the way, digging his knees into the air, gesticulating, talking,
pointing to a kestrel above or a cormorant black as soot on a rock."
And: "The old man was a strong walker, bending to it, but when
he stopped he straightened, and Rowena smiled at his air of detach-
ment as he gazed at distant things as if he knew them."

AS A CRITIC, PRITCHETT was a descendant, or perhaps a cousin
once removed, of non-academic practitioners like Gissing, Wells,
and Priestley, who brought an unflagging, sparrowlike attention
and precision to the experience of letters. He wrote about classical
authors and young arrivals with an equal degree of respect, and
took up French and German and Spanish not only to read writers
in their own languages but as preparation for travel. Russian and
Russia itself eluded him, but he was not disconsolate about that. "I
have an imaginary Russia in my mind that I owe entirely to Russian writers," he once said. "How splendid and kind and generous
writers are in their intellect, in spilling over in this way and in
carrying us into their minds and into their experience." Something
of his usefulness and his range is conveyed when one runs an eye
down the seventy-seven reviews he contributed to this magazine
from the fifties to the late eighties, and finds pieces about Arnold
Bennett, E. M. Forster, Edmund Wilson, Picasso, George Sand,
Swift, Flann O'Brien, Borges, Rushdie, Lewis Carroll, Betjeman,
Turgenev, Rebecca West. A secret about Pritchett, I think—and
perhaps not enough of this has been made in the recapitulations—is
that his own bottomless reading ("I am appalled by the amount I
have read," he cries in "Midnight Oil") did not dull the eagerness
of his mind. Never lofty, he was able in his critical work to convey
his excited participation in this three-part agreement—writing to

reading to writing again—and, in turn, to link on the next reader, the one now taking in his review, as an indissoluble part of the process. And he could *write*. Again and again, he is capable of the acute perception, the absolutely convincing illumination of thought, that can transform the eye's journey down a page into a sensual and startling experience. In a piece about Mark Twain he says, "The peculiar power of American nostalgia is that it is not only harking back to something lost in the past, but suggests also the tragedy of a lost future." Writing about John Updike's Rabbit Angstrom novels, he takes note of the attention Updike pays to television commercials, the Sears, Roebuck catalogue, vinyl car seating, and the like, and ventures, "It has always seemed to me that in his preoccupation with the stillness of domestic objects Updike is a descendant, in writing, of the Dutch genre painters, to whom everything in a house, in nature, or in human posture had the gleam of usage on it without which a deeply domestic culture could not survive its own boredom."

It is riveting to read him on Wilson, another non-academic who had a long, work-stuffed life as a writer, and was another venerated contributor to this magazine. They could not have been more different. Wilson, a mandarin in every sense, was an intellectual aristocrat and snob, an indefatigable partygoer, and a daring solo voyager into scholarship. Pritchett never produced anything on the order of Wilson's obsessive studies of the Dead Sea Scrolls, the Iroquois, Pushkin, or revolutionary history, nor did he possess the gossipy, alcoholic sociability that went into Wilson's five decades of diaries. But Wilson, who was impatient with strangers and scornful of the sort of people who went to the movies, could never have written a Pritchett story.

Here, in any case, is Pritchett looking back to "To the Finland Station," a work that he believed was perhaps the only book on the grand scale to come out of the thirties: "[Wilson] was an enormous reader, one of those readers who are perpetually on the scent from book to book. . . . He is a critic in whom history is broken up into minds. And despite the awkwardness of his prose, he is a coherent artist in the architecture of his subject. I mean that he is an artist— this is evident in so much of his writing—in the sense that he is a man possessed. The effect is all the stronger because he is not exalted; he is, indeed, phlegmatic, as if his whole idea were a matter of grasp. . . . An egotist himself, he understands that the egotism of his conspirators is a passion and a fate."

What in the world would Edmund Wilson have made of this? He is called an awkward, phlegmatic, egotistic writer but at the same moment becomes the recipient of a rush of world-class com- pliments that say things about him which even he himself has per- haps not perceived. He can't complain, because he has been taken seriously and originally; the contract has been observed, and he will never be quite the same again.

PRITCHETT BELIEVED THAT HE had portrayed himself best in his critical works, but for me the stories convey a richer sense of the man, and perhaps more of his unconscious self. They are crowded with sexual passion and an almost pagan happiness in the unexpected turns of life. His characters tend toward the eccentric; they are all elbows and attitude, and puffed with hysterical self- regard. They share an off-center British strain that connects with the Ealing comedies, those weird interviewees on "Monty Python," and the wrangling families in a Mike Leigh movie. Pritchett had a fondness for British middle-to-lower-middle-class professionals and survivors—hairdressers, landladies, landscape gardeners, rag- trade merchants, butchers' widows, decorators, club stewards—and their gabble and confidence contribute to the thick impasto of talk and distracting side events which makes his fiction surprising and

familiar at the same time. He drew on everything he knew for the
stories, down to the smallest prop or gesture. "Just a Little More"
gets its title from the murmur of its gluttonous old gentleman as
he helps himself to another serving of beef—the same greedy catch-
phrase that Pritchett's plump, self-indulgent father says at table in
"A Cab at the Door." A temperamental fig tree that used to stand
in the back garden of Pritchett's house in Regent's Park Terrace—I
can recall Victor complaining about having to sweep up its huge
yellow leaves each November—also droops and drops its leaves in
"The Fig Tree"; and a Victorian glass case full of stuffed birds which
I remember in their first-floor sitting room turns up in the Noisy
Brackett trilogy. "Cocky Olly," a story about a fourteen-year-old
girl falling in love with a bohemian, art-suffused family next door,
takes its name from an invented, dash-about indoor game that the
children of the house play—the same game, as Oliver Pritchett has
pointed out in his foreword to "The Pritchett Century," that he and
his sister, Josephine, sometimes played as young children. Nothing
odd or distinctive has been forgotten; the same opulent memory
that illuminated "A Cab at the Door" works to dress the sets and
write the dialogue in this unreeling vivid show of fiction.

Pritchett was eighty-eight when he wrote "Cocky Olly," which
shares with his other late stories a strain of penetrating affection
while omitting the imperious, world-well-lost exclusivity that the
young require when they are in love. In "On the Edge of the Cliff," a
pair of elderly former lovers have met again by accident but quickly
agree not to see each other anymore: each is clinging to a much
younger lover, and though they know that these arrangements can't
last they don't want to hurry the process by throwing the young
people together. The former lovers part without regret, almost
blithely, each recognizing the stratagems and kinds of acceptance
that are necessary to keep hold of such luck. Pritchett's lovers aren't
particularly lovable: the middle-aged, long-since-abandoned wife

and the shouting, preposterous widower who are park neighbors in "Did You Invite Me?" have every conceivable reason not to get together, including their two dogs, who fight. We don't like the pair enough to want a happy ending, but they know what they have seen in each other, and must have. Almost apologetically, Pritchett tips us off at the end: their houses are up for sale, one of the dogs has a new owner, and the other has disappeared somewhere.

Summing up fiction is a losing game, of course, and if I persist here it is only to suggest the exuberant disorder that blows through the Pritchett stories. "Cocky Olly" puts two children on the wrong train—a huge mess, involving misunderstandings, lies, the police, and a headline murder case. We can barely follow it, but the children don't care. They love every minute because this is what life is like to them at its best; they are at home in muddle. In one of his last stories, "A Change of Policy," a brainy, grownup couple—he an art publisher, she the recent editor of an intellectual journal—are almost too busy to fall in love. He has a wife who has been in a deep coma after an accident, and a young son; the woman, Paula, is uneasy—it's all too much for her. In delayed, glancing, elegantly circumstantial fashion, they do become lovers. Then he is killed in a horse-riding accident, which we hear about, disbelieving, through a garbled overseas telephone call. There is a shift, a little pause of years, and then a quiet ending that contains a turnabout. It's almost an O. Henry–esque surprise. "Come *on*," we want to say, but something holds us back. Fiction need not always confirm our knowing, irony-abraded wariness; sometimes we need it to motor along life's outer possibilities, to provide the jolts and swerves that keep us awake, against all odds, and up for the next part of the trip.

The almost visible sweetness that surrounded Victor Pritchett in his later years flowed from a happy sixty-one-year marriage, and the glances and flashes of attention that he and Dorothy directed toward each other in the company of friends were a caution. She was his amanuensis and translator—he wrote in a squiggly, mystifying private Cyrillic—and his most trusted editor. I remember the look of blissful pride that overtook him one night when some extro-verted Welsh topers in a London pub we were in spotted a Cymry strain in Dorothy's calm, intelligent face and coaxed her into the inevitable singalong.

I can't quite place the London restaurant where Carol and I had our last lunch with the Pritchetts, but I remember a little swatch of afternoon sunshine lying across our table as we finished our coffee, and the happy, unstopping flow of talk: about absent friends (my splendid colleague Edith Oliver); about Wimbledon (Dorothy was mad for Navratilova); books (Trollope, I think); and times gone by (the broiling-hot July in the mid-sixties when, by coincidence, they had ended up subletting the walkup apartment directly over ours, on East Ninety-fourth Street, and how the odd, bumping footsteps we kept hearing overhead were finally explained when they told us that they stayed cool up there by going naked all day). Perhaps this was also the lunch when Victor told us about calling upon Yeats, years and years before, in Dublin, and about the great man's coming out onto Merrion Square wearing only one sock; he drew its mate out of his pocket and, leaning on his young visitor, pulled it on. So we ended another meal with laughter, and did not lin-ger long, much as we wished to. Pritchett never showed the dazed, half-there look of the mid-book author—he was too considerate for that—but it was understood by everyone who cared about him that his main engagement always awaited him. After our goodbyes and their cab ride home that day, there might be a nap for him, but soon he would climb the four flights of stairs to his top-floor study, fire up his pipe, and pick up his book or writing board. He was back on the road.

Books, December, 1997

LONG GONE

LIFE AND LETTERS

Christmas has flown, and mail at home this week will produce shiny bargain-sale notices, some bills and invitations, an early thank-you note for a gift, and a late Christmas card or two, but perhaps not an actual letter. There's nothing new about this, but a bit of sadness, a pang, has remained since the Postal Service announced, last month, that it will soon drop any promises of next-day delivery for first-class letters. The post office is broke, and the forty per cent of the first-class mail that currently reaches us within a day will now arrive in two, or even three. Two hundred and fifty-two local post offices are being considered for elimination, and only congressional approval is delaying the termination of Saturday mail service. We've done this to ourselves, of course, and done it eagerly, with our tweets and texts, our Facebook chat, our flooding e-mails, and our pleasure in the pejorative "snail mail." Well, yes, O.K., but where's the damage? Why these blues?

Letters aren't exactly going away. Condolence letters can't be sent out from our laptops, and maybe not love letters, either, because e-mail is so leaky. Secrets—an expected baby, a lowdown joke, a killer piece of gossip—require a stamp and a sealed flap, and perhaps apologies do as well ("I don't know what came over

me"). Not much else. E-mail is cheap, and the message is done
and delivered almost as quickly as the thought of it. The sense
that something's been lost can produce the glimmering notion that
overnight mail itself must have been a sign of thrilling modernity
once. The penny post (with its stamps and its uniform rates) arrived
in the United Kingdom in 1840, and in the decade that followed
Anthony Trollope, a postal inspector, was travelling all over Ireland
on the swift new express trains and persistent locals, to make sure
that every letter, wherever bound, was actually being delivered the
next day. On those same trains, he sat and wrote novels, and in the
novels dukes and barristers and young M.P.s and wary heiresses and
country doctors were writing letters that moved the plot along or
reversed it or tilted it in some way. The restless energy of Victorian
times, there and here at home, demanded fresh news and lots of
it. I myself can recall the four-o'clock-in-the-afternoon arrival of
the second mail of the day at our house when I was a boy, and the
resultant changes of evening plans.

If we stop writing letters, who will keep our history or dare
venture upon a biography? George Washington, Oscar Wilde, T. E.
Lawrence, Virginia Woolf, Oliver Wendell Holmes, E. B. White,
Vera Nabokov, J. P. Morgan—if any of these vivid predecessors still
belong to us in some fragmented private way, it's because of their
letters or diaries (which are letters to ourselves) or thanks to some
strong biography built on a ledge of letters. Twenty years ago, many
of us got a whole new sense of the Civil War while watching and
listening to Ken Burns's nine-part television documentary, which
took its poignant tone from the recital of Union and Confederate
soldiers' letters home. G.I.s in the Second World War wrote home
on fold-over V-Mail sheets. Troops in Afghanistan and, until lately,
Iraq keep up by Skype and Facebook, and in some sense are not
away at all.

Writers can't stop writing, and it's cheering to think which of them would have switched over to electronics had it been around. The poets Robert Lowell and Elizabeth Bishop conducted an enormous correspondence—four hundred and fifty-nine letters, between 1947 and 1977 ("What a block of life," Lowell said), spanning three continents and, between them, six or eight different lovers or partners—but one need read only a few pages of these melancholic literary exchanges to know that the latest BlackBerry or iPhone never would have penetrated their consciousness. The best account of London under siege during the early years of the Second World War came from Harold Nicolson, a British diplomat who knew everyone in the political and literary and social scenes, kept Pepysian diaries, and wrote incessantly to his wife, Vita Sackville-West, at Sissinghurst Castle, their home in Kent. When their sons Ben and Nigel went off to war, he added them to the list. It's my guess that the avidly busy Nicolson would have relished e-mail but would not have skipped a single letter.

Losing the mixed pleasures of just-arrived letters may not mean as much in the end as what we're missing by not writing them. Writing regularly to several people—a parent, a friend who's moved to another coast, a daughter or son away at college—requires one to keep separate mental ledgers, storing up the weather or the idle thoughts or the disasters we need to pass on. We're always getting ready to write. The letters out and back become a correspondence, and mysteriously take on a tone of their own: some rambly and comfortably boring; others cool and funny; some financial; some confessional. They stick in the mind and seem worth the trouble. A few years ago, I began exchanging letters with a celebrated baseball biographer, Robert Creamer, who lived in Saratoga Springs, New York. I first knew him when he was a young writer for *Sports Illustrated*. Our letters started with news about old friends and maybe something about Roger Clemens; later, because of our age, there were paragraphs about loss.

John Updike was the last *New Yorker* writer to use the mails. He wrote his stories and novels and reviews on a word processor but avoided e-mails. He reserved a typewriter for his letters and private postcards. These last mostly contained compliments—a good word to an unknown writer whose novel he'd happened upon; a piece he'd liked in the magazine—but he also permitted himself room for a whine or something cranky. Somewhere he complains about a sprained right pinkie that's messed up his typing—the finger that has all the best letters. What's certain also is that he expected to be preserved; every jam-packed small card touchingly begins with the full date—Oct. 24, '03, and so on—in the top right corner.

These collected and delivered messages need not come from the gifted or famous few, or even from someone we know, in order to hold attention. Until recently, tourists stopping in a roadside antique shop could expect to find stacks of anonymous old local postcards lying in a box: relics of family yard sales, no doubt. I know one that depicts a stiff-sided, two-story summer structure, with a narrow porch and a printed "The Mountain Ash Inn" label. It was mailed in 1922 or 1932: the circular cancelling stamp is smudged and it's hard to be sure which. The two-line address, in a nice cursive, is "J. M. Voss" over "P.O.," nothing else, and the message reads, "Ida and her uncle went to Swans Isl after all but return tomorrow. Supper Tuesday." It's signed "Do."

This would be an e-mail now but an invitation without a future. I've kept the original—it's in my summer cottage in Maine—and I'm accepting. How was Swan's Island, Ida? What's for supper?

Comment, January, 2012

MORE TIME WITH THE BRITANNICA

Last week's announced cancellation of any future printed editions
of the Encyclopaedia Britannica came as another dull shock—a predictable shock, if that's possible—but it woke me up today with a
clear vision of myself at the age of twelve sitting in our living room
in New York, with my nose deep inside Volume XXIV ("Sainte-
Clair Deville to Shuttle") of the Eleventh Edition and once again
perusing my favorite entry of the entire twenty-nine-volume work,
"Ship." I was a sailor only in a metaphoric sense, which is to say
that I was a curious reader and a boy, and thus eager to embark
upon any multi-paged, profusely illustrated and diagrammed
chunk of information that came my way. My wakeup brought with
it some remembered black-and-white photographs of Lord Nelson's
stripe-decked *Victory* and those plumb-bowed dreadnoughts of my
father's generation. The Eleventh, of course, was the most popular and acclaimed edition of them all—the Koh-i-noor, the Cary
Grant of the genre. It was published in 1911, the same year my old
man graduated from college, and I think he must have picked up
ours early on; by the time I got into it—and into "Aboukir" and
"Armor" and "Muscular System" (great drawings), "Reptiles" and
"Zanzibar," along with "Ship"—each slender, blue leather-bound
volume would leave a crumbly dust of learning in my lap when I
got up to put it away.

I'm a Wikipedia user now, like everybody else, but an impulse
took me into the quiet back corners of this magazine's Checking
Department Library, where, on a back shelf, I found, holy smoke,
this magazine's own Eleventh Edition, or what's left of it. The spines
were gone and some of the boards came off in my hands when I
began to pull out the first volumes, and the lap debris now included
fragments of gold title-lettering. The thin, high-grade paper still

felt strong in my fingers, though, and the gray twin rivers of text flowed steadily and thrillingly downward, as before.

"Ship," when I got there, was even better than remembered. It blew me away: sixty-three pages (pp. 860 to 922) of text, diagrams ("The Arrangement and Armour of the Austrian *Erzherzog Franz Ferdinand*"), tables, cross-sections, *cf.s,* footnotes, and, by my quick count, fifteen thousand words of maritime text, plus ninety-five photographs. Here was the *Victory,* yes, and here was the five-masted schooner *Helen W. Martin;* the bows on the heavily gunned H.M.S. *Inflexible* and H.M.S. *Agamemnon* and the rest now bore a Monty Pythonish resemblance to the Morgan Guaranty Trust Building on Fifth Avenue, but almost retained their menace. I moved along to the sleek Chilean *Chacabuco;* to the Nile gunboat *Sultan;* to the Cunard liner *Mauretania,* with an attached nosing tug, as I had sometimes seen her. I had actually been aboard "The American River Steamer *Hendrick Hudson*" once, on a day excursion up the Hudson, but never, worse luck, on the smoke-belching French *Jules Michelet.* There were a dozen or more submarines, but none so stylish, surely, as the French *Vendémiaire,* whose crew, in those pom-pommed hats, stood at smiling attention along her narrow deck.

I was spending too much time with the photographs, just as I did when I was a kid, and not nearly enough with the thick and daunting text. "On one point it is necessary to insist," I read at random, "because upon it depends the right understanding of the problem. *The ancients did not employ more than one man to an oar.*" Got it, I thought. Farther on, I read about a memorable 1866 race between British barques in the tea service, in which the *Ariel,* the *Taiping,* and the *Sirica* left Foo Chow, China, together, and then "separated and lost one another till they reached the English Channel, when the *Ariel* and *Taiping* got abreast and raced to the Downs, the former arriving some ten minutes before the latter. . . . These three occupied 99 days on the voyage." Ninety-nine days? Ten minutes! I closed the book, promising myself I'd have to get back to all this very soon, perhaps via the quicker and much neater online Britannica.

Only I won't. What's gone, and what I miss most, isn't the Eleventh Edition in type, or a grand document of the last days of maritime empire, but my careless, spongy twelve-year-old mind, which saw time stretching away endlessly ahead and plenty of room in it every day for something absolutely astounding.

Post, March, 2012

PAST MASTERS: WILLIAM MAXWELL

Tribute at the Century Association

Bill Maxwell greeted me with kindness and amazing trust when I first arrived as an editor with *The New Yorker*'s Fiction Department in the autumn of 1956. Along with an assemblage of other remarkable editors, we worked together every day for twenty years, in the utmost happiness. We disagreed on occasion, sometimes passionately, but with never a harsh word and—what's more startling—never a staff meeting. Bill and I were different but it didn't bother us. He once wrote that there are editors who are natural "yes" sayers and others who are natural "no" sayers, and he and I would agree, I think, about where we each belong in that lineup. I also recall a day when I came back from lunch carrying a parcel from the Music Masters store, down in the lobby, and when Bill asked I said it was a record for my younger daughter, who was then about five years old. His daughters, Brookie and Kate, were a few years older than my two, and I knew that they had been raised from the cradle on Brahms and Heifetz and Chopin, so I was embarrassed when I took out my purchase, a Little Golden Record that featured Tom Glazer singing "The Little Red Hen." Bill looked at this object with wonder—he'd never seen such a thing—and he said, "Oh, Roger, you're so worldly."

I'm going to read a brief passage from "So Long, See You

Tomorrow," which was published in 1980. It's a long story or a short novel, of surpassing power and sadness. Like so much of his fiction, its setting is Lincoln, Illinois, his childhood home. One of the protagonists is the narrator, William Maxwell, whose voice you will recognize:

> My father was all but undone by my mother's death. In the evening after supper he walked the floor and I walked with him, with my arm around his waist. I was ten years old. He would walk from the living room into the front hall, then, turning, past the grandfather's clock and on into the library, and from the library into the living room. Or he would walk from the library into the dining room and into the living room by another doorway, and back to the front hall. Because he didn't say anything, I didn't either. I only tried to sense, as he was about to turn, which room he was going to next so we wouldn't bump into each other. His eyes were focused on things not in those rooms, and his face was the color of ashes. From conversations that had taken place in front of me I knew he was tormented by the belief that he was responsible for what had happened. If he had only taken this or that precaution. . . . It wasn't true, any of it. At a time when the epidemic was raging and people were told to avoid crowds, he and my mother got on a crowded train in order to go to Bloomington, thirty miles away, where the hospital facilities were better than in Lincoln. But even if she had had the baby at home, she still would have caught the flu. My older brother or my father or I would have given it to her. We all came down with it.

It sometimes surprises me that I remember the settings and events of Bill Maxwell's childhood almost better than my own: the house on Ninth Street, Grandfather Blinn, Hattie Dyer, Aunt

Annette. The fabled short-fiction writer Alice Munro once told me that she had been in the habit of visiting the towns and cities that were closely connected to the works of great American writers—Oxford, Mississippi, for Faulkner, for instance. Lincoln, Illinois, she said, meant the most to her. Every street corner seemed intimately familiar and close at hand. It was like coming home. We feel the same way, incidentally, about John Updike's boyhood town of Shillington, and its people and places—Grandfather Hoyer, Pep Conrad's store, the sandstone farmhouse. But we shouldn't be much distracted by this appropriation, nor attribute it only to the skills and obsessive attention of these wonderful writers, who have circled back over these same trails again and again in their work. I believe, rather, that their stories are the same stories that we tell ourselves, each of us, over and over, every day and every night, returning to our own distant or recent past, possibly in search of happiness but much more often in the hope of finding an unexpected window or bend in the path there. We want our stories to come out differently, but they never do. Except in the detail, what we find so often in the writings of William Maxwell is our lives relived—with the same questions asked, and with answers or the chance for amends still elusive—but now illuminated with the courage and persistence of a great companion. This is perhaps the very first purpose of fiction and, most assuredly, one of the rewards of art.

Thank you, Bill.

October, 1998

SIX LETTERS

⁰⸻⸻ˏ

TO ANN BEATTIE

October 29, 1985

Dear Ann,

I'm sorry—extremely sorry—to say that we're sending back "Another Day." No one here could recognize these people; they don't seem to have any connection with real life. The story is written with wonderful clarity and intensity, but the gigantic egos and destructive behavior of your characters are presented so bluntly and coldly that they blot out everything else; no one is left alive, except the victims, and they are almost grotesques, too, because of what has been done to them. It seems to me that fiction of this sort flattens one's interests in the events and discoveries of a story, because one knows that what comes next will be equally deadly and bitter. Two people here who read the story said that they expected that someone would shoot the dog next.

This sounds as if we're looking for pleasant fiction or a particular view of life, but I don't think we are. It may be that you know people who are as horrific and destructive as this and

that I don't, but I still would expect them to be recognizable
to me in some intuitive fashion. Many of your stories have been
about people who were living a very different life than my own,
and thinking and saying things that I didn't expect or know in
advance, but there was an instant and unabashed recognition; they
seemed alive and important, and no matter what they said or did,
I cared about them. It seems to me that I could even care about
Harry and Jo-Beth and Oren and the rest, if I felt that you cared
about them too, but that doesn't come across here.

I don't know how it has happened that we are so far apart
just now in our view of fiction, but I know it will correct itself
somehow. I hate to write a letter like this, but it's probably best if
we try to be clear. Whatever you think (and please do think about
all this, even if you don't agree), please keep writing stories and
sending them to me. I count on you always, you know.

Love,

TO NANCY FRANKLIN

November 18, 1999

Dear Nancy,

I suppose you know that your great piece about my mother is
in the forthcoming Profiles collection, and I suppose further that
you've already seen the book. I was looking at a copy the other
day, and read your KSW Profile all over again, front to back,
and was struck again by its great reporting, its thoroughness, its
elegant concision, its daring perceptiveness, its fairness, and—
well, its love. I think I wrote you a note when it first came out,

but I want to say again how much it means to me that you wrote it in the first place, and how happy I am that it's in a book now, for keeps.

The piece is also a big fat relief for me, because I'll never have to write one of my own about my mother—or at least not a major, all-points effort like yours. I feel no need to correct or to amplify what you've done, because you've got so much of KSW into yours, in a way that feels both level and intimate. I'm also pleased in a wise, satisfied way because of your "As an editor, she was maternal, and as a mother she was editorial." If I'd heard this in 1965, let's say, I would have saved about $20,000 in psychiatrists' bills—no, make that $25,000. I would have invested that sum in Xerox, then Microsoft, and I'd be telling you all this right now, this minute, while driving us to the Villa Angellino in Cap Ferrat in my mauve Jaguar XV-I6 two-seater. Pity.

Love again,

TO JOHN HENRY ANGELL

July 16, 2000

Dear John Henry:

Here's a late, well, I hope not too late, but heartfelt happy birthday to you, my dear—with wishes for a happy, sunny day, happy summer, happy whole year, and many more. I won't say decade because thinking in those big blocks is sort of gloomy, I've found. One always tries to weigh the meaning of those ten-year chunks, and the only answer is mortality, which we knew about before we started. But I think you're a million miles ahead of where you were ten years ago—I remember you then, of course, and also with joy—and more at home in the world. . . . There, see what I mean: heavy thinking: I'm sorry.

I wish we could be with you to watch your thirties come up the bay with the tide, but we'll catch up with you soon. Hope you can find your way back again in August, since there always seems to be a little more time there for us all. Meantime, I'm enclosing a check, as usual, with my love—as usual only more so. Buy a new paddle or something.

I imagine you can pick up a general tone of frazzlement between the lines here. It all comes from [David] Cone—the book, the man, the decline, the money, the late hours, the terrible pitching, the unknown future, the unorderly notes, the passing and often lost ideas, the need to get along with it and the need to get it right, and more. I think he may actually retire at almost any point—or least disappear to another team after some sort of buyout from the Yankees. It's killing him that all this is happening in full view, here in the big city. I think it's his worst dream come true. He seems to pitch a little less well each time, while trying harder, and I think he's run out of ideas. But his behavior in the face of all this is nothing less than extraordinary, and that alone makes me glad I got into this big, weird mess.

I'm sorry, by the way, to stick this into your birthday letter, but it's sort of natural, since talking with you is natural to me, and gives me confidence. You have no idea, I think, of the place you have in my thoughts all the time now, and how often I find myself wanting to tell you things, and waiting to hear what you think. It's one of the great rewards of me being my age and you being yours.

Happy birthday, my dear, and welcome to whatever is coming along for you next. It's great to have you around.

All my love,

TO WYLIE DAUGHTY*

February 7, 2008

Dear Wylie (if I may):

How very kind of you to think of me! I read your father's unpublished pages with far more attention to the author, of course, than to *The New Yorker* stuff. I'm *always* interested in O'Hara, which puts me into an exclusive club of about a hundred thousand. I felt the old and undeserved proprietary affection, and got a kick when I saw that he'd made his hero a Harvard man this time. But Stephen learns and remembers more than anyone at Harvard would have bothered to do—and actually more than anyone except John O'Hara would have. Everyone is here—Andy and Thurber and Lobrano and Sullivan and Ross—along with some made-up lesser figures, but the real presence is the author, burning up the pages once again and pouring the dialogue around like gasoline.

I kept thinking of him writing this, and the noise his typewriter would have made, and got a thrill when I noticed that the ribbon is getting a little pale by the time he gets to the last page.

Thanks again, Wylie, and all the best,

P.S.: Please let me know if this does get published so I can get hold of it again.

---

* Wylie Daughty is the daughter of John O'Hara.

TO HERBERT MITGANG

February 17, 2010

Dear Herb:

Thanks for your letter and the kind words. *Brief* was a
skinny slick-paper G.I. magazine published in Hawaii—we used
the *Honolulu Advertiser* presses and distributed around the four
million square miles of the Central Pacific by ATC planes. It
cost 15 cents per copy and looked sort of like *Life*. We actually
made a small profit in the end but conscientiously drank it all
up in a series of magnificent postwar parties. Circulation was
around eighteen thousand per week, as I recall it. It started as
a small G.I. weekly for the 7th A.F. but I was sent out early
in 1944 by the A.A.F. with three other writer-reporter guys to
make it better, since they knew that the theater would become
huge once the war ended in Europe. It was called *Brief* because
of "briefings"—you know, wartime intelligence distributing.
We did O.K., scored some beats, but ran into trouble with an
editorial attacking Ernie Pyle (he came late to the Pacific and
was only associating with Navy brass, etc.), which came out the
day before he was killed on Ie Shima. I remember a guy in my
barracks stopping by and saying, "Wake up—you just killed
that old man."

I wrote a lot and had a weekly column, and helped put
the thing to bed every week, so I never got to the Marianas or
anywhere else. But I liked the job and was pretty good at it. I was
in my early twenties.

Glad you're hanging in there, Herb. I'm still at work here
every day but don't work very long hours, thank God. But I'm

way younger than you. I won't be 90 till September. I'm glad you like *The New Yorker*.

All best, as ever,

TO RAY SMITH

February 18, 2010

Dear Ray Smith:

Thanks for your letter and thank you in particular for reminding me of Andy White's thoughts about the Xerox matter. What hurts now, in a time when newspapers and other publications are dying off in such scary numbers, is his sentence, "Not all papers are independent, God knows, but there are always enough of them to provide a core of integrity and an example that others feel obliged to steer by."

Not so, it turns out, and who can believe that blogs and tweets will fill the gap? I worry about this every day. You and the *Gardiner Gazette* are the exception, and congratulations to you both.

Yours & best,

WEST SIDE STORY

Home in the city on a broiling Saturday, Carol and I threw in
the towel early, opting for an afternoon full retreat to the sixplex
on Broadway at Eighty-fourth Street, where a "Parsifal"-length
submarine-warfare drama (ping-*tongg!* ping-*tongg!*) might keep us
cool until almost sundown. On the way, we would stop at Harry's
Shoes, just across Broadway from the theatre, where I'd try to snap
up a pair of unfashionable, low-gunwale Keds for our upcoming
vacation. Weekend afternoons at Harry's can remind you of a Mar-
rakesh souk, but when at last, sneaks in hand, I spotted a vacant
try-on chair and threw myself into it, the man sitting to my right,
putting on *his* new sneakers, was Alfred Kazin. City etiquette in
these circumstances calls for silence, but he and I had met, now and
then, at book parties and the like, and I introduced myself.

"Oh, sure," Kazin said, giving me an engaging smile. Though
he is seamed and white-haired, there was a lot more student than
prof in his gaze. He made a little swishing gesture through the
air with one hand, and I nodded yes, right: I was the baseball guy.
Our wives were introduced—both of them, I think, enjoying the
odd situation, with the seated gents now lacing and stomping like
kids and the women standing momlike before them, looking stern
about size and fit. The wives went off together, hunting for a salesman and perhaps for some less bankerish choices for their guys,
footwear-wise, while Kazin and I, thickly surrounded by the Ree-
boky hordes, chatted about our boyhood ballparks, here in the city.
I offered the Polo Grounds, name-dropping the likes of Mays and

Mize, Ott and Hubbell, but he topped me when he said that he remembered Ebbets Field but not for the Dodgers.

"We used to go to the opera at Ebbets Field when I was a kid," he told me. "I went to 'Faust' with my father once. Nobody knows it now, but the mayor—the first one I can remember, from back in the twenties—sometimes arranged for free opera there for a few summer days. I don't know which opera company—I can't imagine they were any good. But he was there in person, walking up and down the aisles and reminding us what he'd done. 'Are you having fun? Are you having fun?' he'd ask. 'It's courtesy of your mayor, John F. Hylan, and don't you forget it!' "

I said that I'd interviewed Mayor La Guardia once, for my school paper, after waiting all day in his office. I could no longer remember anything he'd said but still kept the vision of his feet, under the vast mayoral desk, not quite touching the floor.

"Yes!" Kazin said. "A small man but a big mayor. The best."

Judith Dunford, Kazin's wife, had arrived with a salesman, and while their order was being written up her husband checked his watch and said, "We're just right."

They were headed for the sixplex, too, it turned out—and for the same underwater epic. "Judith wanted 'Little Odessa,'" Kazin said, "but I had a different plan. Anything not to think!"

After we said goodbye, Carol and I looked at each other and said, "Isn't New York great" at the same instant. Just after that, while I was standing at the cashier's counter, the Kazins came past me, with the critic carrying his Harry's parcel under his arm. "In New York," I heard him say, "you go for shoes and meet a writer."

All this happened exactly a year ago. The name of the movie was "Crimson Tide." I recall nothing about it except Gene Hackman losing his cool and Denzel Washington really keeping his. Remembering the Kazins at Harry's Shoes is a different story: that's easy.

Talk, July, 1996

CRYING MAN

Walking my dog last week, I came upon a man crying in the street. He was sitting on the raised stone ledge of a back-yard fence separating two small apartment houses, his back against the iron bars, with one hand up to his face. The dog gave him a glance and we moved on by, but when I stopped after a decent distance and looked back he'd bent forward in his misery and I could hear sobs. A thin, tall man, perhaps in his late forties, his pale face now glistening with tears. Black jeans, gray shirt, some sort of jacket. My first thought was to go back and ask if there was anything I could do. My dog is a young fox terrier, and I thought that his charm might perk up the poor guy for a moment. I held back, though, immobilized by New York's code of privacy and because I was embarrassed. He hadn't noticed us, and the soft sounds of his grief now seemed to be the main event on the block we were on. What had happened? What rotten news had come his way? His mother had died. His girlfriend—they'd have been together for three years, come January—had gone away to São Paulo for good, leaving a note on the kitchen table and a longer message on his e-mail. His cat Max unaccountably fell down the airshaft. His lover, who runs an art-moving business, had been hit by a bicycle on Greenwich Avenue and required neurosurgery. His job—he was a furniture restorer; an anesthesiologist; an associate curator; a cloud-computer analyst and designer; a private-school gym teacher—had been terminated by budget considerations. His father, the retired oboist, urgently needed a live-in companion with experience in dementia. I didn't know or need to know. But I had patronized this sidewalk neighbor with my imaginings. His loss was his own, and unimaginable. The dog and I resumed our tour, and I was surprised by unexpectedly remembering what crying is like.

Not that I shouldn't have known. Weeping is visible just about every night on the evening news, around bombing sites or after violent weather events, also at memorials and candlelight vigils, or, more locally, near the end of the half hour, from neighbors of the abruptly deceased. (Women who cry in movies nowadays, and even some on the TV news, often wipe away dampness with a delicate gesture of their fingertips, to preserve eye makeup.) But my man had been crying for real, with no one else around. Men don't want to cry, of course, because it's unmanly. Women cry more warily than they once did, perhaps, weighing the implications. We cry at the shrink's office, or choose not to. For grownups, tears, when they do arrive, come from a considerable distance but startle us with their familiarity. Crying has not been in the conversation, but, yes, we know how to do this. This is an old dance step; it's swimming resumed. What's also been forgotten and is now quickly and strongly restored is the comfort of giving way to these awkward seizures and shakings, the swift flooding and thickening of sinuses, and then our sense of shame and need for apology also giving way, if we're lucky, to acceptance and perhaps more and still more tears, more Kleenex, and a bit of peace.

When the dog and I came back to the same place fifteen minutes later, the man had gone, and my generous thoughts about him had stopped, too. No crying today, please. No more reminders around here about this magical ten-cent restorative, and the million waiting reasons we'll be needing it. Not right now, or next week, either. Spare us, mister—O.K.?

Post, November, 2011

STORYVILLE

Do anything long enough, and you hang up a record. Just go to bed every night, and before you know it you've passed Sleeping Beauty. Set down the cat's dinner, day by day, and pretty soon he's put away enough Meow Mix to feed the Dallas Cowboys on Thanksgiving. "Hey," said a colleague of mine, sticking his head in my office door the other day. "Did you know that you've rejected fifteen thousand stories here? I just figured it out. Fifteen thousand, easy."

Well, thanks. I got out a pencil and did some figuring, and decided that twenty thousand was probably more like it. I tried to envision that many manuscripts trudging back home again in the rain, and to imagine the reception they got there when they rang the bell—"Oh. You again"—and, wincing, I heard the mumbled apologies and explanations. Then I added on all the other mournful regiments of rejected fiction sent back from this salient, down the years, by fellow editors of mine in the same line of work: a much larger body of the defeated and the shot-down—a whole bloody Caporetto. "We regret . . . ," I murmured unhappily to myself. "Thank you for . . . " I sounded like a field marshal.

The regret is real, though it may vary in depth from one manu-script to the next. What is certain is that no one can read fiction for thirty-eight years, or thirty-eight weeks, and go on taking any pleasure in saying no. It works the other way around. You pick up the next manuscript, from a long-term contributor or an absolute stranger ("Prize in Undergraduate Composition; two summers at Pineaway under Guy de Maupassant; stories in *Yurt, Springboard,* and *Yclept;* semifinalist in . . . "), and set sail down the page in search of life, or signs of life; your eye is caught and you flip eagerly to the next page and the one after that. Can it be? Mostly, almost always, it is not—or not quite. You read on to the end (well, not always to the end) and then make a note to yourself about what you will say to your old friend who hasn't sold a story here in two years, or what to put, in some lines scribbled at the end of the printed form, to the young or not so young author who has laid his or her soul out on these eighteen pages but somehow not in a way that makes you want to slow down and enter this particular bar in company with Jay and Hugo and Lynn, or hear more of what was said on the back porch on a particular night of recriminations and fireflies. Sometimes there is a little descriptive passage or some paragraphs of dialogue, or the tone or tinge of a page or two, to single out for praise or encouragement, but even these responses, let it be said, may go into a return letter as much to make yourself feel better, a bit less of a monster, as in any great hopes of getting a primo manuscript from this same author in a month's time.

THERE SEEMS TO BE a lot of misunderstanding about fiction. "How do you get a story published in *The New Yorker?*" somebody asks. "Send it in, and if we like it we'll publish it," I reply, and my interlocutor shoots me a knowing look and says, "No, *seriously*—"

"Are you looking for the typical *New Yorker* story?" someone else asks. "Sure, lady," I want to answer back. "The one that's exactly like Borges and Brodkey and Edna O'Brien and John O'Hara and Susan Minot and Eudora Welty and Niccolò Tucci and Isaac Singer. That's the one, except with more Keillor and Nabokov in it. Whenever we find one of those, we snap it right up."

A distinguished reporter here, the author of long, ferociously researched articles, stopped by to see me one day in great excitement, to say he was giving up all this drudgery and would write only fiction from now on. "Fiction writers never have to leave their desks, do they?" he said.

"Well, no," I said. "Except for one thing."

"What's that?"

"They have to get up to vomit," I said.

A visiting reporter from a media journal once asked, "What are you people looking for in the fiction line? What are your standards?"

I stalled for time. "I don't know what they are," I mumbled at last. "We've never decided. We want something good—you know, something we like."

"No, *seriously*," she said, but when she saw that we were serious (I had cunningly laid on some colleagues) she closed her notebook. Her piece never appeared.

THE WRITERS ARE THE main players, which means that we can hurry past such esoterica as the opinion sheet, on which two or three or more fiction editors weigh in helpfully or warily or stubbornly ("Hate to disagree, but—") on an incoming manuscript; often the process turns up some structural flaws, and the work is shipped back to its creator for minor or major repairs. Or rejected. No contributor is spared this blunt possibility, which may explain why certain celebrated authors have attempted to negotiate an acceptance before a story of theirs is sent along, or have stopped submitting altogether. Lack of unanimity on an opinion sheet is not uncommon, nor is the brave or truculent silence of a dissenting editor in the face of a story that has been taken in spite of his or her fervent objections: a turn of events that brings brief, rushing doubts about the future of Western civilization, or about the sanity of the Editor, who has had the last word. This is a weekly, thank God, and a few days later we fiction people are out in the hall exclaiming over a new manuscript, by an old standby or a total unknown, that has just gone the rounds: "Have you *read* it? Isn't that terrific!" Some writer has made our day, and we are collegial once again, gleaming in reflected brilliance.

Just as there is no one way to write a story, there is no one way to edit it for publication, or to deal with its author over an extended period of time. What is being set down here, I mean, is one editor's experiences and recollections of these semi-private matters—a selective history that cannot give proper honor to my departmental colleagues, past and present, or to writers whose work did not happen to come my way. What I noticed about bygone fellow fiction editors at the magazine—among them, Robert Henderson, William Maxwell, Robert Hemenway, Rachel MacKenzie, Frances Kiernan, Pat Strachan, and Veronica Geng—was how much alike they were in their passion for their work, and how different in the ways they went about it. The same holds true for my present friends and everyday companions here, whose devoted attentions continue the long line of *New Yorker* stories—over six thousand of them so far—while properly encouraging its alteration, almost issue by issue, in directions unforeseen. Fiction is special, of course, for its text must retain the whorls and brush-splashes of the author: the touch of the artist. At the same time, the editor should not feel much compunction about asking the writer the same questions he would put to himself about a swatch of his own prose: Is it clear? Does it say what I wanted it to say? Is it too long? Does it *sound* right—does it carry the tone that I want the reader to pick up right here? Is it, just possibly, too short? And so on. (It's no coincidence, by the way, that so many *New Yorker* fiction editors have also been writers.)

Some distinguished editors here have forsworn most such meddling, particularly with young contributors, on the theory that the writer almost always knows best. My own instincts lean the other way, for the obligation to preserve the sanctity of a neophyte's script is counterbalanced by my hope that he will, by life habit, come to ask himself those short, tough questions as he writes along, never omitting the big question at the end: Is it good enough? Is it any good at all? Lifelong practitioners—the best ones, I've noticed—

ask themselves this every day: that's why they look the way they do (hunched over their word processors, or at the bar next door), which is like morticians.

That new story we exclaimed about will be brilliant, but perhaps not right away. A week has gone by, and its author—a young man in his twenties, let's say, not previously published in *The New Yorker* or anywhere else—is in my office. We are sitting side by side at the desk, with his manuscript between us, and on its top page he finds some light pencillings and question marks. What's this? The joyful, sunstruck expression he has worn ever since he got the good news fades a fraction; middle age, one could say, has just begun. They *edit* fiction here? "Don't worry," I say. "Let's take a look. Down here, do you want these three whole lines about the dog, who doesn't turn up again in the story until . . . until over here on page 11? Do you want to say something quicker about the dog? Up to you. . . . But before this, up here at the top of the paragraph, I'm not sure why the father seems so bitter. Do you need to explain that, or have you made him seem angrier than you meant to? Well, let's mark that and move on. . . . Over here on page 4, just after Lucinda goes off in the truck, you've used this same construction for the third time in a row—you've got awfully fond of those dashes. Want to do it some other way? And then here's your 'dirgelike darkness,' right in the middle of this wonderful scene. Can darkness have a *sound*? What should we do about that?"

I pause and look at him. He is trying to decide whether I'm simply a bully or someone out to steal his writer's soul. Perhaps it's neither. How can he be persuaded that these are the same wireworms and dust balls that every writer discovers in the corners of his beautiful prose, no matter how carefully he has woven it and laid it down? The young man looks pale, and who can blame him? He feels himself at a brink. He wants to be an artist, but he also wants to be a pro. His words, which once seemed so secure, so right, are beginning

to let him down. Why is this all so hard? Why has the language
suddenly turned balky? He needs time to think it over.

"Never mind the dashes," I offer now. "I think they'll work
fine. And you can look at that 'dirgelike' later on, when this is all
in type."

We go on to the next page, and I have a passing brief memory
of other writers, sitting just here to my left, as we bend over a
manuscript or a proof together. William Maxwell, cheerfully X-ing
out a proposed line change (marked "for clarity" at the margin of
the galley), smiles and says, "I don't want to be *too* clear." Donald
Barthelme, encountering a short paragraph with my "Omit?" at its
flank, sighs and reddens. He is the cleanest of writers, and proud.
"Well, yes, goddam it, if you say so," he mutters at last. "I count
on you to get the hay out." And then it is my turn to wonder if I'm
right. Later on, I may recall some words of William Shawn's—the
only advice about editing I ever heard him put forward. "It's very
easy to make somebody's manuscript into the best story ever written," he said. "The trick is to help the writer make it into the best
story he can write on that particular day."

If I could do it, I would invite the first-time author to come
back on a day when I am sitting here with John Updike, going
over the galley proofs of a story of his, or discussing them with him
on the telephone. Updike has rewritten (in his angling pencilled
handwriting) some lines of his, up on top of a long paragraph, and
we are trying to decide about a word in the middle of one sentence.
"Well, you may be right," he says in his soft, musing way. "Which
do you think *sounds* better?" He says the phrase with the word in it
over to himself once or twice and makes a decision. The following
day, after this and a dozen other burning trifling matters have been
resolved, I overnight the revised page proofs to him at his home in
Massachusetts, and two days later—on the morning the story must
go to press—the proofs come back to me with the word and the

whole section we discussed crossed out. The top of the paragraph has been redone in pencil, done differently: the content is the same, but the tone, the feeling, of the passage has shifted. Elsewhere on the proofs, Updike has altered some bits of punctuation, crossed out things, reworded something else. This is the way the story will appear in the magazine, and, later on, the way it will read in the next collection of Updike's stories. The book will go into libraries and into some school and college curricula, I imagine. The way the story reads—the words that students will find in the book and will believe were put down that way from the beginning, cut in stone—is only another stage in the struggle to get the writing to do its work: the version that the author and the editor had to let go of in the end.

The young writer's own galleys (with some of the queries and suggestions taken, others not) will be finished up, too, one day, and he and I will shake hands, out by the elevators. The story will appear next week—a great moment for us both. He is launched, and his tippy little canoe will soon disappear round the bend, on a journey whose duration no one can tell. I don't think he knows how short it may turn out to be, or how unimaginably long. "Let us hear from you," I say.

READING SHORT-FICTION MANUSCRIPTS CAN be wearing and wearisome from day to day and week to week. Every human situation, every sort of meeting or conversation, is something you have read before or know by heart. But then here comes a story—maybe only a couple of paragraphs in that story—and you are knocked over. Your morning has been changed; you are changed. A young woman and her sister, a nun, are talking in the back yard in the evening, and Sister Mary Clare says that she is going to take a vow of silence. "Do you think it's a bad idea?" she asks, and her sister says no, it's a good idea.

> "If you care, I'm not very happy," Sister said.
> "You were never happy," Melissa said. "The last time I saw you laughing was the day that swing broke. Remember that day?"

Spare and pure, the story murmurs along to its ending. It is intimate and painful and then it stops, and these particular lives go on. It is Mary Robison's "Sisters," her first acceptance here—though not, I believe, her first submission. It was written in 1977 and now feels like part of its time, but what I felt when I came to those lines is still fresh and strong. Every fiction editor here has had such an experience, and eagerly waits for the next one.

That same era brought a freshet of striking fiction from Ann Beattie: along with the painful, sensual feelings of loss in those stories came assemblages of characters apparently insatiable for company but increasingly alone—young men and women talking and cooking, arriving from somewhere, telling stories, picking up on ironic details, patting the dog, getting drunk, changing the music, driving to town for pizza, waking up in the night, waiting for something else to happen. The titles—"Vermont," "Tuesday Night," "Shifting," "Downhill," "A Vintage Thunderbird," "Colorado," and the rest—are a generational montage now, but the stories remain vital news for anyone who read them when they were just written and just out.

"Epiphanies" became the chic, dismissing word for scenes of this kind, but other forms of the short story, arriving here in due course, seemed only to reach the same ends by a different route. Bobbie Ann Mason's scrupulously detailed accounts of a younger

Kmart generation of Southerners, living in mobile homes and shabby condos and making do with the remnants of their parents' lost rural America, brought characters less inclined to linger on what was happening around them but perhaps no less aware that something had been going wrong in their world. Mason is such a sharp noticer of down-home detail—her people make "Star Trek" needlepoint pillows, own cats named Moon Pie, unexpectedly find the name "Navratilova" floating in their heads, and know that "Radar Love" is a great driving song—that we sometimes don't give her her full due as a chronicler of American loss. I remember once asking whether her men and women felt emotion without always finding ways to show it, and she said, "I don't understand. I thought these stories were nothing but emotion." Then, a year or two later, while she was finishing her poignant post-Vietnam novel, "In Country," a section of which ran here in 1985, she called me and said, "The emotion has turned up. I don't think I can *stand* much more of this."

We editors wait for whatever it is that the writers are trying to discover, and sometimes it arrives here in surprising forms. Once, it arrived in a flash—a gas explosion in a parking lot, where some kids were listening to Bruce Springsteen over their radios and had flicked their lighters during "Born in the U.S.A." That 1988 story, Alan Sternberg's "Blazer," was the first of his gritty, eloquent panoramas of southern Connecticut mechanics and builders and carpenters and cops and landfill inspectors toughing out hard times and industrial decline, along with their wives—who, all in all, were handling it a lot better than they were.

Stories and groups of stories work differently, and may require editors and readers to learn their particular tone and language before they can reach us, sometimes while an author is also struggling to find a direction or an opening that is not yet clear. Now and then, a writer stakes out an entire region of the imagination and of the countryside—one thinks of Cheever, Salinger, Donald Barthelme, and Raymond Carver, and now Alice Munro and William Trevor—which becomes theirs alone, marked in our minds by unique inhabitants and terrain. Writers at this level seem to breathe the thin, high air of fiction without effort, and we readers, visiting on excursion, feel a different thrumming in our chests as we look about at a clearer, more acute world than the one we have briefly departed. Reading Alice Munro's tales (the old word fits here) presents us always with the wholly unexpected moment—an inner "What?" that is quickly replaced by an accepting " . . . but of course." It's magical and brings back for me, strangely, the mood of thrilling expectancy with which I read the entrancing events in all those variously tinted fairy-story collections of my childhood—"The Blue Fairy Book," "The Yellow Fairy Book," "The Grey Fairy Book," and the rest. Trevor's stories, by contrast, are quieting, but with the awful calm of acceptance: his precise, deadly stitchings of country or family circumstances and cruelties leave their victims, for the most part, silent or almost decorously murmurous in resignation.

Ruth Prawer Jhabvala's stories, arriving here (on crinkly, tightly typed airmail paper) from India in a steady stream through the sixties and seventies, moved at a pace that sometimes made me fidget or sigh impatiently for more action and swifter developments—but only while I was still in the early pages. Reading along, I would find myself slowing, and listening to the sounds and hours of a different continent, as I grew aware of the grinding societal weight with which lives were being fixed, in comical or gruesome or affecting fashion, in the multilayered modern India she knew so well. Mrs. Jhabvala, who is Polish but is married to an Indian architect, wrote, in the introduction to her last collection, "Out of India," of her deep discomfort with the hypocrisies and ironies of her second country. "I have no heart for these things here," she said, and, "All the time I know myself to be on the back of this great animal of poverty and backwardness." Almost in self-defense, it appears, she watched and wrote. Her stories can be satirical (a wealthy, Anglicized young Indian, making out with a similarly modernized girl on a date, thinks, I am kissing a Parsee), or simultaneously touching and tough-minded (an old woman attempts to explain the lifelong passion that keeps her close to the elderly, Dutch-born sahib who has been her careless lover), or scarifying (in a similar situation, a police superintendent sexually mounts his Muslim mistress while encouraging her to pray out loud, after her fashion, on her knees). Jhabvala's fiction runs more to novels these days, and since leaving India she has given most of her attention to screenwriting, as her Oscar-winning screenplays for the long-established Merchant-Ivory production company attest. It would be ungrateful to complain.

The movies have almost snatched away a different but no less valued contributor, Woody Allen. Most of his work for this magazine, to be sure, came in the form of wild parodies and casuals, which isn't quite what we're talking about here, but at least one submission, "The Kugelmass Episode," is a dazzling short story, a Fabergé of the form—not the first attribute that would come to mind while one is wheezing or pounding one's thigh in happiness over the C.C.N.Y. humanities professor Sidney Kugelmass, who, through the ministrations of a magician, is able to bring the live Emma Bovary to New York (he stashes her at the Plaza) and, conversely, to visit her at Yonville. Allen's modest early submissions here so resembled the work of his literary hero S. J. Perelman that I had to remind him that we already had the original on hand; he saw the point and came up with the remedy, almost overnight. Those first casuals also seemed to carry a joke, or sometimes two or three jokes, in every sentence—something that didn't work as well on the page as it did when one heard the same stuff during one of Woody's standup routines at the Bitter End. *"Fewer* laughs?" he said doubtfully, and, horrified at the thought, I nodded yes—yes, please.

"Whatever Works" should be the sampler that a fiction editor keeps affixed to his wall, or up over the water cooler. Mary Robison's story "Yours" seemed to have some missing manuscript pages when it turned up in the mail in 1980, but after I'd read its seven hundred and ninety words it was plain that a single line more would be much less. "We" was the title of Mary Grimm's 1988 story about a Midwestern working-class neighborhood of young newly married women friends, and the pronoun was repeated through multiple scenes, in paragraph after paragraph, as the group became less obsessed with sex and more with children, tried out recipes and new jobs, and grew older and more private together. The "we" was an impossibility, a trick, but one that became more pleasing and useful and right as the story moved to its terrific conclusion.

You never know. Edith Templeton's engaging first-person stories of her childhood in the grand-monde nurseries and castles of Czechoslovakia in the nineteen-twenties, which ran here thirty years ago and more, offered no preparation for "The Darts of Cupid," in 1968, a rending erotic love story about a married British woman working in the United States War Office outside London during the Second World War: a novella of power and perfection. Twenty-three years passed, and then here came her "Nymph & Faun," a twisted tale about money and wills and antique silver and marital cruelty that unfolds, at length, in a writhingly intimate conversation between an art dealer and a reclusive older woman, a widow, who understand each other because each can speak the drawling, edged, deadly language of the British upper crust. Mrs. Templeton, who lives in Bordighera, on the Italian Riviera, readily admits that most of her stories are true stories, but this time the mining and extraction of a clear line of events from her many pages of manuscript, and then her early and late galley proofs (on which her interpolations, done in green ink, ran to dogs and artists, British naval parlance, psychiatry, Mayfair scandals, quotations from Dante and Isaac Singer and Thomas Mann, visits to a Maharaja and the King of Nepal, Hemingway's suicide, and the workings of international art dealerships), produced from each of us long letters filled with questions and explanations but set down in tones of trust and mutual pleasure over the work we were engaged in together. It almost made me wish I'd been an antiquarian, so that I could concentrate on keeping hold of things instead of taking them out. We parted at last (we have never met), after exchanging a final thick set of airmailed galleys and agreeing that it was time to push this child out the door to fend for itself. I have at hand a page of her correspondence, discussing point 14, on galley 20, where she describes a figure of Dürer's, in the story. "I'd like it to stand—hood, scythe, hourglass . . . death being alone, and not wanting to be had up for speeding." And she adds, "As Goethe said of a painter, 'He doesn't paint red velvet, but the idea of it.' " Her stories, she wrote to me farther along in this letter, were "outside facts underpainted with subjective feelings"—a definition of fiction that will do as well as any other.

WHAT BECOMES CLEAR IS that we can't sum up this tough, shifting, indefinable medium with these samplings, or talk about a few *New Yorker* story writers while excluding the vital many, including those scores of contributors who gave us one or two or three wonderful works of fiction and then, for one reason or another, or for no apparent reason, could not or did not write more. To convey some idea of the long flow of fiction here, I can do no more than list a handful of splendid contributors, whose names and work will have to stand for the rest: Eudora Welty, Mavis Gallant, Gabriel García Márquez, Nancy Hale, Brian Friel, Jean Stafford, Jean Rhys, Edward Newhouse, Robert M. Coates, Peter Handke, Roald Dahl, Deborah Eisenberg, Milan Kundera, Mark Helprin, Michael

Chabon, Tom Drury, Doris Lessing, Shirley Hazzard, Frederick Barthelme, Peter Taylor, Laurie Colwin, Jamaica Kincaid, Alice Adams, Cynthia Ozick, Nicholson Baker, Thom Jones.

There have been stories in this magazine that felt like nothing in the language that had come before, and there is great pleasure for me in thinking back to some of our predecessor fiction editors—among them Katharine White and Gus Lobrano and William Maxwell—and imagining what they must have felt when they first read John Cheever's "The Enormous Radio" (or "Goodbye, My Brother" or "The Country Husband"); Frank O'Connor's "My Da"; Shirley Jackson's "The Lottery"; J. D. Salinger's "A Perfect Day for Bananafish" and "For Esmé—with Love and Squalor"; Vladimir Nabokov's "Lance"; Harold Brodkey's "Sentimental Education"; Muriel Spark's "The Prime of Miss Jean Brodie"; and many others.

It's funny, too, to look back at myself: thirty years ago, opening the stories from Donald Barthelme (with his name typed at the top left corner of the manila envelope) that first brought us his pasteups and headlines, the falling dog, the pitched street battles with bands of Comanches, the lost fathers, Eugénie Grandet, and Montezuma, the seven men—Bill, Hubert, Kevin, and the others—living with Snow White while she dreams of princes and pushes her shopping cart. "What *is* this?" subscribers asked indignantly, and though it wasn't always easy to frame an answer, what we all knew for certain, editors and readers (most of them) alike, was that we were lucky.

The new is alluring, but not always what matters most. What is more pleasing to a long-term editor or a loyal subscriber than to watch a master of fiction—a Prospero or a Jefferson of the form—as he walks his thematic acres and then, once again, falls to work? John Updike, unfailingly curious and spirited and reflective, circles back to the Maples, or to his native Pennsylvania small town, or to his mother and her death, reopening and revisiting lives and connections he has been setting down in these pages for forty years; and some of the late stories—"A Sandstone Farmhouse," "His Mother Inside Him," "Playing with Dynamite"—carry a grave power not touched by him before. William Maxwell goes home to his boyhood in Lincoln, Illinois, still again, to bring back a shocking sixty-year-old murder (that novel, "So Long, See You Tomorrow," ran here in 1979), or to tell about his brother's terrible accident, or to reconsider the complex, silent lives of the black servants in his family's house and in other houses then, and, if we think at first that we have been there before, the story, without fail, will show us why this trip was essential for him and for us.

WEEKS AND STORIES GO by, and one of the records that are being run up, one realizes, is a life's work. V. S. Pritchett is as old as the century, and, while there is little about him that feels monumental, he is England's grand master of the short story and our language's presiding man of letters. Sir Victor has always insisted that he is more craftsman than artist, and claims that plots are almost beyond him, but he is too modest. The three interconnected Noisy Brackett stories, which begin with "The Key to My Heart," are made up of car chases, crooked business dealings, drunkenness, gossip, class snobbery, and comic invention: the ingredients of a Feydeau farce, one might say, except that they are also stuffed with heartbreak and sexual suffering. Rereading them, you relish the craftsmanship, but then your eye is caught, once again, by something else. Birds, for instance. I had remembered ". . . and the rooks came out of the elms like bits of black paper," in "The Key to My Heart," but not "A soft owl flew over the lane." The short adjective, instead of the expected adverb, is art itself, and makes a place and a mood and a time of day, an entire scene, out of seven words. Call back the interviewer. This is what we're looking for in the fiction line: we want that owl.

Onward and Upward
with the Arts, June, 1994

POSTLUDE

This trade talk is more than twenty years old, and there have been a few changes. I am no longer reading and editing and rejecting fiction, and about time, but the process at *The New Yorker* remains about the same. That list of regular fiction contributors has turned over, as well, with my old varsity gradually being replaced by George Saunders, Richard Ford, Zadie Smith, Tessa Hadley, Roberto Bolaño, T. Coraghessan Boyle, Tom McGuane, Lorrie Moore, Chimamanda Adichie, Junot Díaz, Donald Antrim, Colson Whitehead, and many others. The incumbent editors, Cressida Leyshon, Willing Davidson, and fiction editor Deborah Treisman, carry on the same intimate day-to-daying with writers—well, perhaps not quite as intimate, since it all happens online now— but editing, I think, remains a mystery to the world. Sometimes it even mystified me. Back in 1991, when we were closing Edith Templeton's "Nymph & Faun," cited above, it was suddenly learned that most of the characters in it still had the same names they'd borne in life: names she'd carried in memory while changing past events into high-style fiction. For legal reasons, we had to fictionalize them, give them pseudonyms. I reached her by telephone at her home in Bordighera, Italy, and explained the little crisis, asking her to call back the next day with fresh names; I would do the same, and we'd write in our fresh cast on the page proofs. The next day, we found that three of the names I'd thought up and attached to different characters were exactly the same as hers. Later, in a citation at the end of her collection, "The Darts of Cupid," she called our mutual understanding "telepathic."

Now and then there are public rewards, as well. When Alice Munro was announced as the winner of the Nobel Prize for Literature in 2013, we *New Yorker* fiction types yelled and hugged each other in the hallway outside our offices. Munro was a short-story writer, nothing else, and now the world's best. She'd never stopped, and she was ours. Deborah Treisman had been her editor for a decade or more, and they counted on each other for everything.

July, 2015

LA FORZA DEL ALPO

An opera in four acts, conceived prior to successive evenings at the Westminster Kennel Club Show and the Metropolitan Opera.

CAST

GUGLIELMO—A dashing fox terrier (*tenor*)

MIMI (Ch. Anthracite Sweet-Stuff of Armonk)—A poodle (*soprano*)

DON CANINO (her father)—Another poodle (*baritone*)

BRUTTO—Companion poodle to Don Canino and suitor for the hand of Mimi (*basso*)

FIDOLETTA—A Lhasa Apso. Nurse to Mimi but secretly enamored of Guglielmo. A real bitch (*mezzo*)

SPIQUE—A comical bulldog (*basso hundo*)

DR. FAUSTUS—A veterinary (*tenor*)

CHORUS: Non-sporting, herding, and terrier contestants; judges, handlers, reporters

(There will be three walks around the block)

After the disastrous failure of his misbegotten early "Arfeo" at La Scala in the winter of 1843, few expected that Verdi would soon return to the themes of canine anticlericalism and the proliferation of Labradors (*labbrazazione*), but his discovery of the traditional Sicilian grooming cavatina—as recapitulated in the touching barkarole "Dov'è il mio guinzaglio?" ("I have lost my leash") that closes Act III—appears to have sent him back to work. Verdi's implacable opposition to the Venetian muzzling ordinance of 1850 is to be heard in the rousing "Again a full moon" chorus that resonates so insistently during Brutto's musings before and after the cabaletta:

At the opening curtain, Guglielmo and Mimi, in adjoining benching stalls, plan their elopement, despite the opposition of Don Canino, who has arranged her forthcoming marriage to Brutto despite rumors about the larger male's parentage. After the lovers' tender duet "A cuccia, a cuccia, amore mio" ("Sit! *Sit,* my love!"), recalling their first meeting at an obedience class, they part reluctantly, with Guglielmo distressed at her anxiety over the nuptials: "Che gelida manina" ("Your icy paw"). Don Canino, enlisting the support of the perfidious Fidoletta, plots to dispatch Guglielmo into the K-9 Corps, and, joined by Brutto, the trio, in "Sotto il nostro albero" ("Under the family tree"), jovially celebrates the value of pedigree.

As the judging begins, Guglielmo, alerted to Don Canino's plot by the faithful Spique, disguises himself as a miniature apricot poodle, but the lovers fail to detect the lurking presence of Don Canino, who has hidden himself among a large entry of Rottwei-

lers in Ring 6. A pitched battle between hostile bands of Lakeland and Bedlington terriers requires the attention of Spique, and in his absence Fidoletta entraps the innocent Guglielmo, who discloses his identity to her. She breaks off their amusing impromptu duet "Non so chi sei" ("I don't know who you are, but I sure like your gait") to fetch the police, but Guglielmo makes good his escape through the loges during the taping of a Kal Kan commercial—an octet severely criticized in its day, but to which Mascagni makes dear obeisance in his later sestina "Mangia, Pucci."

Guglielmo, not realizing in the darkness that he has found his way back to his natal kennel in Chappaqua, delivers the dirgelike "Osso Bucco" while digging in the yard, but is elated by news from Spique that he has uncovered certain documents in the back-door garbage compactor. Fidoletta, puzzled, trails the valiant pair as they hasten back to the Garden.

In our turbulent final act, the wedding of Mimi and Brutto is interrupted by the arrival of Dr. Faustus, bearing the purloined A.K.C. documents unearthed by Spique. The good vet declares that the nuptials must halt, because Brutto is in fact not only Mimi's father but (through a separate whelping) her uncle as well. Don Canino, horrified at his own depravity, vows to enter holy orders, and, in a confession, reveals that Brutto is no purebred—"Mira l'occhio azzurro" ("Ol' Blue Eyes")—thanks to a Pomeranian on his dam's side. Dr. Faustus removes Brutto to his laboratory for neutering. Guglielmo, still in disguise, unexpectedly wins a Best of Opposite Sex award in his breed as the lovers are at last united. Guglielmo serenades his Mimi with the "Sono maschio" ("I am a young intact male") as the happy couple, renouncing show biz, envision their future as a breeding pair with a cut-rate puppy mill in the Garden State Mall. Spique, exhausted by so much unlikelihood, falls asleep on the emptied stage, where his sonorous snores ("Zzzzz") are joined by those of the audience.

Shouts & Murmurs,
February, 1994

THE DARIEN CONNECTICUT DEF POETRY JAM

2 HAIKU

Kick him in the groin
And get that yellow, baby:
Mom's late for yoga.

Bo's header in net
Beats Mamaroneck 1–zip.
Early admission?
—*Sokkamom*

SITTER

Changin yo Huggies
Baby honkee muhfuh
So don do me no trix
Got a Calculus I test
Tomorrow second period
And if I turn Tupac way low
You go'n sleep
Sweetie babe?

> —*LASOUL*

ON FIRST LOOKING INTO CHAPMAN'S SECOND DRAWER

I hear you Vanessa and Aly:
French cuffs are so
McOut.

> —*M. Moi*

RPM

ogetoffmyassgetoffmyassgetoffmyassmisterbigfatlexus
high on latte here on the dewy do we merritt
i'm askin'—you wanna play games?
you wanna play bumperpool?

You wanna play the lil game i taught
my poodle name of renoir: rollover and play dead?
looks like it. . . .

                  rumrum rummedyrum.
Uhohwasthatyouflashingyourhighbeamatmejustnow?
                  —*Walter Putnam Stebbins*

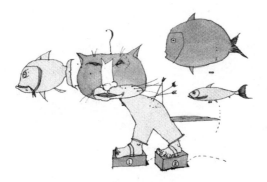

A GOOD MAN

Right beyond the Whiskas and stuff
2nd left after Dependency Needs
Straight along past the Goldfishes
Balsamics Baking Supplies Batteries Bottled Waters
Now left again before Party & Poolside
+ look w. care thru Other Herbs (Rt. Side) and if not
ASK!
But what the hell is
—can't make out your writing—
"Filé Powder"?

                  —*Yupster*

INTIMATION AT WEE SPINNEY

My Title—
1st from a boggy
Lie sailed O sunlit
Orb slightly trapward
Ere my deft in
Sideout 6-iron
Draw
Plunked it just on the second
Cut at 17 from
Where it rolled
Sweet slight bend
Yow exclam cried Herb
To within 2' 8" but
What's left for me
Now eye ask?

—Biff III

12:31 A.M.

You 'wake?
Listen what came between the Accord hatchback
And the yellow Volvo DL wagon? Sort of
Gray with a little ding
Low on the door on your side?
Funny to ask when I'm looking at my dad's
Malibu here plain as day.

—Ambien

GREEN AS GREEN

We are crabgrass. Up up up up up up up
Grow grow grow grow grow—
HOLD IT! QUIET GUYS!
mnmnmnmnmnmnmnn
Yep, it's Rider-man. Heads down, everybody:
. . . *mnmnmMNMNMNMNmnmm mn m n* . . .
There he goes—did you catch that *hat*?
Well, back to the old salt mines, I guess.
Grow grow grow grow up up up up up
Their Shih Tzu died

—*S. Ward*

Verse, June, 2003

PAST MASTERS: WILLIAM STEIG

THE MINSTREL STEIG

The rule about age is never to think about it, so let us instead pack "two suitcases, the first with food, the second mostly with food," and be on our way. The travel tip comes from Zeke, a gifted young pig who leaves home in the middle of the night, upset because his harmonica-playing invariably puts his family to sleep—"out like a light, no matter how merry the music." The story is continued in "Zeke Pippin," a book for children published on November 14th, the day its author and illustrator, William Steig, turned eighty-seven. It was his twenty-fifth children's book since he first took up the work, a quarter century ago; almost all of them remain exuberantly in print, with several still popping up here and there in new editions and surprising languages—Hawaiian, say, or Xhosa—and with sales, foreign and domestic, that now total close to two million. Steig, of course, is this magazine's own William Steig, who sold his first drawing to *The New Yorker* in 1930 and his most recent one last month, which makes him our longest-running active contributor. The magazine has published sixteen hundred and fifty drawings of his and a hundred and seventeen covers, and there are more of each in the bank. He is probably still best known here for his extensive series "Small Fry," which concerned the rowdy doings and pleasures of inventive and pugnacious young boys and girls: street kids, for the most part, who all bore strong resemblance to one another—stubby and snub-nosed, with bright eyes and tough, tipped-up chins—and thus, inescapably, to Steig himself. His most celebrated cover, I imagine, is the one for May 9, 1953—a portrait of a five- or six-year-old boy artist, brush in hand, leaning against the runny, color-bursting tree he has just painted, under a yellow-ray sun that would make van Gogh squint: Kid Steig forever.

Most of Steig's art, though, has been for and about adults, and it has not always been lighthearted. In some of the cartoons, men and women yell and quarrel, snap at their kids, glare inkily at each other from old armchairs. In one drawing, a sour-looking widow standing in front of a gravestone, her mouth open and her finger in the air, is continuing the argument. Other Steig people, alone and captionless, stare out at the reader from faces that are masks or Rorschach blobs or blotter lines; the style is hard to describe, because it keeps changing, sometimes almost from week to week. Courtship and love (and plenty of lust) turn up, mostly in classical guise: broad-hipped nymphs, tattered knights, satyrs, men as roosters, lions as kings. Everyone seems to have dressed up, in the child's sense of the word, perhaps in hope of more fun. Animals and flowers and masks abound, but almost sadly. The titles of some of Steig's collections sound like warnings: "The Lonely Ones," "Ruminations," "Strutters and Fretters," "Our Miserable Life." It's amazing how different, how direct and open Steig is when he turns to the difficulties and adventures of children.

Not children *exactly*. In most of the books, one notices, the dramatis personae are boys and girls in disguise—junior pigs, mice, dogs, geese, donkeys, and frogs—with parents (in coats and pants, hats and dresses) of the same breed; and before long the switch, which looks only charming at first, takes on a more useful purpose. "I realized that I could get crazier with animals and have them

Launched by Steig's flowing pen, Pearl, of "The Amazing Bone," happily sets sail
(above and on following pages), on dire and colorful adventures.

do stranger things," Steig said not long ago. "And I put them in
clothes, as other writers have done."

Steig's heroes and heroines, young and innocent as they appear,
keep running into appalling obstacles and troubles. Roland (of
"Roland the Minstrel Pig") is almost garrotted, narrowly misses
being crushed by a boulder, and then is strung up from a tree
limb. Sylvester, a donkey, is turned into a rock. Amos (the mouse
in "Amos and Boris") falls overboard in mid-ocean, and Boris (a
whale, *ibid.*) is stranded on a beach by a hurricane. Abel, the mouse
hero of "Abel's Island," is marooned for a year, and Pearl, a very
young pig in "The Amazing Bone," is nearly cooked and served

(with a nice green salad) by a fox. So it goes, but these small critters remain valorous, and they come through in the end. Survival, we begin to understand, is the main event. These animals aren't just sweet; they're tough and active and optimistic. They love to get going. They're battlers. Dominic, the eponymous dog hero of Steig's picaresque novel, carries a spear and routs the rascally Doomsday Gang again and again. When he's buried in a deep hole, with the foxy and ferrety gang members licking their chops up above, he starts to dig his way out at once. "Working away, he was happy he had gone out into the world to seek his fortune. So many interesting things to do! With four sets of claws and the spear, and a bountiful supply of energy, he burrowed a long tunnel away from the hole and under the crowded roots of a large tree. Then he worked his way upward to the surface."

I AM A FATHER of children who are widely separated in age, thanks to a second marriage, and when, in the mid-nineteen-

seventies, my wife and I first took turns reading aloud "Sylvester and the Magic Pebble" and "Amos and Boris" and "Caleb & Kate" and "Farmer Palmer's Wagon Ride" to our young son, I sometimes felt a brief pang for my daughters, who were by then well into their twenties, because they'd come along too early to get that first-hand, child's-eye view of such treasures. Is there a word for this phenomenon—"postchronism," or some such? It's like being sorry for Sophocles's audiences because they missed out on "The Tempest," or pitying the monks who first stared up at the freshly painted Giotto frescoes in the Basilica of St. Francis in Assisi because they never got to think about Cézanne. It is my own view that we dismiss children's literature too readily, perhaps because young readers are always poised to move along to the next stage, but also because we suspect that anything that appeals so strongly and pleasurably to us, as parents, is too easy to be taken seriously. How many of us do not still believe in our secret hearts that with a little luck we could have played major-league baseball or written a first-class children's book. Dream on.

Many friends of mine, I discovered, have kept the Steig books on a special shelf in their memories even after the prime consumers of the books have grown up. Mention a title or a hero to them, and their faces light up. "They're so *clear!*" is a common response, and the erstwhile reader-aloud sounds no different from a contemporary young parent in the midst of the same happy experience. "I think Elizabeth loved 'Gorky Rises' best," a newspaper editor said to me the other day, speaking of her eight-year-old and an intrepid Steigian frog aviator. "All that floating and zooming around."

Other friends recalled Steig himself, along with the books; there seemed to be no dividing line. Warren Miller, a younger colleague of Steig's at the magazine, and himself the illustrator of two works for children, said, "I love his books. I remember him years and years ago, in the Village. I'd be playing my trumpet in some jazz cellar and I'd see him sitting over in the corner, listening intensely." Miller hunched over slightly and drew in his elbows. "You know, he's always paid such attention. And I like the writing in his books almost as much as the illustrations. There's one phrase I've never forgotten, from 'Amos and Boris,' when the whale is stranded on the beach—"

" 'Breaded with sand,' " I said, breaking in.

"That's it!" he cried. " 'Breaded with sand'—what a writer!"

Frank Modell, a *New Yorker* artist and children's-book writer who is a little closer in age to Steig than the others I talked to, said, "He's always worn dark clothes and sneakers. Even among the artists, he was informal. I always felt that he stood aside from the rest of us and watched. He and I used to live near each other in the Village—he had a place just off Sixth Avenue. I was there one day when he suddenly told me that he liked his apartment better than mine. I was living on Ninth Street then, in a ninth-and-tenth-floor apartment that had a terrace and a view, so I was surprised. Steig drew me to a window in his place and pointed, and then I realized that we were on the second floor and that what he saw, just below us, was men and women and kids and dogs and traffic going by. It was as if he had a television set that brought in the whole world."

In Steig's books, clarity and comedy feel as easily conjoined as words and pictures, and a little magic sometimes helps as well. In "The Amazing Bone," the garrulous object that Pearl puts in her pocket previously belonged to a witch, from whom it picked up almost more powers than it knows what to do with. After it has disposed of that gourmet fox, it stays on with her and her family: "Pearl always took it to bed when she retired, and the two chatterboxes whispered together until late in the night. Sometimes the bone put Pearl to sleep by singing, or by imitating soft harp music. . . . They all had music whenever they wanted it, and sometimes even when they didn't."

Foxes fare poorly in the *Steigwerk,* usually after a brief losing battle with their consciences. "I regret having to do this to you," the fox says to Pearl as he totes her toward the cookstove. "It's nothing personal." In "Doctor De Soto," the fox is grateful to the tiny mouse-dentist who has pulled his bad tooth. (The deft, white-smocked D.D.S. does the extraction with a winch, working, with his wife-hygienist, from the top of a tall ladder.) "I really shouldn't eat them," he muses. "On the other hand, how can I resist?" Fortunately, De Soto is a top mouse in his field, and he requires only the magic of science to handle the situation. Dentists can do anything these days.

Steig's second book, "Sylvester and the Magic Pebble," which won the Caldecott Medal (the most prestigious American prize for juvenile-book illustration) when it appeared, in 1969, is still his masterpiece. In the story, Sylvester, a young donkey, collects pebbles for a hobby and one day comes upon a strange red one, which has the power to grant him any wish. On the way home, he

encounters a lion and saves himself by rashly wishing to turn into a rock. It happens, and then he is stuck—a rock in a field, with no way to wish himself back or to call out for help. He is searched for everywhere, mourned by his parents, almost forgotten, but then one day . . . The inexorable quiet of the tale is deepened by the simplicity of the underpopulated landscape illustrations: the rock that is Sylvester seen under a blazing firmament of stars; the rock in a winter snowstorm; the rock in the springtime. The text is just as spare: "Night followed day and day followed night over and over again. Sylvester on the hill woke up less and less often. . . . He felt he would be a rock forever and he tried to get used to it. He went into an endless sleep."

The book is about death, nothing less, but it is death in the way that young children first think about it. What can it be like to be still and not speak and never move again? Steig himself does not entirely agree with this interpretation. "I think Sylvester's being that rock has to do with his relations with his parents, too," he says. "Sylvester inside that rock is an armored creature, but when he realizes how loved he is, he can come back. Coming back to a family in the end is natural for kids. These things are symbolic, but never in a thought-out way."

Steig is an artist of sunlight (in contrast to Maurice Sendak, for instance, who is an artist of night), but he has a fondness for starry skies and the long thoughts of small creatures alone under the heavens. Amos, lying out on the deck of his sloop, the *Rodent,* thinks himself "a little speck of a living thing in the vast living universe," and then, "overwhelmed by the beauty and mystery of everything," rolls off his boat and into the sea. Dominic, off on his own adventures, is susceptible to moonlight, at one point forgetting his doggy daytime self to the point where he declares to the heavens, "Oh, Life, I am yours! Whatever it is you want of me, I am ready to give." It's all too much for him, and he falls into a good, long bout of howling.

"Dominic," which was Steig's seventh book, was an achievement of a different order. Encouraged by Michael di Capua, his editor at Farrar, Straus & Giroux, Steig set out to write a novel, rather than a book told largely through pictures, and he pulled it off with élan. It is illustrated with lively pen-and-ink instead of his customary watercolors, but the writing picks up the added burden without strain. It's a book for slightly older kids—to be read, perhaps, rather than read aloud—and part of why it works is that Steig never writes down, never patronizes his audience. The younger books are full of words ("discombobulated," "lunatic," "sinuous") that a parent may have to stop and explain; and in the books for, say, ten-year-olds, "palsied," "sequestration," "ensconced," "circumstantial," "rubescent," and the like show up, with no more than a trail of context to help out. Good writers and painters, I suspect, compliment their audiences by expecting only the best of them; the responding thrill of understanding is what art is all about.

IT IS CLEAR THAT Steig's stories and small creatures speak for him. It's harder to say how his line and his opalescent watercolors do the same thing. Perhaps because he puts colors and inks directly on paper, with no preliminary sketches or pencillings, his paintings always feel as if he had just placed them in your hands. The Steigian palette and medium, in any case, shift freely from book to book, in response to each new story. "The Real Thief," his third—and shortest—novel, concerns a sentry goose wrongfully accused of stealing the royal jewels, and its darker tones, of injustice and suffering and forgiveness, are conveyed in ink and a gray watercolor wash. Pearl, of "The Amazing Bone," is Steig's youngest ingénue, scarcely more than a baby; the world is new and fresh to her, and what she sees are springtime swards of yellow, lavender, and the palest green. When she is accosted by a band of small brigands, possibly cats and dogs, they are wearing brilliantly colored Japanese masks.

"He's such an observant artist," Frank Modell said to me. "Everybody thinks that people with artistic ability can draw anything, but that isn't true. You can't draw a dog unless you know dogs. His pictures are full of things that other artists avoid—horses, dogs, rocks. He knows them all. Steig has never been afraid of being alone—you can tell that."

Lee Lorenz, Steig's *New Yorker* art editor and longtime colleague (and fellow children's-book writer, as well), says, "I don't know how he does it. You're never conscious of the medium, but it has occurred to me that the only romantic thing about him may be his colors. He's not circumspect, and his approach is so personal that you can't learn or borrow from him. You can only admire. Along with Arno, Addams, and Steinberg, he's one of the heroes around here."

There was an echo in this—a clang of considerable proportions. Just days before my conversation with Lee Lorenz, I had been talking with Mary Pope Osborne, who has written more than thirty books for children (she is also the president of the Authors Guild), and when I told her that I was writing a piece about Steig's children's works she said, "You know, he's been a hero for a whole generation of writers like me. Somehow, he managed to accomplish the feat of writing in a strange and different way that you instantly understood. I never knew how he did it. He helped me take chances with my own writing. For me, he's been like E. B. White and Arnold Lobel and James Marshall—the band of young people's writers that I always put together in my mind. I wanted to be in their company."

.   .   .

LATE IN DECEMBER, I pressed a call on Bill Steig and his wife, Jeanne, at their roomy, sun-filled apartment in the Back Bay section of Boston; they moved there in 1992, giving up what had been their home for many years in Kent, Connecticut, after they reached an age when they foresaw that driving would become difficult. Steig says he does not miss Kent or country life at all. Jeanne is an artist, too, busy at the moment with a collection of small panels containing elegantly detailed near-Romanesque figures which she assembles from street-found bits of wood and metal. (She has also been a writer, supplying light-verse texts for three books that she and Bill did together.) Their place feels stuffed with art, but there's not much Bill Steig on the walls. "He won't have it—it makes him uneasy," Jeanne said. "He says his work is made to be reproduced." She did point out a couple of small, bright tapestries that have his unmistakable touch. "He had to have something to do while we were watching the Watergate hearings," she said. "He invented the stitching as he went along."

Bill Steig attended the National Academy of Design as a youth, but he claims not to have learned anything there. "I enjoyed playing touch football in the yard," he said. He is short and solid-looking, with blue eyes and a calm, workmanlike air. His hair, still in a boyish, upstanding brush, is gray now, but he doesn't look like a man in his eighties—or a man of any particular age. He looks like a student. He speaks quietly, in tentative sentences, sometimes throwing in an unexpected question or a fresh idea that imparts a swervy, back-roads feeling to the conversation.

"I like change," he said at one point. "But I try not to do it deliberately. I'm trying to have fun. I used to use different materials a lot—try thicker pens or brushes, or bamboo pens—with the idea that that'd make me change. If the pen stutters on the page, that's a new thing." He said that finishing drawings for the children's books was sometimes daunting for him, because he had to put the same characters down on the page again and again.

He got into children's books in the mid-sixties, at the urging of a fellow *New Yorker* artist, Bob Kraus, whose entrepreneurial fervor also inspired juvenile books from colleagues like Charles Addams, Whitney Darrow, and Lorenz. (Nowadays, *New Yorker* artists become children's-book authors in even greater numbers, and a stroll through the juvenile section of a bookstore can turn up works by the likes of Warren Miller, Ed Koren, Frank Modell, Roz Chast, and—in brilliant profusion—James Stevenson.) "Bob Kraus got me to write 'Roland,' which was great for me, because it got me out of advertising work," Steig said. "I was almost in my sixties and I was supporting a lot of people."

I said that family seemed to be a recurring chord in his books.

"I've always felt that family was a nuisance," he said. "My parents were very dependent—in fact, I supported them all my life. When I started working, instead of going out in the world I had to begin supporting my family. But I did it with good will."

Steig, who grew up in the Bronx and still carries a whisper of it in his consonants, was the third of four brothers. His father was a housepainter. After Steig finished writing "Dominic," it came to him one day that the spirit of its eager, adventurous hero was a portrait of his father. "I was never read to as a child," Steig told me, "but reading was big back then. We had no radio, no TV. The movies were big, too. We went to the Nickelettes—so called because you could get in for a nickel. There was one of them that would let two of you in for a nickel if you sat in the same seat. We used to go to the library—only we said 'liberry'—on Tremont Avenue, where they allowed you to take out two novels and two nonfiction books on each visit. Sometimes you tried to find a novel that *looked* like nonfiction, so you could beat the rule."

"Were you a street kid?" I asked.

"Sure, I was, along with the other guys in the Claremont A.C.,"
he said. "My part of the Bronx was between Crotona Park and
Claremont Park, but the gang was just the boys who lived in our
building. We were very small kids. We admitted a couple of girls
later on—Sophie Kozanski and Pearl Bimlich—and then we called
it the Claremont Athletic and Social Club."

He seemed surprised when I said I felt that these kids seemed
familiar to me, but then he brightened up and said, "Oh, yeah,
sure—'Small Fry' came from all that. And maybe Pearl, in 'The
Amazing Bone,' came from Pearl Bimlich. On the other hand,
Jeanne and I had a dog named Pearl when we lived in Kent, a dog
that died just before we moved up here." He paused, thinking it
over. "Maybe the dog was named after Pearl Bimlich, too."

Steig, one notices, is never guarded in conversation but never
loquacious; he seems unwilling to draw attention to himself by
sounding wise or consequential. He said at one point that he had
enjoyed writing "The Real Thief," because it dealt with more difficult and more adult ideas—his only book with a message. "Unfor-
tunately, I made a mistake in it," he added at once. "The second half
of it goes back in time and repeats the same events in a different
context. It confuses things. I ran into the same thing once in a Conrad book I was reading—as an adult, I mean. Then I had to go and
give kids the same problem. As somebody once said, you've got to
remember that you're writing for kids—otherwise, you might end
up writing 'War and Peace.'"

We had moved into the dining room by now, and the three of
us were demolishing a luncheon salad, with beer and pickles and
Italian bread on the side. Steig suddenly said, "Are you the kind of
person who pays attention to birthdays and anniversaries?" It was
one of his swerves. I said yes, I was, and Jeanne, across from me,
began to laugh. "Our anniversary was yesterday," she said.

"I knew it was around the end of the year," Bill said cheerfully.

Jeanne broke the piece of bread she was holding in half and handed a morsel to him. "Happy anniversary, Bill," she said.

"What are your feelings about Picasso?" he asked me, chewing.

I did a quick inventory and ventured that he was clearly the premier artist of my lifetime—the right answer, I learned later on, because Picasso, another artist who thrived on change, has been Steig's artistic idol, his one and only. Steig once ended an extended friendship with a man who'd expressed some revisionist doubts about the Master.

MY VISIT WAS FLYING away very quickly, and I did not want to overstay. Steig had told me that he suffers from emphysema, which saps his energy. "Some days, I go to my workroom and just do a crossword puzzle," he said. His attention, I noticed, did not weary, for our conversation had also ranged to sports (he misses the Giants—the New York football Giants—on television now that he's moved to Boston) and to his children: his son, Jeremy, a celebrated jazz flutist; and his daughters, Lucy, who is a psychologist and a painter, and Maggie, an actress now also employed as a party planner, who lives in Boston. Frank Modell had told me that he recalled Steig's talking about Jeremy one day, many years earlier, and saying, "My son is one of the nicest people I know." And Frank had said to me, "I wonder how many of us wish our fathers had ever thought something like that."

For Steig, apparently, the emotional and spiritual sectors of life were no farther away than the daily and offhand. I knew that he had been a patient of Wilhelm Reich, the Viennese radical psychologist, and he told me now that he still regularly climbed into his Orgone Accumulator, a metal-lined, telephone-booth-like container in his workroom, as part of the therapy to which he attributed his own long survival, as well as his mother's recovery, years before, from a serious cancer invasion. "I've been an ardent Reichean," he said. "Just the other day, I read somewhere that guys who think about the universe say that seventy-five per cent of it is still beyond their ken. Well, I think that seventy-five per cent is orgone, which, for some reason, we refuse to get in touch with."

The talk went back to his work. "Drawing is something I feel impelled to do, but I don't feel an undeniable urge to write these books," he said. "I've done more than I originally intended. It's not inspiration, but I take it seriously, writing for kids."

I asked the obligatory question. Was writing the books perhaps a way for him to remain a child?

"I enjoyed my childhood," he said. "I think I like kids more than the average man does. I can relax with them, more than I can among adults. I'm what you call shy—it's been a lifelong problem. Children are genuine, which is such a big problem with grownups. After we're about thirty, we have to give up being children. You can't try to stay young—that would make you old in no time—but I like to think I've kept a little innocence. Probably I'm too dumb to do anything else."

WHEN I GOT HOME that evening, I looked through my little stack of Steig books, and noticed once again how many different dedicatees there were. Jeanne was there, and so was Michael di Capua, and so, of course, were Steig's children and his two grand-daughters, but the list seemed to grow from year to year and from book to book. "To Maggie, Melinda, Francesca, and Nika" was the dedication in "The Amazing Bone." The next book is "To Delia, Nika, Abigail, and Francesca," and the one after that "To Delia, Sidonie, Nika, Sylvain, and Estelle."

Jeanne had told me that she was part of a large, Chicago-based

family that included a son and daughter of hers from an earlier marriage, four grandchildren, and also nieces and nephews and cousins in profusion, and she said that a number of these kids had been cited by Bill in his later books. The son of a woman who'd worked in a grocery store in Kent was in one of the books, and so was Chuck Close's daughter Maggie. Jeanne thinks that getting their names into Bill's books is almost a new fad or craze for kids. Bill, smiling, said that he'd begun to impose a visa system: three or four repeats and then you couldn't expect to find yourself in there anymore. But now, looking over the thin, different-shaped volumes, and the gatherings of names up at the front, I got the feeling that the message here was more complicated: real children climbing their way into books where they had so clearly and so often been made to feel interesting and important. "To Delia, Sidonie, Sylvain, Estelle, Kyle, Molly, Reid, Tina, Serena, Zachary and Zoe," and "To Alicia, Charlotte, Curran, Evan, Geneva, Georgia, Kate, Maggie and William." And others waiting.

Onward and Upward
with the Arts, February, 1995

FOUR FAREWELLS

EARL WEAVER

Earl Weaver, the banty, umpire-contentious, Hall of Fame manager of the Orioles, who died Friday, was the best naked talker I ever heard. Deadline-aware writers, seeking him out in his office shortly after another last out, would often find him behind his desk gnawing on a chicken wing, sans uniform and undies: a five-foot-seven, birthday-suited unsentimentalist still alight with the complexities and hovering alternate possibilities of the trifling game we'd all just attended. His seventeen-year—1968–86—run at the helm in Baltimore (he retired at the end of the 1982 season, then thought better of it a couple of years later) produced teams that won ninety or more games in twelve seasons, along with four American League pennants, and one World Championship: the second-best managerial record of the century. He will remain most famous for his red-faced, hoarsely screaming set-tos with the umps, which produced hilarious photos, thanks to the size differential, but even here he was an intellectual at heart, having discovered that tipping the bill of his cap to one side would allow him to get an inch or two closer to the arbiter's jaw, without incurring the automatic ejection of the tiniest physical contact.

What Earl wanted, what he battled for and talked about and

thought about endlessly, was that edge, the single pitch or particular play or minuscule advantage that could turn an inning or a day or a season his way. Long before Billy Ball, he had his coaches keep multicolored pitching and batting charts that told him which of his batters did well or poorly against each righty or lefty flinger in the league, and where on the field well-hit enemy line drives against one of his starters' or relievers' sliders or fastballs would probably land.

He relished eminent, top-performance players—Frank Robinson, Brooks Robinson, Mark Belanger, Ken Singleton—played them every day, and barely spoke to them for games and seasons on end. Perhaps he was secretly even happier about his left-field platoon of the right-handed-batting Gary Roenicke and left-batting John Lowenstein, since they presented an irritating little difficulty for the other manager when making out his starting lineup. Most of all, I think, Earl loved his perpetually available left-handed pinch-hitter Terry Crowley, the primo late-inning, other-manager's dilemma of that era.

"Oh, I *love* this stuff," Earl would exclaim, perhaps only talking about the trifling game when he'd tried an outfielder, John Shelby, at second base for a few innings, in place of the slumping Rich Dauer: "Shelby at second gives us an extra move, and I'll go with it. . . . If you're losing, go for offense. Look for that move."

Talent mattered, too. In 1982, raving about his rookie infielder Cal Ripken, whom he had lately shifted from third base to shortstop, he said, "Wherever he plays, you can write him in for the next fifteen years, because that's how good he is." Yep—and thanks, Earl.

But let me tack on one more exchange, just before his retirement, which I initiated with the suggestion that he'd surely be back in baseball again before long, perhaps as a coach with a college or even a high-school team somewhere.

"I *hate* kids and I hate fucking kid baseball," he barked, startling us both to laughter. All he wanted was the real thing, the edge and nothing less.

Post, January, 2013

GARDNER BOTSFORD

Memorial at the Century Association

We've come to the end of the line, and my only duty is not to say anything that would appear to sum up our old friend. As an editor, he didn't trust heavyweight last paragraphs and liked to make them shorter or drop them altogether. What he'd say right here is enough already—let's stop the speeches and have a drink. Pieces of him are still turning up—flashes and bits of talk that come unexpectedly into my mind: his way of plumping his hands onto the dinner table, palms down, before the soup arrived—a gesture of satisfaction about where he was and what was to come. A noontime swimming party at the pond at Four Fields, before the pool was built, with several of us treading water or standing in the ooze, up to our chins in the dark, cool water. Arms and shoulders are barely visible and the impression is of a collection of floating white balloons—one of them, at the center, still wearing his eyeglasses—all talking and spouting, and stopping only now and then when a young frog comes breast-stroking by. And a moment of Gardner at the wheel of our Italian Rent-a-Car, twelve years ago, when we were driving home from Assisi, and the others of us babbling along the Lower Basilica and Cimabue and Giotto and Santa Chiara. We're working hard on our accents—"Chi-mah-BOO-aye" . . . "Ghi-YAH-to"—and there's almost an air of conversion hovering about, and then Gardner saying, "Oh, well, yes, but it's all just Disneyland."

After he'd left *The New Yorker* we'd see each other a couple of times a week—mostly at the Coffee House, where we bored the pants off the younger members with our talk about old New York late-night radio stations and Edith Oliver and FDR and Charlie Addams and Margaret Sullavan and Fiorello La Guardia and Carmin Peppe, and a number of breathtaking young women we'd both known and danced with sixty years before—Gardner knew them better than I did and was a better dancer. When we talked about the magazine he was sometimes unhappy about how it had changed, but he was never one of the mooners about *The New Yorker*'s past grandeur. He was alert and generous about what was new in the magazine—a terrific piece this week from some writer he'd not heard about before. And if I mentioned an exceptional story or a lively department column or Comment piece that he'd missed he'd write himself a note and look it up later. His name still came up at the office, and after he died Rick Hertzberg wrote me a note saying how much he'd loved Gardner's book. "To read it," he said, "is to see what was right about certain sons of the American ruling class of the early twentieth century—the modesty, the confidence, the straightforwardness. I felt real affection for him."

Gardner's gift to us was to keep himself elegant. He was aware of the dark side but preferred lightness and emotional economy. He knew all about the collapse of our cities and our politics, and the glazing-over of American good will, but assumed that we did, too. Because he was knowing and grown-up and good-looking it was easy for us to accept the invitation and try to be suave and optimistic when in his company—the way we used to feel when we came out of a Fred Astaire–Ginger Rogers movie, each of us quicker on our feet now and looking around for the next party, just down the street.

One morning a few weeks after he'd retired from *The New Yorker* in 1982, I had a phone call from him, and he said, "I can *see* you! You're sitting at your desk. In a blue shirt—right?" He'd just rented a one-room Midtown office for himself, over on Madison Avenue, near Forty-second Street, and when he'd looked out the window he was startled to find that he could see our old digs on the nineteenth and twentieth floors, away across Fifth and halfway up the next block on Forty-third Street. He told me to look out *my* window, but I couldn't find him. "Hold on," he said, and then, "Now look." I stared across the great chasms and palisades of stone and glass, and then, sure enough, there was Gardner: a tiny figure flapping a dust-rag or maybe his raincoat from a side window, with the phone in his other hand. "Wow!" I said. "I can't believe this!" he said, and we laughed and, I think, agreed to meet for lunch. Another little piece of Gardner—farther away now but still waving hello.

September, 2005

JOE CARROLL

When word came the other day that Joe Carroll had died, old *New Yorker* guys (or this old *New Yorker* guy) had a flash of taking a right off our nineteenth-floor office corridor and walking into Makeup, where everyone, it seemed, was cheerful and conversational, and worked standing up. Writers hid away in slot-like offices, hunched miserably over their typewriters; cartoonists came in on Tuesday mornings and went home again after lunch; and fiction folks did their thing upstairs; Makeup was a mostly Irish, mostly male enclave—John Murphy, Bill Fitzgerald, Bernie McAteer, John Broderick, Pat Keogh, et al.—that you hurried into to plead for another seven inches for your copy, which already lay pinned out on a corkboard delivery table, with beautiful runarounds enclosing blank spaces that would soon hold a cartoon or a spot drawing. Joe Carroll—leaning and smiling, with a dashing light beard—ran the place, and after he'd provided the blessed relief ("For you, of *course!*") there would be time enough for him to pass on a joke that just had come in over the phone from the R. R. Donnelley printing plant in Chicago, where the magazine was printed. Everyone in Makeup looked young but had been there forever; there's a 1982 photo of Joe and six of his boys—all in white shirts and dark or striped ties—who together represented a hundred and eighty-six years' service, or nine thousand six hundred and seventy-two closings.

Joe Carroll, who came to work at *The New Yorker* in 1936, and succeeded the fabled Carmine Peppe as top Makeup man in 1977, always seemed to have that extra beat of time that great athletes retain in mid-play; late on a Thursday night, when a piece or a Comment had fallen through, he was the quiet, smiling guy in the midst of curses and raised voices who somehow knew that we'd be O.K. again soon. He was a reader of the magazine as well as one of its makers, and along the way also found time to write a couple of Talk of the Town pieces, draw a cartoon that got published, and sire eleven children. He was ninety-one when he died last week in Virginia, and he still took pleasure in the ongoing newer and quicker, silently produced *New Yorker.* His magazine took form more slowly each week, after a process that required the skills of craftsmen or guild masters to put it together, and when the thing arrived at the office on Monday morning (with "ROUGH COPY" stamped on the cover) it promised pleasure and quality and a long future.

Post, January, 2011

ELWOOD CARTER

Read by Alice Angell at Elwood Carter's memorial, Brooklin, Maine

I'm extremely disappointed that age and disability prevent me from joining Nota and Lisa and Troy and the rest of you here this afternoon to remember Elwood and celebrate his splendid life. He looked after our Wells Cove cottage for about thirty years, but I think it's fair to say that we were friends all that time. We may have disagreed from time to time about what needed to be done to the shed roof or part of a seawall or a porch gutter, but we took our time about it, and it generally turned out that he had been right all along. His work for us was dedicated and professional, and much more. There's scarcely a screen door or rusty lock or sickly spruce or stretch of shore or driveway on the place that we haven't watched over and talked about together, and tried to fix. He cared about that point of land and the shore and that old house fully as much as we did. He loved it all and took pride in it, and our feelings about the place were touched and deepened by his pride in what he'd done.

Elwood was also a caretaker of our town and land, and the people in it. I loved the way he talked about dogs and children and the weather—he was a great noticer—and I hope I learned from listening to him. He was modest or moderate in everything. Six or seven years ago, the ancient flagpole out by the point collapsed, after decades of patching and propping. I was a little shocked by the cost of a replacement, and we postponed a decision until spring. But when June came around Elwood let me know that he'd been working on a new flagpole through most of the winter while at home—a slender but shapely pine that he'd cut down, trimmed and sanded and painted for weeks on end, without a word to me. He was shy and nervous about it when I turned up—he called it "my starter flagpole"—but of course it was perfect, and all the better for a gentle bend at midpoint and the hint of a stem or nub of a branch here and there along the shaft. It's been up and working for years now, and it will stay up forever.

We bought a smaller, new flag, and I folded up the tattered old one and put it away in an old bureau in our little house, along with some others. I'm telling you this because it leads up to one of the rare moments when I took Elwood by surprise—a summer morning when I took him out to that same bureau, pulled out a drawer of folded old flags, and showed him what I'd just found: a red, white, and blue mouse nest.

I wish Elwood were here this week to enjoy the Red Sox and maybe see them win the World Series. Not that he'd exactly enjoy it. I'm supposed to know a bit about sports and sports fans, but in all this time I could never cheer up Elwood about the Sox or the Patriots or the Bruins. If the Red Sox do beat the Cardinals, and I think they will, he'd say, "Well, all right, but next year don't look too good, does it?"

When I first got to Brooklin, more than eighty years ago, I noticed that men around here like to call their old friends "dear." "Howard de-ah" . . . "Charlie, de-ah." I feel the same way. Thank you, dear Elwood.

October, 2013

INNINGS

BARRY AND THE DEATHLY NUMBERS

Barry Bonds, the Lord Voldemort of baseball, has prevailed in the end, rapping the enchanted No. 756 and, for the moment, closing a complex tale that has held us too long and (here in Eastern Daylight Time, at least) way too late. The image may not hold up, since it casts baseball commissioner Bud Selig as Harry Potter, but for half a decade now a dank moral haze and a sense of unlikelihood have surrounded the Giant slugger Bonds as he pursued the famous seven-hundred-and-fourteen lifetime home-run mark established by Babe Ruth, and then Hank Dumbledore's all-time seven hundred and fifty-five. An irritated non-reader (or non-fan) who happened in on this story three days earlier and saw Commissioner Selig standing up in his box in San Diego but *not applauding* Bonds as he circled the bases after his tying seven-hundred-and-fifty-fifth poke, against the Padres, would sense at the same moment that footnotes or a movie version would not begin to clear things up. You had to have read the books.

Bonds's record dinger, in the fifth inning of a night game against the Washington Nationals at Petco Park, in San Francisco, came in his third at-bat of the evening, succeeding a loud double and a single. One vacationing Maine-coast cottager with a dinky

© The Saul Steinberg Foundation / Artists Rights Society (ARS), New York

summertime TV set—this cottager—had recently fallen into the
habit of going upstairs to brush his teeth and put on his pajamas
after watching Bonds's first at-bat, returning before the second one,
and tottering back up to bed when it was over, never mind the
rest of the game. This time, the vision of Barry's locked-in, more
characteristic swings kept him awake, and brought him back down
again minutes before midnight: just in time for the blessed three-
and-two solo blast, four hundred and thirty-five feet to right-center
field, and the clenched fists to heaven; the slow but not too slow
base-circling; the extended-family hugs (including one with Willie Mays, who is Bonds's godfather); a careful but placating prere-
corded concession by the saintly and now deposed Hank Aaron,
delivered on the Jumbotron ("I move over now and offer my best
wishes to Barry and his family on this historical achievement"); and
locally—on the stairs once again, with the set turned off at last—a
"Yesss!" in the dark.

The rejoicing here is not just over an expected natural decline in the booings and editorializings about Bonds's inferred but unproved use of steroids during the 2000 to 2003 seasons, late in his career (he is forty-three), when his customary thirty-seven or thirty-eight homers per season jumped into the upper forties and, in 2001, produced the all-time single-season record of seventy-three. Another hope is for less piety, a shift in the altogether mystifying popular notion that the lifetime home-run mark is somehow sacrosanct— "baseball's most hallowed record," as the news reports called it the other day. Hallowed but hollow, perhaps, since home-run totals are determined not just by the batters but by different pitchers, in very different eras, and, most of all, by the outer dimensions of the major-league parks, which have always varied widely and have been deliberately reconfigured in the sixteen ballparks built since 1992, thus satisfying the owners' financial interest in more and still more home runs. Bonds has been called a cheater, but the word should hardly come up in a sport whose proprietors, if they were in charge of the classic Olympic hundred-meter dash, would stage it variously at a hundred and six meters, ninety-four, a hundred and three, and so forth, and engrave the resulting times on a tablet.

The weight of records and their breaking could be seen in Barry Bonds's vapid swings and feeble pop-ups and dribblers during the six homerless games he endured before tying Aaron's mark. By coincidence, the same frailty overtook Alex Rodriguez, the Yankees' celebrity thumper and third baseman, who is leading all comers in home runs this year but fell into a career-worst, oh-for-twenty-two stretch at the plate while he attempted to deliver the round-tripper that would put him into the élite five-hundred lifetime home-run club, with every pitch to him now weirdly illuminated by the glisten and flare of thousands of digital cameras. The same strain, for that matter, lay within the preoccupied, baggy-eyed stares of Tom Glavine, the slim elder lefty of the Mets,

as he went for his splendid three-hundredth lifetime victory. The
reprieves almost overlapped—A-Rod's first-inning homer against
the Royals arriving on Saturday afternoon, and Glavine's win the
next night, against the Cubs—and two days later Barry set us free.
He is not much liked—"churl" and "churlish" have had a wide
revival in the media lexicon when he is under discussion—but his
smile after the homer and the hoopla was benign. This was Opening Day.

Talk, August, 2007

NOTHING DOING

With the Yankees' pitching in a perpetual flummox and the distraction of a home All-Star Game looming into view in the last
summer of baseball up at the Stadium, this is a good time to bring
up a vivid, semi-obscure Yankee team record that almost rivals
those fabled thirty-nine pennants and twenty-six World Championships. Telling it only takes a minute. On Sunday, August 2, 1931,
the Yanks were shut out on the road by the Red Sox, 1–0, in a game
played, mysteriously, at Braves Field, the home of Boston's National
League club in those days. The Yanks were not shut out again, away
or at home, until August 3, 1933, a span of three hundred and eight
games, or, as measured back then, exactly two seasons. Zeroes are
baseball's most insistent number, but no other major-league team
has come anywhere close to this astounding skein. The parallel
record in the National League, for instance, is the Cincinnati Reds'
two hundred and eight games not-shut-out, between April 3, 2000,
and May 23, 2001. Last year's Yankees were shut down eight times,
while last year's Twins were goose-egged fourteen times.

The statistically minded might suppose that the endless con-
nivings of chance played a role in the Yankees' great run, but any

eleven-year-old interested enough to punch up the 1931–33 Yanks
on his bedroom iMac would know better the moment he saw that
their starting lineup in those days included six regulars subsequently voted into the Hall of Fame: catcher Bill Dickey, first baseman Lou Gehrig, second baseman Tony Lazzeri, third baseman Joe
Sewell, and outfielders Earle Combs and Babe Ruth (who was near-
ing the end of his career). There were also three future Hall of Fame
pitchers on the Yankee roster—Herb Pennock, Red Ruffing, and
Lefty Gomez—although, with one exception, the Yankee pitchers
didn't play much of a part in avoiding shutouts. The exception is
Ruffing, who, on August 13, 1932, blanked the Washington Senators over a scoreless nine innings—scoreless for both teams—in
their home park, Griffith Stadium.

Allowed to bat again in the tenth (he was good enough at the
plate to be called on regularly as a pinch-hitter), Ruffing hit a solo
home run, and then closed out the Senators in the bottom half, to
preserve the win and the string. Ruffing, the Yankees' ace, had slit-
ted eyes and high cheekbones, and held further interest for every
New York boy fan of that time because he'd lost four toes on his
left foot in a mining accident, back home in Illinois, at the age of
fifteen. Now he had accounted for both scores in the same game.
No other pitcher has matched this extra-innings deed in the ensuing seventy-six—well, almost—years.

But how come the Yankees played at Braves Field on the day
of their last previous zero? For the answer, we called up Seymour
Siwoff, the founder and proprietor and chief enthusiast of the Elias
Sports Bureau, the Fort Knox of sports statistics, and put the question.

"Back in a minute," he said, and 2.316 minutes later he was
back. "Sunday blue laws!" he cried. "Oh, I love this place—we have
everything! You couldn't play ball on Sunday at Fenway because
there was a church within a thousand feet of the park. Maybe more

than one. So they'd go over and play at Braves Field instead. The Monday game, back at Fenway, was the beginning of the Yankee streak. Listen, do you know who ended it—who shut them out finally? Should I look that up?"

"It was Lefty Grove," we said, naming the Philadelphia Athletics grandee, the primo starter of his era.

"Grove, of course!" said Siwoff. "I had an inkling. I almost knew."

Talk, July, 2008

YAZ'S TRIPLE CROWN

Tigers slugger Miguel Cabrera's new triple crown—he led the American League in batting, home runs, and runs batted in this year—has brought Carl Yastrzemski back in the news again, and about time. Yaz was the last player in either league to turn the grand trick, in 1967, when his deed helped propel the Red Sox into the World Series and won him an M.V.P. award as well. Cabrera's M.V.P. will have to await the postseason balloting, but there shouldn't be much news in it this time around: a feat outweighs an honor any day.

Yastrzemski carried the Red Sox on his back through that month of September, collecting twenty-three hits in his last forty-four at-bats. On the final weekend, with the Twins, the White Sox, and the Tigers also still in contention for the pennant, he went seven for eight in the season's last two games, at Fenway Park, against the visiting Twins, hit a game-winning home run, and threw out a base runner at second with a rally-killing peg from left field. I was elated by all this but not exactly surprised. Earlier that month, when Yaz came up to bat in a critical moment against the Tigers in Detroit, the *Globe*'s Clif Keane, then the reigning baron of the Boston media, addressed him from behind my seat in Tiger Stadium. "Go ahead!" he cried. "Prove that you're the M.V.P.! Prove it to me! Hit a homer!" Yaz hit the homer.

He played on for another sixteen years, retiring in 1983 with the third most at-bats and the seventh most hits in the history of the game. One of my poignant private regrets when he departed was the same one I felt when Nikita Khrushchev stepped down: I knew how to spell their names without looking. I also knew about an honor of his that never came to pass. A Sox-smitten friend of mine had determined to name his awaited new baby boy Yaz, and was only thwarted by his wife's absolute veto. Pity. The kid, grown up now and a valued colleague and pal, could have shared his zingy byline with the likes of Jay-Z, Dizzy Dean, Itzhak Perlman, and Zooey Deschanel: Yaz McGrath.

Post, October, 2012

THREE AT A TIME

The Yankees' triple play last night, which came in the second inning against the home-team Tampa Bay Rays, received the customary tepid buildup in the ensuing media recountings. Customary because triple plays, despite their rarity, are over almost before they begin, and rarely involve a great play or a close call anywhere. Someone grabs a line drive, steps on a base, and gets off an everyday infield fling: one, two, three, the inning is over, the teams are changing sides, the TV goes to a commercial, and the mini-event is done in less time than it takes to read this sentence. Last night's play came after a second-inning leadoff double against Yankee starter C. C. Sabathia by the Rays' Evan Longoria, then a walk to the right fielder Wil Myers. The next batter, Sean Rodriguez, hit a bouncer to third baseman Yangervis Solarte, who backed up and touched third, flipped to second, where the pivoting Brian Roberts stepped on second and got off a poor throw to first, where Scott Sizemore uneasily swiped at and held on to the one-bounce relay. Bang-bang-bang. Not much news there, so let's quickly add that Sabathia was also on the mound for the Yanks on the occasion of the previous Yankee triple play, at Baltimore, on April 12, 2013. And then, wow, let's not forget that Sizemore was playing first base for the first time ever in his career.

Triple plays are rare—they happen three or four times a year, on average—so it's a good bet that you never saw one. What's great about them isn't really their scarcity but the fact that they beautifully illustrate the invisible force that hovers about each pitch and play and inning and game in this pausing, staccato, and inexorably accruing pastime: the laws of chance. Neither Sizemore nor Roberts nor Solarte had ever been involved in a triple play before, and there is an excellent chance that none of the three ever will be again. The only triple play I ever witnessed came at Yankee Stadium on May 29, 2000, when Oakland second baseman Randy Velarde grabbed a mild liner from Yankee outfielder Shane Spencer, took a step or two forward to tag out the oncoming runner from first, Jorge Posada, and, without hurrying or changing direction, stepped on second to easily triple-off Tino Martinez, who had been heading for third. Yay, wow—I mean *Wow!*—but Velarde, arriving at the visiting team's dugout, appeared almost embarrassed: Geez, guys, it just *happened*. I stood up at my press-box seat to yell, but everyone else was still seated and at work. Unless it's the lottery, you can't scream over a number that's fallen out of the sky.

I wasn't on hand on August 23, 2009, when Phillies second baseman Eric Bruntlett grabbed a low liner, tagged a nearby runner, and almost dazedly stepped on second for a game-ending unassisted triple play, becoming the first player to pull off this caper since 1927. The abruptly losing team against Bruntlett's play was

the Mets, which simultaneously and perfectly illustrated the opposite of unexpected.

Post, April, 2014

ZIM

Don Zimmer, who died yesterday at eighty-three, was an original
Met and an original sweetie pie. His sixty-six years in baseball were
scripted by Disney and produced by Ken Burns. (Grainy black-and-
white early footage, tinkly piano, as he marries for life at local home
plate in bushy, front-porchy Elmira, New York; smiling baggy-
pants young teammates raise bats to form arch.) As a stubby, ear-
nest third baseman and utility infielder, he compiled a .235 batting
average over twelve seasons for six teams, including the Brooklyn
and Los Angeles Dodgers, the Chicago Cubs, those 1962 ur-Mets,
and the Washington Senators. In the off-seasons, he played ball in
Puerto Rico and Cuba and Mexico. Turning coach, he was hired
eleven times by eight different teams (there were three separate
stints with the Yankees) and along the way managed the Padres,
Red Sox, Rangers, and Cubs. Two championship rings as a player
with the Dodgers, four as a coach with the Yanks. He finished
up with the Rays, in his home-town Tampa: a coach, then a local
presence.

But never mind Disney: only baseball could have produced a
C.V. like this, and it's not likely to happen again. I think Zim is
best remembered as the guy right next to manager Joe Torre on the
right-hand side of the Yankees dugout in the good years: a motion-
less thick, short figure, heavily swathed in Yankee formals. The
bulky dark warmup jacket and the initialled cap neatly and monas-
tically framed his layered white moon-face, within which his tiny,
half-hidden eyes remained alive and moving. He could also run and

yell, of course. Boston fans—no, fans everywhere—will not forget the night he charged Pedro Martinez on the mound in that Fenway Park playoff fracas in 2003—and instantly wound up on his back, like a topped-over windup toy. Zim burned hard, and the hoots and yells and laughter that ran through the fiercely partisan Back Bay stands were familial and affectionate.

Zim sitting is the way he comes back to mind, for me. Like a few other old coaches, he had converted clubhouse silence and immobility—elbows on knees, hands folded, head aimed forward and downward, lips zipped—into something like a regional religious practice. If he caught your gaze as you walked past the coaches' little anteroom on your way to Joe Torre's office after another late game—he was down to sweats and clogs by now—he might manage an infinitesimal nod of recognition. Yep . . . same old.

Our affection for Zim is complicated, beginning as it does with our childlike joy in his bald cannonball head and stumpy bod and jack-o'-lantern grin, but encompassing as well, I think, a deep trust in and respect for his decades of exemplary competitive service, without stardom or contemporary distraction. He was a baseball figure from an earlier time: enchantingly familiar, tough and enduring, stuffed with plays and at-bats and statistics and anecdotes and wisdom accrued from tens of thousands of innings. Baseball stays on and on, unchanged, or so we used to think as kids, and Zimmer, sitting there, seemed to be telling us yes, you're right, and see you tomorrow.

Post, June, 2014

CLASS REPORT

When the news came, not late on Tuesday night, we did some hugs and high fives at my place, drank a little champagne, and dampened up at the sight of Jesse Jackson in tears amid the crowd of a hundred and fifty thousand or so in Chicago. In bed but not asleep, I thought back predictably to Selma and Birmingham, Oxford (Oxford, Mississippi), Martin Luther King, Jr., and Lyndon Baines Johnson, and tried but failed to remember another name. In the morning, it still wouldn't come—an old college classmate of mine. His name wasn't far from mine in the alphabet, which meant that he sat close to me in a couple of classes. I could almost see him, and though I never knew him or exchanged a word with him, he had been in my mind all this time—and in the minds, I'm almost sure, of most of the 1,097 of us in the Harvard Class of 1942.

I found him again in an old reunion report, and filled in the blank: Lucien Victor Alexis, Jr., of New Orleans. In our junior year, he'd been briefly in the news, when the Navy lacrosse coach refused to allow his team to take the field at Annapolis, because of Lucien's presence as a player on the visiting Harvard team. Lucien was black—the only black player on the team, just as he was the only black member of our class. The Harvard lacrosse coach refused to withdraw him, but was overruled on the scene by the Harvard athletic director, William J. (Bill) Bingham. Alexis was sent back to Cambridge on a train; Harvard played and lost, 12–0. There was a subsequent campus protest at Harvard, a petition was signed (I can't remember if I signed it), and soon afterward the Harvard

Athletic Association announced that Harvard would never again withdraw a player for reasons of race. Harvard's president, James B. Conant, had been away in Europe at the time of the lacrosse incident, but when he came back he apologized to the commanding admiral at Annapolis for the breach of cordial relations that Harvard had occasioned by bringing Lucien Alexis along.

Alexis graduated and went into the service, as most of us did then. When he came back, he was accepted at Harvard Medical School but then told that he couldn't attend after all, because there was no other black student in the entering class and thus no one he could room with. He went to Harvard Business School instead. He got his degree, went back to New Orleans, married and had children, and became the head of a small business college there. He died in 1975, at the age of fifty-three. He and I belong to what has sometimes been called "the Greatest Generation." If most of us have felt uncomfortable about the honor, it may be because we've known that in some ways we haven't been all that great. The election of Barack Obama as President could mean that all of us in the United States belong to the Greatest Generation now, and though this astounding event seems to have happened all of a sudden, for some people my age it wasn't soon enough.

Talk, November, 2008

JACKIE ROBINSON AGAIN

I'll catch the new Jackie Robinson movie, "42," over the weekend—it's great, friends say—but I need no sports-clip reminders or careful re-creations to bring his front-footed swing or his shouldering, headlong style on the base paths clearly back into view. I will keep some of his games forever—in particular, that final meeting with the Phillies, in 1951, to force a playoff for the pennant, which he saved with an astounding dive and stop behind second base in the twelfth, and won with a home run in the fourteenth. But that was just baseball; my first thought about him to this day was never a play or a famous hit but an idle, almost inexplicable midsummer, mid-game moment at the Polo Grounds in June or July of 1948.

I was sitting in a grandstand seat behind the third-base-side lower boxes, pretty close to the field, there as a Giants fan of long standing but not as yet a baseball writer. Never mind the score or the pitchers; this was a trifling midseason meeting—if any Giants-Dodgers game could be called trifling—with stretches of empty seats in the oblong upper reaches of the stands. Robinson, a Dodger base runner, had reached third and was standing on the bag, not far from me, when he suddenly came apart. I don't know what happened, what brought it on, but it must have been something ugly and far too familiar to him, another racial taunt—I didn't hear it—that reached him from the stands and this time struck home.

I didn't quite hear Jackie, either, but his head was down and a stream of sound and profanity poured out of him. His head was down and his shoulders were barely holding in something more. The game stopped. The Dodgers' third-base coach came over, and then the Giants' third baseman—it must have been Sid Gordon—who talked to him quietly and consolingly. The third-base umpire walked in at last to join them, and put one hand on Robinson's arm. The stands fell silent—what's going on?—but the moment passed too quickly to require any kind of an explanation. The men parted, and Jackie took his lead off third while the Giants pitcher looked in for his sign. The game went on.

I have no memory of who won, but that infinitesimal mid-inning tableau stayed with me, quickly resurfacing whenever I saw Jackie play again, in person or on TV, over the next eight seasons and then again on the day he died, in 1972. He was fifty-three years old but already white-haired and frail. We all knew his story by heart, of course, and took a great American pride in him, the very first black player in the majors: a carefully selected twenty-eight-year-old college graduate and Army veteran primed and prepped in 1947 by Dodger president Branch Rickey, who exacted a promise from him that he would never respond, never complain, never talk back, no matter what taunts or trash came at him from enemy players or out of the stands.

He did us proud, but at a cost beyond the paying.

Post, April, 2013

SIX LETTERS

TO DANIEL MENAKER

After a twenty-five-year career as a New Yorker *fiction editor, Daniel Menaker shifted to book publishing in 1996 and became executive editor in chief at Random House. He is the author of five books.*

Dear Dan:

My plan was to tell you tomorrow how much I like your book—but second thoughts tell me that I'll forget something or, more likely, that talk at your table about "A Good Talk" might feel too self-conscious to make for good talk. Anyway, all I want to say is that the book is a very quick read, because of its pleasures and surprises, and also a slow one because you want to stop and go back and think about some of the things going on there. One of the surprises is the Fred and Ginger conversation, which I strongly resisted at first because I wondered how either one of them could talk without extreme caution or embarrassing over-performance since they knew they were being taped. But they do gabble away quite easily and the talk immediately carries the day and gets the reader eager to know what they'll say next, thus instantly proving the book's value and excitement. This is true even during your interruptions or digressions, which are compelling but also make one eager to get on with the talk.

Carol read the book too, and I noticed that she kept laughing as she read along, proving how much she liked it even before she said that she did.

Speaking of which. After we'd read the book I asked C if she ever thought about those moments when someone at dinner is about to stop talking and everyone else there starts gunning their mighty engines a little, like drivers at a red light, hoping to win the breakaway jump into the next conversation a fraction of a second before the last one is quite over. And she said no, because I always hope I won't be the one who has to talk next.

So now we can talk about that.

Actually I'm going to try not to say a word at your house tomorrow night because of the things people will be thinking about me now, thanks to your book. And now I have to stop and look for typos. Thanks for that task, pal.

Yrs. of course,

TO RON FIMRITE

April 21, 2010

Dear Ron:

I've heard your miserable news and I couldn't be sorrier. David tells me you want no wailing at the bar and I will forbear, although this will be the first bar date with you I've ever passed up. You have been a true friend, and even though we've met rarely in recent years I've always thought you were in the next room and

available at a moment's notice for lunch and light discussions.
Whenever we talk on the phone, we're simply resuming our
conversation, even if the previous one was back last year. Thanks
for that and a whole lot more.

I can't remember exactly when we became lifetime pals, but
I suspect it was some time in the mid-seventies when I made my
first spring training trip to Arizona. On your invitation, I joined
you at the—duh: some desert name—on (I think) Van Buren
Street, and learned how to play Pong and how to leave ballgames
never later than the seventh inning, in favor of more civilized
doings at poolside. I think that was the year that Jack Mann left
his shoes outside his door at night to be polished (in a motel?) and
went around barefoot for the next day or two. Days and nights
and eventually years went by in this delightful fashion, with Chub
and Steph and Rig and David and Linda and Carol and Lesly and
others joining the company for jokes and talks and sweet times.
All your doing, really.

I have the same feeling about my stays in San Francisco,
where you were always the host, the Grover Whelan, of each visit,
making me feel as if I was simply taking my place in a large and
friendly family of mine that wanted me around for every meal.
How else could I have felt when you and Linda took me in right
after the earthquake in 1989, and I came to breakfast crying,
"Something really serious has happened: I've lost my notebook."

You know all this by heart, Ron, as do I, and many pages
more of it will go unsaid for the time being. My plan is to call you
tomorrow—I understand you're coming home from the hospital
today—for a brief chat. I'm told that you don't have a walk-around
phone (is yours the party-line wall model, with a crank?)—and if
you don't feel like coming down the hall please don't bother.

Carol sends her love and some major hugs. John Henry sends

his love, and says he holds very clear memories of good times in your company. (He lives in Portland, Oregon, now, which is too far away, but he'll be around here for a few days later this week, along with his wife Alice and their eight-month-old daughter Clara, who is making her East Coast début.)

Hang in there, Ron. This whole thing is a hell of a note, because you've been pencilled in for years to speak at my memorial. Who's going to take your place—Bobby Valentine? See what I mean?

Yrs, ever, dear Ron, believe you me,

TO TRACY DAUGHERTY

December 9, 2006

Hi Tracy,

Thanks for your message. I enjoyed our meeting and felt that we both enjoyed talking about Donald Barthelme at such length. I think your book "Hiding Man: A Biography of Donald Barthelme" is off to a great start. I was glad to see you making a note about my little observation that the only thing a biographer should beware of and eschew in writing about Don B. is that hovering, omnipresent sense of awe and reverence that seems to surround him still.

I don't think that the swift offer of a first agreement came from any sense of mine that we were on some special wavelength or would always understand each other. Rather, it was because he could write funny stuff, as we had seen from those early casuals.

Reliable writers of humor were always at a very high premium
for us, because of their rarity. I had little or no idea what sort of
writer Donald would turn into, and doubt that he did, either.

I want to emphasize again the influence and importance of
editor William Shawn through all the *New Yorker*'s dealings with
Barthelme. I enthusiastically admired what he was and what he
became, and we two did work together happily and productively,
but none of that would have meant much and little of it would
have happened were it not for Shawn's daring and intuitive
understanding of what sort of an artist had turned up when
Don began submitting his amazing early pieces. As I said the
other day, many people on the magazine did not share this deep
admiration, either, and there were always complaints and puzzled
murmurings as we began to publish him pretty steadily and to
find space for his oddly illustrated semi-abstract casuals, and to
run the longer stuff like "Snow White" at full length. Some *New
Yorker* writers and staffers did cotton to him from the outset, of
course, and loved what he brought to the magazine and to all of
us in that place and time.

There was little mention of this in the small flood of books
about Shawn that appeared after he died; it was as if Shawn's
genius as a fiction editor was held to be secondary to his other
gifts and not an integral part of his influence over the writing and
thinking of that time. I've pointed this out over and over in the
past few months, while talking about my own little book, but
not many people seem interested. Fiction and art don't belong,
for some reason. This misapprehension predates Barthelme, to
be sure. The early books about Harold Ross, including Brendan
Gill's popular but patronizing view of him, "Here at *The New
Yorker*," treat *New Yorker* fiction (Cheever and Salinger aside) in a
somewhat offhand way, even though for many years we used to
run three or at the very least two stories or casuals in each issue,

with the leadoff or "A" story always appearing in the primo slot, right after the Talk of the Town.

It also seems to me that people forget now how significant—how much admired and imitated and talked about—Donald's stuff was for a stretch there. Did you by chance come upon the long analytic and admiring piece about him by Richard Schickel in the NY *Times* Magazine for August 1, 1970, which is written in a Donald-like Q.-and-A. format?

Sorry to go on so.

Best,

TO CHARLES MCGRATH

Charles (Chip) McGrath was a long-term fiction editor at The New Yorker, *and was named managing editor in 1988. He became the editor of the* New York Times Book Review *in 1995, and has subsequently served as a* Times *writer at large.*

February 28, 2008

Dear Chip,

Our gloomy lunch talk made me realize steroids are finally getting to me—not so much the practice but the sordid denials and evasions. I still can't get over Clemens before that Congressional Committee the other day. Deeply weird drama—the bulging Spaceman phiz and whoever lives behind it lying and lying, and the skulky drug provider telling nothing but the truth. I'll never forget it.

Your line to me that if there was a little something you

could take that would turn you into John Updike you'd do it in
a nanosecond has brought back that three-day visiting-writer-gig
I had at the U. of Penn a few years ago, where I was in the hands
of a lively English prof named Al Filreis, who taught writing.
I did a reading, went to some comp classes, met his bright and
talented students . . . well, a few were talented. The last morning
there was sort of an open house where I took questions and read
a little more. A mixed audience, undergrads and grad students,
with some faculty and Penn staff people drifting in and out. Forty
or fifty people there at a time. About half the questions were
about steroids, and I finally said, "Let's say you're a lawyer or an
architect or a veterinarian, and there's this little something you
can take that will make you not just a better lawyer, architect, or
veterinarian, but the best one in the world. It's illegal but if you
take it nobody will know. How many of you would take it—put
up your hands."

About half the bunch put up their hands—almost all of them
faculty or staff types, folks in their thirties or forties. When I
asked the other question—who would never, never take the elixir,
all the kids stuck up their hands vehemently. This poll depressed
me at first, but thinking about it later I decided that what we'd
seen wasn't about idealism and its loss as much as innocence:
young people with no idea yet about how tough and grungy the
world was going to turn out to be for them.

I think fans still don't have any notion of how hard big-league
baseball really is—how the season gets to you. Other sports beat
you up—this one happens every day and it grinds you down. It's
by far the hardest sport to play at a high level. .230 hitters get
desperate just trying to keep up to their own level, then get ready
again for another game tonight. A lot of them, I think more than
half, used to take greenies, amphetamines, to keep that edge. Joe
DiMaggio, not exactly a struggler, drank fourteen or fifteen cups

of coffee every day. There's also lingering pain, and daunting or disabling injury awaiting you, especially for the pitchers. A lot of them used to soldier on while in horrific pain. I wrote about this in an old piece, "The Arms Talks."

I think I told you about the time in spring training a little while ago when I found myself sitting on a back bench at ————, a couple of yards away from ———— and ————. No one else there. Two famous closers, one the fabulous veteran home stopper and the other his opposite number, there with the visiting ————s for that afternoon's game. They were shop-talking pitching and pharmacology, what they took every day to get ready. (They gave me a glance, but ———— knew me and probably said I was O.K.) What I picked up from the murmured converse was their strong interest in the proper order of self-medication— "Man, you take that in the *fifth* inning? I always wait till the seventh, middle seventh, *then* the Blurto top of the eighth." Etc. It was all nicknames and prescription shorthand, no Ben-Gay or Bayer in it anywhere.

Talk to you next week,

TO CHARLES SIMMONS

March 31, 2010

Dear Charles:

Please forgive my delay in responding to your "Once More About Anatole Broyard," which was caused by its predictable popularity among my colleagues. This did not produce a decision to publish the piece, I'm sorry to say, so this letter is an apology.

We're letting it go, I'm told, because it would be so odd for us to run two separate Broyard memoirs. I understand this verdict even if I don't agree with it, and this impels me to ask whether you have any other *Times* memoirs in mind or in the works. If so, I'd love to see them, and would expect though can't promise a better outcome.

The Broyard piece has changed my view of the *Times,* which I now see as a steamy souk or hothouse of sex. I thought of this place in the same way, years ago, but we were just preppy fooler-arounders compared to you folks off to the west. I put all this in the past tense only because of my age; for all I know there may be more action than ever on these floors, though I think it more likely that harassment issues and Facebook and the cell and the tweet have combined to produce a new Puritanism among journalists—a terrific loss to life & letters.

It was good to hear from you, Charles. Please write back anytime.

Yrs, and best,

TO ROBERT CREAMER

March 10, 2009

Dear Bob:

I love the tale of the blackberry brandy, or pre-Imodium. I myself recall a couple of storied evenings on Frank's porch [Frank Sullivan], when those five or six rocking chairs of his were refilled two or three times over in the course of the conversations. My eternal repayment for his kindness was one of the few really good ideas I've ever had in my life. I called up Jock Whitney* at the *Trib* (and somehow got through to him right away) and after identifying myself suggested that he arrange to name a race at the current Saratoga meeting as "The Frank Sullivan," in honor of the great man. I also explained that I'd been told already that the NYRA never, never named a race after a living person.

"It will be done!" Whitney cried, in imitation of the Pope, and it was. When "The Frank Sullivan" made its début as a modest, mid-card Saratoga event the following August, Frank was delighted. He went with a passel of friends and made a bet on every horse in the race, so he'd be sure to have the winner. I think he died later that same year.

Best again,

———

* Philanthropist John Hay (Jock) Whitney was the last editor and publisher of the *New York Herald Tribune.* As co-owner (with his sister Joan Payson Whitney) of the Greentree Stable, he was also a major figure in American turf circles.

HERE COMES THE SUN

With Opening Day gone by, a visitor to the recent spring-training camps can expect to keep no more than a handful of memories of the short season, such as a low line-drive homer in Tampa by the Yankees' new import, Hideki Matsui, intensely annotated by a horde of visiting Japanese media; or a Mo Vaughn sailer at Port St. Lucie, over the right-field fence and into a sandpit, where it was excavated by an exclaiming pack of boy archeologists; or Renee Conley's birthday party in Lower Box 105, Row D, at Scottsdale Stadium, in Arizona. Renee and four slender, well-tanned friends of hers—Laura McDermott, Angie Ray, Angie Cronk, and Ann Chaillie—were dressed in jeans, tank tops, and a scattering of forward-facing baseball caps, and their occupation of this sector, close behind the backstop screen, a bit over toward the visiting-team dugout, brightened the afternoon almost as much as the sun, which had been hiding behind chilly rain clouds for the past couple of days. The women put out the news that this was Renee's twenty-first birthday, and Renee, bowing and blushing a little—she had cropped dark hair and a nice strong nose—accepted the good wishes of the old fans and kid fans around her but then said, well, no, she was *thirty*-one today. This seemed to put her about in the middle, agewise, in her bunch, who turned out to be servers from the nearby Bandera restaurant. "The best margaritas in town," said Laura, who is a bartender there. "Only don't go today, because all the staff will be rookies."

The game began—the Giants were hosting a split squad of Seattle Mariners—but the young women were distracted by party-favor comical cardboard eyeglasses, with a jagged "Happy Birthday" in exuberant colors above the frames. Putting these on could be done only by reversing the caps, and once this was done, to cascades of laughter, it was time for a round of Bud Lights and the first of a dozen or so group shots, with the girls hugging up in a tight bunch and showing their perfect teeth to each helpful, "cheese"-urging neighbor fan wielding a borrowed camera. Fan parties can turn into a royal pain if you're there for the game, but, c'mon, this was spring training, and it was a kick to see how rarely this part of Row D ever actually looked at the field.

By the time the women had slipped on pacifier-sized candy rings (more snaps), you began to pick up some of the conversations and sort out the principals. Angie Ray had serious crimson lipstick and wore a cap with "Alien Workshop" over the peak, while Laura's cap said "Lucky Brand" in script astern. Angie Cronk was the one with a cluster of small silver rings in her right ear and a lavender silk scarf fashionably twisted around her short, white-blond hair. She looked a bit like Jean Seberg. One of her friends said, "Angie, your ring matches everything—God, you always look so great!"

"Ooo, look, the bases are loaded," somebody said—we were in the fifth by now—but Rich Aurilia's grand slam over the left-field fence was more or less missed because the friends were so busy with the birthday cake: two Hostess cupcakes, side by side, with a candle "3" stuck in one of them and a candle "1" in the other. Renee instantly blew them out, to a screaming that became part of the wild game noise as Barry Bonds, the next man up, delivered a monster blow over the berm in right. Nobody ate the cupcakes.

Not all the hitting was on the field. When a tall, not-so-young volunteer cameraman regrouped the friends for another album shot, he made lifting motions with his hands and said, "Come on, ladies, gimme some cleavage. In Venezuela, you'd be wearing way too many clothes."

"This is the U.S. of A.," Renee said.

Ann Chaillie, who had crinkly blond hair and was wearing a fetching straw cloche hat, had by now moved down front, in the hope of snagging a discarded game ball, and, after one was gently rolled her way across the roof of the visiting-team dugout, she screeched and danced. When a towheaded eight- or nine-year-old boy in a red T-shirt said, "If I gave you a hug and kiss, would you give me that ball in return?," she said sure. More balls were found and the hug-and-kiss barter system was quickly established, to heavy local applause. These women were not Yankee Stadium types, you saw at last. No cursing, no dishing, and a lighter coat of cool. Laura McDermott said, "Well, if you can't find an older man, go for the younger ones," and she moved down with Ann and the kids too.

All that remained was the next stage of the party. Because of the anticipated beers, the young women had parked their cars at Renee's place and safely biked to the park. The last party treat was a drawing of slips with various possible post-game destinations inked on them, including Zorba's Adult Shop, on Scottsdale Road, and a long-shot Las Vegas. "We could totally do Vegas," Angie Ray announced, but they all had to be back at work tomorrow. Laura was holding down three jobs between Thursdays and Tuesdays each week. Renee's party would soon end, possibly wrapping up at Billet Bar, a nearby biker joint, with adjoining tattoo facilities. When the friends had last been in there, a bouncer said, "Next time, ladies, back your bicycles into the rack. That way you're real bikers." The ballgame was running out—it was 7–3, Giants, in the end—though nobody wanted it or the sunshine and hurrying warm clouds to go away. The night before, President Bush had announced that Saddam Hussein had two more days in which to depart or face war. But this was still spring training, where nothing counts. We had this one coming.

Talk, April, 2003

OVER THE WALL

Carol doesn't know that President Obama won reëlection last Tuesday, carrying Ohio and Pennsylvania and Colorado, and compiling more than three hundred electoral votes. She doesn't know anything about Hurricane Sandy. She doesn't know that the San Francisco Giants won the World Series, in a sweep over the Tigers. More important, perhaps, she doesn't know that her granddaughter Clara is really enjoying her first weeks of nursery school and is beginning to make progress with her slight speech impediment. Carol died early last April, and almost the first thing that she wasn't aware of is that our son, John Henry, who is Clara's father, after saying goodbye to her about ten hours before her death, which was clearly coming, flew home to Portland, Oregon. Later that same night, perhaps after she'd gone, he had a dream, which he wrote about briefly and beautifully in an e-mail to the family. In the dream, she is hovering close to him, and they are on 110th Street, close to the Harlem Meer, at the northeast corner of Central Park. The Park is bursting with spring blossoms. She is walking a dog that might be our fox terrier Andy. Then she falls behind John Henry. He turns to find her, and she has become an almost black shape and appears to be covered with feathers or black-and-dark-gray Post-its. She and the dog lift off the ground and go fluttering past him, and disappear over the low wall of the Park.

What the dead don't know piles up, though we don't notice it at first. They don't know how we're getting along without them, of

Carol and Roger Angell, Brooklin, 1966

course, dealing with the hours and days that now accrue so quickly, and, unless they divined this somehow in advance, they don't know that we don't want this inexorable onslaught of breakfasts and phone calls and going to the bank, all this stepping along, because we don't want anything extraneous to get in the way of what we feel about them or the ways we want to hold them in mind. But they're in a hurry, too, or so it seems. Because nothing is happening with them, they are flying away, over that wall, while we are still chained and handcuffed to the weather and the iPhone, to the hurricane and the election and to the couple that's recently moved in downstairs, in Apartment 2-S, with a young daughter and a new baby girl, and we're flying off in the opposite direction at a million miles an hour. It would take many days now, just to fill Carol in.

There's a Kenneth Koch poem, "Proverb," that begins "Les morts vont vite, the dead go fast, the next day absent!"

Later, it continues:

> The second after a moth's death there are one or two hundred
>   other moths
> The month after Einstein's death the earth is inundated with
>   new theories
> Biographies are written to cover up the speed with which we
>   go:
> No more presence in the bedroom or waiting in the hall
> Greeting to say hello with mixed emotions.

Yes, but let's stay with Carol a little longer. She was seventeen years, nine months, and seventeen days younger than me (we had a different plan about dying), but now that gap is widening. Soon our marriage will look outlandish or scandalous, because of the age difference. I'm getting old, but I'm told almost every day that I'm keeping up, doing O.K. What Carol doesn't know by now is shocking, let's face it, and I think even her best friends must find themselves thinking about her with a certain new softness or sweetness, as if she were a bit backward. Carol, try to keep up a little, can't you?

All right, I take that back, and I also feel bad about those moths getting in here. Carol had a serious moth and bat phobia, dating back to childhood. She was a teacher at the Brearley School, an eminent New York academy for girls, and one day one of her students got an urgent telephone call from her in algebra class. "I need you down here right away," Carol said.

"But, Mrs. Angell, I'm in math class," the girl said.

"Never mind that," Carol said. "There's a moth in my room, and I need you to come down and remove it right now."

Anecdotes sweep away time, and are there to cheer us up, but just as often they work the other way, I'm finding out. Let's get to my unstartling theory, which is that it may not be just years that make you old or young but where you stand on the treadmill. Shakespeare possessed an astounding knowledge of history and of his own times, it's agreed, but missed out on Newton and Napoleon and the Oreo sandwich. Dickens joined the conversations of his day about Darwin, but stayed mum about Freud and Cézanne and Verdun. Lincoln never understood Auden. Verdi just missed Louis Armstrong, leaving the room before the first runthrough of "Mahogany Hall Stomp." Donald Barthelme's fiction was known for its flashing and ironic references to contemporary names and styles of thought; he died in 1989, however, at the age of fifty-eight, and under the regulations was forbidden ever to mention Michele Bachmann or the Geico lizard. Carol knew Donald well, and loved his writing. She was also a fan of John Donne, an even more sternly handicapped genius, and one evening got us into an extended conversation—I remember almost every word of it— about his poem "Aire and Angells" (note the spelling), which she was unravelling with an eleventh grader.

What do these people have in common: William Shawn, Nancy Stableford, Bill Rigney, Joseph Brodsky?

Well, for one thing, I knew them all, though Brodsky, the poet and Nobel Laureate, only passingly or socially: he was a fabulous conversationalist. Shawn was my boss, the decades-long editor of *The New Yorker;* Nancy Stableford was my older sister and a biology teacher; and Bill Rigney—a onetime major-league infielder and then a manager of the Angels, Twins, and Giants—my best friend in baseball. Each of them was a grownup, and, in their different ways, vibrantly intelligent. What else did they have in common?

Why, all of them died before September 11, 2001, which is to say that all of them, in company with many hundreds of my bygone and deceased schoolmates and office friends and relatives and summer acquaintances, and their parents and my parents, had no inkling of the world we live in today. I think of them often—my seniors, my innocents, my babies—and envy them, and believe that many others my age have had this passing thought as well, and have from time to time felt a flow of protective love for them, and even a bit of pride that we can stand in for them, or stand up for them, that rational and more hopeful old gang of ours, and so put up with this dismal flow of violence and schlock and complicated distant or very near events that makes up our daily and hourly menu.

Clara and the baby downstairs in 2-S (her name is Quinn, I've learned) are scarcely aware of irony or bad news yet, but they'll catch up and be O.K. with it very soon. Thinking about them the other day, I remembered a poem called "Conch," written by my stepfather, E. B. White, back in the nineteen-forties. He wrote light verse, but took it seriously. Here it is:

> Hold a baby to your ear
> As you would a shell:
> Sounds of centuries you hear
> New centuries foretell.
> Who can break a baby's code?
> And which is the older—
> The listener or his small load?
> The held or the holder?

Quite a lot of time has gone by since Carol died, and though I've forgotten many things about her, my fears about that are going away. There will always be enough of her for me to remember, and some of it, to my surprise, comes back with fresh force. I've been thinking about her hands, for instance, which are visible, of course, in the hundreds of photographs we have of her, often lightly touching someone else in a family setting. Her hands in repose were strikingly beautiful, their resting or down-angling familiar shape somehow expressing both confidence and a perfect ease that a great ballerina could envy. I go back to look at that again and again.

E. B. White—we called him Andy, and, yes, the dog is named for him—and Carol are close to each other now, in the Brooklin, Maine, Cemetery. His and my mother's graves are side by side, under a tall oak tree that Andy planted there when my mother died, in 1977. Their gravestones are made of bluish-gray slate, but Carol's and mine, though they have the same shape and old-fashioned narrow body, are in white Vermont marble. They carry the same lettering that Mother's and Andy's do: a suave contemporary style called Centaur that was recommended to us back then by an art-director friend of mine named Hank Brennan.

My decision to have my gravestone put in at the same time as Carol's, in early August—it only lacks the final numbers—wasn't easy, but has turned out to be comforting, not creepy. Brooklin is much too far away just now—I live in New York—but the notion that before long my familiar June trip back there will be for good is only keeping a promise.

I visited Carol's grave every day during the rest of my summer stay, often in the early morning, when the oblong shadows of my mother's and Andy's markers nearly touched hers. There's more family nearby: my brother Joel White's gray granite marker (he died in 1997) and that of my daughter Callie, who died two years ago. The two of them had their ashes put into the sea at almost the identical place: an upper sector of Jericho Bay from which you can see the steep mountains of Mount Desert, to the east, and, in the other direction, the rise of Isle au Haut. Token cupfuls of their ashes were saved and went into the cemetery later. This is a

currently popular option, but Carol and I passed it up. There are
ten cemeteries in Brooklin, which is a lot for a population of eight
hundred; many are family plots, half-hidden in fields or brush now,
and the little Mount Eden Cemetery, on Naskeag Point, is probably the most beautiful. The Brooklin Cemetery is the largest, and
lies right in the middle of town: across Route 175 from the Baptist
Church and a couple of hundred yards down from the library and
the Brooklin General Store, where the road bends.

My visits to Carol didn't last long. I'd perk up the flowers in
the vase we had there, and pick deadheads off a pot of yellow dai-
sies; if there had been rain overnight, I'd pick up any pieces of the
sea glass that had fallen and replace them on the gentle curve and
small shoulders of her stone. We first thought of this tribute in the
family on the day of her burial. Good sea glass is getting scarce,
now that everybody has learned not to throw bottles overboard, but
Carol's collections were made long ago, plucked from a stone beach
of ours on Eggemoggin Reach and an even better spot, just to the
east, that belongs to a neighbor. There are dishes of sea glass in
different sizes all over the house. Carol's favorite pieces (and mine)
were small pale mauves and those smoothly rounded gray shapes,
probably from old milk bottles, worn to sensual smoothness by the
actions of tide and time. In recent years, when she knew that children of friends were coming over to visit us, she'd sometimes grab
a small handful and secretly seed the beach in places where she'd
bring the kids later.

I often took Andy along on my visits—a violation of cemetery rules, I'm sure, but we almost never saw another soul, and in
any case he only wanted to rocket about in the vacant fields, away
from the graves and their flags and plantings. On our way home, I
sometimes stopped in the oldest part of the cemetery, closest to the
road, and left the dog in the car while I walked among the graves
there. These are marble or granite headstones, for the most part,

but all are worn to an almost identical whiteness. Some of the lettering has been blackened by lichen, and some washed almost to invisibility. These aren't old graves, as New England cemeteries are measured—there's nothing before 1800, I believe—but their stories are familiar. Many small stones are in remembrance of infants or children who died at an early age, often three or four in the same family; there are also names of young men or old captains lost at sea. There's a low gray column bearing lowercase lines of verse in memory of a beloved wife who died in 1822, at the age of twenty-seven. Many of the names—Freethey, Eaton, Bridges, Allen—are still well represented in Brooklin today. What I noticed most, though—the same idea came over me every time—was that time had utterly taken away the histories and attachments and emotions that had once closely wrapped around these dead, leaving nothing but their families and names and dates. It was almost as if they were waiting to be born.

Personal History, November, 2012

THE WRONG DOG

Dogly type deposes to take mild exception to a line in Tad Friend's Talk of the Town piece, "Sound of Silence," in the current issue of *The New Yorker*, in which he states that the Jack Russell terrier that appears in the new movie "The Artist" is "the breed that once cocked an ear to RCA Victrolas." I don't think so. The dog sitting attentively and eternally next to that old-fashioned phonograph horn on RCA Victor records is a pooch named Nipper, who looks to me like a fox terrier or something close. The canine belonged to a Royal Academy British artist, Francis Barraud, who painted "Dog Looking at and Listening to a Phonograph" sometime in the eighteen-nineties. The picture was acquired by the Gramophone

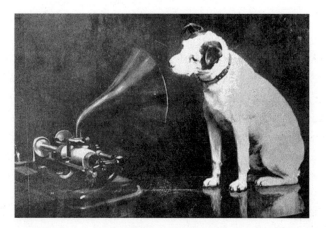

Company in 1900, and shortly thereafter rights to it went over to Victor, where the painting was edited into its famous His Master's Voice trademark. Only lately has anyone suggested that Nipper might have been a Jack Russell, but a good second look at those elegant Ionic forelegs dismisses the claim.

Jack Russell terriers are the wildly popular, intense, short-legged cutesters now probably visible (and audible) on a taut leash in your apartment lobby or around the nearest shopping mall. Fox T.'s, which come in the smooth or wire-haired model, are taller and narrower, and, by a fraction, more staid. Though probably out-numbered by Jacks just now, they are the older, more established breed; one version of Jack Russells, a country cousin, was developed in the eighteenth century by a British divine who gave the breed its official moniker, the Parson Russell Terrier. The American Fox Terrier Club was founded in 1885; the Jack Russell Terrier Club of America in 1976. I grew up in close proximity to dogs, but the first time I ever heard of a Jack Russell or laid eyes on one was in 1965, when an old Boston friend of mine, Kornie Parson (yes), introduced me to a delightfully waggling football he'd just picked up on a business trip to England.

A smooth fox terrier, Ch. Warren Remedy, won the Best in Show award at the very first Westminster Kennel Club Dog Show, in 1907, and repeated in 1908 and again in '09. Between them, smooth and wire foxes have won seventeen Best in Shows at Westminster, more than any other breed (Scotties are second, with eight). The most famous fox terrier was Asta, a wire who stole scenes from William Powell and Myrna Loy in all those "Thin Man" movies in the nineteen-thirties and early forties, and the next-best probably Ch. Nornay Saddler, who won fifty-one Best in Show awards (then a record) between 1937 and 1940, but somehow never the top Westminster prize, and became the subject of the very first *New Yorker* dog Profile, written by E. J. Kahn, in 1940.

Dogs have been getting a lot of attention from colleagues of mine in the magazine lately, what with the selection from Susan Orlean's book "Rin Tin Tin: The Life and the Legend," which ran in the issue of August 29th, and Adam Gopnik's Personal History, "Dog Story," which recounts his recent conversion to the world of dogs, thanks to a charming Havanese named Butterscotch. My own claim to distinction in this arcane area began when Carol took our fox terrier Willy out for a walk one morning in 1990, and encountered a fashion shoot in progress in Central Park: a photographer working with a chocolate-brown Lab and a tweeded-up male model for a Paul Stuart advertisement. When Carol and Willy came past again, on the way home, the photographer asked if he could please borrow our dog for a few minutes, and heartlessly made the switch. The resulting Paul Stuart ad ran in the issue of October 29th. My only disappointment was with Willy's commission, which turned out not to be a fifteen-hundred-dollar Italian silk-Irish-tweed-mix jacket for his owner but a free copy of the Paul Stuart catalogue.

Fox terriers were bred for foxhunting, but not on foot. After the much bigger, no-relation foxhounds (with their floppy ears and waving tails) had driven the fox to earth, the F.T. would be handed down from a bag or basket on the Master of Hounds' saddle and would instantly dig out the poor beast. Foxhunting has pretty much been abolished now, even in England, but more than one owner of the breed must have noticed that somewhere along the line fox terriers—with their long faces, straight front legs, and pricked ears—had been selectively bred to look a lot like horses. The young incumbent at my house, Andy, has yet to encounter a fox or a horse, but doesn't seem to mind. My son, noting his unusual patching, thinks he looks a lot like a cow.

Post, November 30, 2011

ANDY'S HAIKUS

Hey, why the long face,
Mr. Smooth Fox Terrier?
Dog jokes never die.

Stay down, crazy pooch!
Stop jumping all over me.
Enough love—O.K.?

Petal ears on top,
Triangles of attention,
Pick us up also.

Aloft and agog,
My old dads, depanniered,
Cancelled fox's plan.

Unacceptable,
4 A.M. nose in my ear.
Oh, well—c'mon under.

Prewash your plates
Is what I do around here:
Lift that door and die!

Circling your cushion,
Settled on your spot to nap:
Curvature ensues.

Black patches on white
Form an archipelago:
Terrierana.

June, 2014

MORE HAIKUS

MARATHON

Six more miles? Oh, God,
Let me die like what's-his-name—
Like Pheidippides.

OSPREY

Still taking on airs,
Making a splash at dinner,
Local star keeps up.

HEY!

It surprises me
That what pigeons keep saying
Is "Hai-kuu" . . . "Hai-kuu."

PILEATED

A pair of redheads
Jackhammering a spruce stump
Got my attention.

SIX LETTERS AND A MEMO

TO ANONYMOUS

December 4, 2009

Dear ———:

Thank you for your letter pointing out that Cliff Lee's 2008 record for the Indians was 22–3, not the 22–2 that we printed. Actually this "error" was intentional, and was inserted into my Sporting Scene article thanks to *The New Yorker*'s collaboration with a joint Brandeis/Harvard Sociology Departments' readership reaction survey: a well-devised format which searches out really objectionable readers and will eventually document more than 32,000 irritating or self-regarding responses to journalistic carelessness in the United States and Canada; a similar study is just getting under way in Great Britain.

Professor Greta Shunway, of Brandeis, is also excited by your closing "Tant pis," pointing out that this qualifies you as a rare double entrant in the study, and guarantees that you may expect a personal visit within the next ninety days from professionals on the survey's board.

Sincerely,

TO TRACY DAUGHERTY

November 26, 2008

Dear Tracy:

Thanks for getting back to me—and many more thanks for your compliments. Please don't agonize over any of this. You've written a tremendous book, "Hiding Man: A Biography of Donald Barthelme," and the thing for you to do now is to enjoy it. I really mean that. The brief experience of publication—the delivery of the m.s., the calls and letters back and forth with the editor, the fixings and rethinkings, the first proofs, the corrected proofs, the talks about the cover and the pub date, the jacket copy arrangements and the blurbs, the book itself in your hands (!!!), the signing and the mailing of copies to friends, the actual pub date and its swift departure, the reviews, the sight of the books in a bookstore, the letters and phone calls, the weeks rushing by and the book suddenly not on the shelves anymore—goes by at warp speed, and my advice is to relish every moment. What Tolstoy thought, five or six days after the publication of "War and Peace," was *Yes, but what have I done lately?*

I hope you're about to have a really great Thanksgiving.

Yrs. & best,

TO BOBBIE ANN MASON

Monday, February 8, 2010

Thanks, Bobbie. I think writing is different for different

people and I know it was always hard for you. It's never easy,
let's agree. But I don't think Salinger's great skills or genius
meant that he wouldn't stop writing, as you speculate. I have two
theories about him and perhaps both are wrong. I think he was
badly damaged by the war, when he had some hard experiences.
Certainly he became more bitter as a hermit, and chose to
interpret his own fame and reputation and preference for privacy
as a test of something or other. But every writer encounters this
to some degree and has to decide how to handle flattery, ego,
agents, money, and the demands of publicists and rival writers and
yearning readers. For some reason this was beyond him, and since
he could find no recourse in irony or humor or semi-detachment
he fell into that deep suspicion of everyone out there—see Lillian
Ross on that "smell" he began to detect everywhere—turned into
deep eccentricity and paranoia. The other strain that occurs to me
can be found in the Glass stories, which begin to fall apart in the
last one we've seen—the Hepworth mess. He's been promising
some semi-religious higher truth in the series, but now can't
deliver. Seymour has been dead a long time and where can this all
go? He's painted himself into a spiritual corner.

I don't trust writers who end up just writing for themselves.
Writing is a two-way process and the hard part isn't just getting
in touch with oneself but keeping in touch with that reader
out there, whoever he or she is, on whom all this thought and
art and maybe genius will devolve. Without the reader you can
do anything, put down anything or nothing—it doesn't matter
much.

But one's own way of writing, which almost requires leaving
the world altogether, demands too much of oneself, and I can see
why you'd seriously think of stopping. I just don't think anything
of the kind happened to Salinger.

Maybe we'll be given a great trove of brilliant untouched Salinger prose now. I hope so but somehow I doubt it.

Love,

TO TOM BELLER

Tom Beller was writing "J. D. Salinger: The Escape Artist" (2014).

May 1, 2014

Dear Tom Beller again:

Sorry to be late with this.

I'm pretty sure that Jerry Salinger would have walked toward Madison, not Lex, in search of that pack of cigarettes. He could have tried at the little Schmidt's Drugstore, two doors north of 91st Street on the NE corner of Park, but probably that was still a pure drugstore. It had one of the pharmacist's vases of mauve water hanging in the window.

You're right: Madison then was nothing like Madison now. The gentrification began in the 1980s, I believe. It was a businesslike avenue before that, and in Jerry's time, with two-way trolley tracks in the middle. All traffic was two-way. It had newsstands, a Gristede's (on the NE corner of 92nd); a liquor store or two; a plumber's store, with a bathtub in the window (mid 91st–92nd, on the east side of the avenue); a florist's (J. D. Flessas, on the SW corner of 91st); numerous drugstores (including Cantor's on NE or SE corner of Mad and 93rd, depending on which year we're talking about, and, maybe a bit earlier, a nearby

Liggett's); plus shoeshine and shoe repair shops, hardware stores (probably Feldman's, even then), etc., etc. The Hotel Wales was already there, east side of the avenue between 92nd and 93rd, but much seedier then.

Lexington was much the same, also with trolleys—the trolley cars on the two lines were not identical in appearance—and with the same stores, maybe more groceries or butcher shops, but all of them cheaper and with a slightly less affluent clientele. More laundries; more of those basement ice, coal & wood places. Maybe some deli's but they weren't called deli's then.

Lexington and I think 93rd had a Lucky Lindy coffee shop. But neither of the two avenues felt affluent; they were useful. Almost all the buildings along them were four-story brownstones. Madison, as you noted, was on the same geographical level as Park; Lex was downhill from Park. There was some construction going on in these blocks all through this time, depression or no depression. The Walter Chrysler and H. Goadby Loew mansions, on 93rd between Park and Madison, both went up in the 1930s or a bit before; the large Brick Presbyterian Church (NW corner of 91st and Park) went up around 1939.

Salinger and the younger me probably passed each other more than once on the street back then, all unknowing. We each knew that the wind was from the east on gray mornings when we woke up with the smell of hops in the air, blown from the huge Ruppert's Brewery, which lay east of Third and north from 90th Street.

I think you're making a mistake to scorn or downgrade Gus Lobrano. He was a major figure in the fiction department, and a top man at the magazine at the time when the Shawn succession was being determined. He died much too young. He handled many significant writers, including Ogden Nash, Frank O'Connor, James Thurber, Ogden Nash (verse), Edward Newhouse,

Peter Taylor, and more, including the younger me. A gentle, determined, and brilliant editor and a sweet guy. He had been a classmate of E. B. White's at Cornell.

I think I'm about Salingered out, but do let me know if you have something specific that you can't quite find. It's good news that the book is almost ready.

Best,

TO PHILIP LEVINE

November 16, 2010

Dear Philip:

Terrific poem this week—thank you. "Turkey" really snuck up on me, maybe because of those short lines. No, it's your shifts: Jean-Claude, then "Indochine," then the Admiral radio. But you know all this. Your stuff never fails me.

It's been a while since my last to you. I turned ninety in September—a huge surprise, though I thought I'd gotten ready for it. I'm still working at the magazine, but suspect that's only because I'm too old to fire. I've been trying to make up for sparse production with my old Christmas jingle, but couldn't deliver this time, thanks to some tough family events. I'm still reading fiction, or some of it, but we in the department have noticed a sudden drying up of submissions since this election. It reminds me of when Nixon got elected for the first time: a horrible event that suddenly produced a flood of funny casuals (not about him), of all things. But I don't think that will happen this time around.

Maybe you noticed that Sparky Anderson died. The obits

made me think of a moment in the eighties when I was in his office in Lakeland, where there was a huge photo of Ty Cobb up on the wall. I was doing a piece on old-time ballplayers vs. the modern guys, so asked him if Cobb would make his team. He took the pipe out of his mouth and lowered his voice when he said, "I know he's not starting for me. I hope he makes the twenty-five-man squad."

All best, Philip, and thanks again,

P.S. I just reminded a young guy next door about your all-time title: "The Poem Circling Hamtramck, Michigan, All Night in Search of You."

TO SAM FIELD

November 18, 2011

Dear Sam:

Thanks so much for your letter. I loved your story about the lost and magically retrieved copy of "Let Me Finish"—a tale that would thrill any writer, including Dickens or Tolstoy. I also enjoyed going to Sebastopol via that link and getting a glimpse of the beautiful houses and setting in your home town. I'm glad you're playing golf now and then, though I stopped some time ago—being ninety-one I don't play anything anymore—but I don't mind passing along the golf shot of my life. This came while I was still at Harvard, and was playing with another hacker pal of mine one weekend at a suburban course in Wayland, Mass. There was a party of three just ahead of us on the course, and

I waited for them to get a decent distance ahead on some hole
before I stepped up and somehow hit the longest drive of my life,
which began to fade ominously in their direction. I started to yell
"Fore!" but stopped because I didn't want them to stop walking.
The ball hit a couple of yards behind them and then I saw one of
them begin to writhe and jump about oddly. He didn't go down,
but when I'd gotten to within his cursing distance we discovered
that the ball had come down *inside his collar* and had ended up
down his back somewhere. I apologized endlessly but couldn't
quite suppress my grin: Wow—greater than a hole in one,
any day!

I see Tad Tomkins a lot but almost no one else from the old
Snedens days. Jack Macrae is still with us, though reduced by MS.
He gets around on a little go-cart but still goes to work at his
publishing house. I'm also able to get to my office almost every
day, but my writing now is mostly via *New Yorker* blogs. I do
enjoy the form.

I had an inquiry by e-mail not long ago from a man who'd
been trying to find the old Snedens waterfall swimming pool
and pergola. He said that people who lived there told him they'd
heard of it but that it had disappeared. He walked around the area
and found the waterfall but no pool or anything else. It turns out
that it was all destroyed by vandals some years ago—they came in
by boat off the Hudson, and hammered it all down in less than an
hour: the pool and the white pergola and the paired steps and that
lovely small reflecting pool with the Roman white marble lion's-
head spouts. A tragic loss, to me.

So good to hear from you.

Best, as ever,

TO DAVID REMNICK

Inter-Office Memo

June, 2009

Dear David,

I'm a lifelong R. Crumb devotee, and while I do admire our scheduled Genesis chapter from his forthcoming version of the Good Book, I fear that seven spreads is going to put us way over our pubic hair allowance for 2009. Wouldn't a six-page selection do the trick and pay him full homage?

Roger

No need to answer . . .

PAST MASTERS: JOHN UPDIKE

JOHN AND THE KID

Tribute at the New York Public Library

Here's a passage that John Updike wrote forty-nine years ago, after watching Ted Williams hit a home run at Fenway Park, in the final at-bat of his career. The date is Wednesday, September 28, 1960, and the lines are from John's "Hub Fans Bid Kid Adieu," which ran in *The New Yorker* three weeks later. Most of you know them already.

> Fisher threw [a] third time, Williams swung again, and there it was. The ball climbed on a diagonal line into the vast volume of air over center field. From my angle, behind third base, the ball seemed less an object in flight than the tip of a towering, motionless construct, like the Eiffel Tower or the Tappan Zee Bridge. It was in the books while it was still in the sky. [Center fielder Jackie] Brandt ran back to the deepest corner of the outfield grass; the ball descended beyond his reach and struck in the crotch where the bullpen met the wall, bounced chunkily, and vanished.
>
> Like a feather caught in a vortex, Williams ran around the

square of bases at the center of our beseeching screaming. He ran as he always ran out home runs—hurriedly, unsmiling, head down, as if our praise were a storm of rain to get out of. He didn't tip his cap. Though we thumped, wept, and chanted "We want Ted" for minutes after he hid in the dugout, he did not come back. Our noise for some seconds passed beyond excitement into a kind of immense open anguish, a wailing, a cry to be saved. But immortality is nontransferable. The papers said that the other players, and even the umpires on the field, begged him to come out and acknowledge us in some way, but he never had and did not now. Gods do not answer letters.

Let's fill in a bit. The game, against the second-place Orioles, was won by the seventh-place Sox, 5–4, an outcome that made absolutely no difference to either team. Attendance at Fenway Park that day was 10,454 and would have been 10,453 if a lady that John Updike had hoped to meet at her apartment on Beacon Hill that morning had not stood him up. He went to the Fens, instead, bought a ticket, and wrote what turned out to be the most celebrated piece of baseball writing ever. In the words of Fats Waller, one never knows, do one? The 1960 regular season continued for three more days, but this was Ted Williams's last game ever. The home run was his twenty-ninth of the season, and his five hundred and twenty-first, lifetime. Here comes a fresh statistic, one you've not heard before. From the beginning of the modern baseball era, in 1901, to the end of that 1960 season, there were 66,112 other home runs struck in the major leagues, all noted and described briefly or at length by a writer or writers in attendance, not one of whom mentioned the Tappan Zee Bridge or feathers caught in a vortex, or conveyed the event with such economical joy.

I think John got a little tired of the attention paid to this piece, down the years. He never wrote about baseball again—golf was his game, as it turned out—and I imagine he had many dozens of other pages or paragraphs that he liked more—parts of "Rabbit Run," for instance, which he'd finished a year before Ted's last blast. When he and I talked about the article, as we did a few times, we each admitted—I with gratitude, he with customary modesty and class—that "Hub Fans Bid Kid Adieu" might have set the tone for my own baseball stuff, which I had not yet begun or thought of, and perhaps also encouraged *The New Yorker* to publish a few more sports pieces than it had so far. Thank you, John.

In the preface to a special edition of "Hub Fans," John wrote that he liked to think that the piece was "suffused with love," because of his boyhood attachment to Ted Williams and his more adult feelings for the woman who'd not kept their date, but I'll settle once again for joy—for the lift and lightness and intelligence that he himself and almost all of his writing conveyed, right to the end. You can go back and read him almost anywhere—this is the consolation he has left us—and see this and find him there once again. And if you think about that feather one more time it may come to you with another gleam of pleasure that the image carries the float and even the mildly lifting and falling shoulders of the contented everyday home-run hitter, suspended in time as he circles the bases and makes it safely back home again.

March, 2009

THE FADEAWAY

Colleagues for more than half a century, writer-editor partners for more than half that time, John Updike and I were close at a fixed distance—he at home north of Boston, I in my *New Yorker* office near Bryant Park—but spoke voluminously by telephone, by man-uscripts and galley proofs, and also via his typed, cheerful two-and-

a-half-by-five-and-a-half
white postcards that bore
his pale-blue name and
address   hand-stamped
in the northwest corner.
Now and then he would
turn up at the office,
startling me once again
with his height and his
tweeds, that major nose,
and his bright eyes and
up-bent smile; he spoke
in a light half-whisper
and, near the end of each
visit, somehow with-
drew a little, growing
more private and less
visible even before he

turned away. The fadeaway, as I came to think of it, may have had
to do with his exile from his own writing that day, while travelling;
the spacious writing part of him was held to one side when not
engaged, kept ready for its engrossing daily stint back home. Infor-
mally august, he stayed young after his hair turned white, but the
additions of fame and a vast work now made him seem Colonial,
ready for the portrait on a postage stamp.

A similar sense of shift and distracting clarity often overtook
a reader in one of Updike's stories when an ordinary enough event
or small-town American scene—a slight earthquake, a 5.4 on the
Richter scale, awakening a man at home in bed in the early morning; a mother on her way to work in the nineteen-thirties running
for a streetcar in Pennsylvania; a man in his late fifties outside his
living room in the winter finding the moons of Jupiter with his

new home telescope—slides to another breadth and meaning in the space of a sentence or two. This is what Updike has had in mind for us all along. He invites us into his story and walks us easily along; all is recognizable and reassuringly alive, but then—we've had no warning—we're seized with a flooding fresh knowledge, in the same fashion that sadness or some ancient night remembrance can sometimes take us in its teeth. Updike was in his twenties and thirties when most of his seventeen stories about the Maples were being written, but his expert and unpatronizing account of a suburban marriage—husband and wife, neighbors and kids, meals and affairs and politics and anxiety—also carried this double view. There's something terrifying about it all, because these young people, parents and children alike, are such beginners, not ready for so much life.

Updike's writing is light and springy, the tone unforced; often happiness is almost in view, despite age or disappointments. He is not mawkish or insistently gloomy. Death is frequently mentioned but for the time being is postponed. Time itself is bendable in these stories; the characters are aware of themselves at many stages. This is Updike country: intelligent and Eastern, mostly Protestant, more or less moneyed. We understand and read on, and then—and then a middle-aged married man named Fanshawe remembers how he had "ceased to fear death—or, so to say, to grasp it"—at the moment when he first slept with a woman named Lorna Kramer. Or the young father, Richard Maple, at the end of a day when he and his wife, Joan, have been explaining to their young children that they are going to separate and try living apart for the summer, ending their marriage at least for now, is telling the news to his teen-age son, in bed and just home from a rock concert, and the teary boy stops him with a word: "Why?" He has forgotten why. Or that young woman from the past—Updike's mother without a doubt, but seen this time as the mother of a man named Joey in a long 1990 story, "A Sandstone Farmhouse"—"running to catch the trolley, the world of the thirties shabby and solid around her, the porches, the blue midsummer hydrangeas, this tiny well-dressed figure in her diminishing pocket of time, her future unknown, her death, her farm, far from her mind."

Updike's sentences are fresh-painted. In all his writing, critical or fictional or reportorial, he is a fabulous noticer and expander; he's invented HD. So armed, he felt free from the start to take up and engage with all that lay within the range of his attention and put it down on paper. As a contributor, he was patient with editing, and pertinaciously involved with his product: an editor's dream. My end of the work was to point out an occasional inconsistent or extraneous sentence, or a passage that wanted something more. Almost under his breath over our phone connection, while we looked at the same lines, he would try out an alternative: "Which one sounds better, do you think?" Sighing, he would take us back over the same few words again and again, then propose or listen to a switch of some sort, and try again. All writers do this, but not many with such a lavishly extended consideration. He wanted to see each galley, each tiny change, right down to the late-closing page proofs, which he often managed to return by overnight mail an hour or so before closing, with new sentences or passages, handwritten in the margins in a soft pencil, that were fresher and more inventive and revealing than what had been there before. You watched him write.

This process sounds old-fashioned, but Updike was probably the very first *New Yorker* writer to shift over to a computer, back in the early eighties. "I don't know how this will change my writing," he wrote to me in advance, "but it will." He was right, of course: the flavor was mysteriously different, the same wine but of another year.

By the end, there were a hundred and forty-six John Updike stories that ran in the magazine, starting with "Friends from Philadelphia," in the issue of October 30, 1954, and finishing with "The

Full Glass," in the May 26, 2008, issue. Another several dozen casuals or works of humor ran up to "A Desert Encounter," on October 20, 2008. All this, of course, was in addition to his five hundred–odd reviews and poems and critical essays in *The New Yorker,* and to one side of or on top of the twenty-three novels, the art criticism for *The New York Review of Books,* and the steady rush of pieces and stories published elsewhere. He often insisted that he was about to run dry. When I became his fiction editor, early in 1976, succeeding William Maxwell, I was alarmed to hear from him that his best fiction-writing days were probably behind him. This was nonsense; his output then was a steady three or four first-class stories per year, but to hear him tell it the end was near. "Fiction is a young man's game," he said querulously. I had not yet understood how much he loved sounding old. Rabbit Angstrom, we might notice, dies of old age, in effect, in "Rabbit at Rest," the fourth and final book of the celebrated work, at the age of fifty-six. By the time his production level did in fact slow a bit, twenty years down the line, I'd found a little trick that he and I enjoyed. Some mornings when we were talking idly on the telephone, perhaps still again about the Sox' pitching, I would tell him that there was a sharp new story coming up in the next issue—something different, by a young man or woman we'd been following for some time now. "*Rea*-lly!" he would cry, his voice rising. He was still a close reader of every issue, and over the years as a reviewer for the magazine he had been amazingly generous to beginning talents. But this was beside the point, as we understood. A couple of weeks would go by and then—not every time, but sometimes—my little pile of morning mail would include a tan manuscript envelope with his name stamped in blue up in the corner: a new story by John Updike.

Talk, February, 2009

MIDDLE INNINGS

MO TOWN

Late on yesterday's dazzling, post-summer afternoon in the Bronx, each batter and infielder moved and ran with his own autumnal sharp-shadow cutout barely attached at the foot. The brilliant, reminding light was relentless; it never let us up, enamelling the grass at the outset, then producing late-inning gateways of alternate shadow and sun between the mound and home plate that made each pitch flicker in its flight. No, no, you wanted to say: Not so fast. Not yet. ("ONE MO TIME," said a fan's held-up plea.) It got late early up there, as Yogi once said, and the outcome we didn't want arrived just the same, in spite of plaques and speeches. Mariano Rivera's pregame "Exit Sandman" final-Sunday ceremonies at the Stadium—he's retiring after nineteen seasons—had been awkwardly merged with Andy Pettitte's recently announced decision to depart for good, too, after eighteen (all but three with the Yanks), but, because Andy would be starting against the visiting San Francisco Giants and was preoccupied with that, it remained Mo's day mostly, and sweetly reassuring. Waterford crystal, the comical rocking chair, parents, family, current teammates and old ones. Paulie, Jorge, Bernie, Derek, Tino, manager Joe, Rachel Robinson (Mo, of course, the last player to sport Jackie Robinson's universally retired

© The Saul Steinberg Foundation / Artists Rights Society (ARS), New York

uniform number, 42). Michael Kay. Speeches, smiles—Rivera won this category, hands down—and an actual surprise: Metallica, live and in person, there to play his entrance song.

All this was happily cheered and clapped for and phone-flashed by the attending forty-nine thousand one hundred and ninety-seven fans (as it had been previously and similarly done in the honoring ballparks where Mo appeared this summer), but, once the game began, these same thousands found themselves for the last time painfully checking off and folding and tucking away their own shared but also private memories of the two, beginning with Pettitte's prayerful, early-Renaissance gaze in at his catcher's signals, with his cap pulled low, his hands up, and his lips touching the top of his upheld black mitt.

Andy was almost great, giving up two hits in seven innings—the first a home run in the sixth by the rookie San Francisco shortstop Ehire Adrianza, and the other a double in the eighth by Pablo

Sandoval, which shortly became the winning run—Andy had gone, with a final hat wave—in the Yanks' excruciating 2–1 defeat. Mariano came on with one out in the eighth, and surrendered a single but no runs, and along the way gave us still again his eloquent entering run from deep center field; the leaning stare-in with upcocked mitt over his heart; the reposeful pre-pitch pause, with his hands at waist level; and then the burning, bending, famed-in-song-and-story cutter. All these, seen once again, have been as familiar to us as our dad's light cough from the next room, or the dimples on the back of our once-three-year-old daughter's hands, but, like those, must now only be recalled.

The game ran down, then ran out, with the Yanks somehow failing to score anybody after putting runners on second and third base with no outs in the bottom of the eighth. The TV camera, sweeping the dugout rail one more time, caught a gallery of derelicts. The last batter, a twenty-two-year-old rookie catcher named J. R. Murphy, went down swinging. Shattered by injuries and with their bullpen worn to a frazzle, the Yankees have lost six of their last nine games. Sagging in the tatterdemalion struggle for that second American League Wild Card in the last week of the season, they will be caught by the heels in the next day or two and gobbled up by the statistical werewolf. Baseball, as Bart Giamatti told us, breaks your heart, but he was thinking of the back-then Red Sox.

Post, September, 2013

SOX TOP SLOPPY CARDS

Game 1, 2013 World Series
Red Sox 8: Cardinals 1

World Series opening games can feel like a sunny day at Camp 6, a deserved picnic where we enjoy the fabulous views we've attained and contemplate the last push to the summit, but all images of the sort flew away quickly last night, when the inept Cardinals gave up five runs in the first two innings at Fenway Park, in the course of an 8–1 pasting by the Red Sox. Jon Lester, the lefty Boston starter, struck out eight Cards over seven and two-thirds innings, and David Ortiz knocked a home run and a single and a sac, driving in three runs: thrilling star material on a better night, but only satisfactory here. The Cards, the best defensive team in the National League, were stinko, with three infield errors, two of them by shortstop Pete Kozma. The pattern of the game became clear when the veteran Cardinal starter Adam Wainwright could only smile wanly after allowing a feeble pop by Stephen Drew to drop like a thrombosed dove at his feet, to begin the Sox' second. No replays, please.

Big Papi's most telling blow may prove to have been his fly ball out to the rim of the Sox' bullpen later in the second—a near replica of that grand slam in the A.L.C.S. sixth game that pinwheeled the Tiger right fielder Torii Hunter. This ball, not quite a line drive, came down a yard or two north of that one, and was plucked back niftily from beyond the barrier by the Cards' Carlos Beltran, who slammed heavily into the four-foot wall there but held on. (Tim McCarver, the sterling Fox commentator, pointed out that that low bullpen wall is safe enough for outfielders when their backs are turned but deadly whenever they raise their arms.) Beltran's contused rib forced him to leave the game, and his absence tonight and perhaps later on, removing his powerful bat from the order, would be worse for the Cards than losing a trifling opener.

The Never Before moment arrived early, when Ortiz, the fourth Boston batter of the evening, hit a soft grounder to the right, where second baseman Matt Carpenter flipped to Kozma to begin a potential double play. When the ball came loose out there, second-base umpire Dana DeMuth signalled that Kozma had held it long enough for the force, even though everyone in the northern hemisphere, including my watching fox terrier and I, could plainly see that Kozma had barely touched the toss with the tip of his glove. The out stood up, *stare decisis*—or would have in an earlier era of umpiric reasoning. Here, though, and to my amazement, five neighboring umps came circling in, like crows or undertakers, and, after consultation, DeMuthed the call—safe on an error, the out cancelled. Justice and common sense had prevailed (along with a snub to the possibility of instant electronic replay to decide such calls next year), but a part of me felt a twinge of loss. Umps should always be right, even when they aren't. In their hearts, as Bill Klem said, they never missed a call.

Post, October, 2013

CHINNY-CHIN-CHIN

Game 4, 2013 World Series
Red Sox 4: Cardinals 2
Series Tied

Last night's game, like Saturday's, ended with a losing-team player disconsolate in the dirt, but this time without an attached ruling to talk about. Kolten Wong, a ninth-inning Cardinals pinch base runner, was cleanly picked off first base by the Boston closer Koji Uehara, for the last out of the game. No excuse: Sox win, 4–2, knotting the series at two games apiece. The play was a fillip, not a filibuster, with the evening's main event remaining Jonny Gomes's three-run homer in the top of the sixth, which broke a 1–1 tie, and held up, guaranteeing that the teams, no matter who wins tonight, will return to Boston on Wednesday, for a sixth and then possibly a seventh and determining contest. Serious stuff by then, with every pitch tense and fraught, and winter now just down the street. No more fun, I mean, so let's pause here and for one last time talk about beards.

In resuming the topic, I don't expect to match or approach the charming and scholarly essay recently posted by my friend and colleague Richard Brody, who said that "one of the beauties of the beard is that its lushness is polysemic, lending itself to an interpretive exuberance to match its flow." Yow, Richard, and excuse me, but might I demur?

Beards are kudzu.

Jonny Gomes's beard—a brown frigate bird's nest—is among the uglier sported by the hairy Sox this year, and when numbers of his teammates began grabbing it and ritually tugging on it upon his return to the dugout after his blast I was among a minority in the land who were hoping they'd pull it off. Gomes, a nice guy from Petaluma, California, has broad sloping shoulders and a pleasant, or O.K.-ish, everyday expression, but he's shaved his head now, too, which doesn't help, unless you're eager to join the crowding recent hordes of the undead. C'mon, Jonny.

Gomes's isn't the worst Sox beard—the title goes to backup catcher David Ross, whose unkempt cabbage includes a clashing streak of white that cascades over his chin—perhaps a relic of a childhood moment when he ran into his grandfather in the narrow back hall outside the bathroom. The other catcher, Jarrod Saltalamacchia, has a raggedy garden-border growth, in keeping with the encircling back-yard shrubbery of his hair. Mike Napoli's beard is thickest; Dustin Pedroia's the weirdest, since it comes with his desert-saint stare and that repeated on-deck or between-pitch mannerism of opening and stretching his mouth into a silent O: a screech owl with laryngitis.

I'm a gentle fellow, and intend no lasting hurts here. I admire Big Papi's plunging mid-cheek parenthesis, which has been there for many seasons, of course, and now feels as familiar and locally reassuring as a statue by Daniel Chester French. I also offer praise for the angle-iron jawline wool sported by tonight's Boston starter, Jon Lester: an aesthetic so clearly modelled on Gunnar Björnstrand's trimmed-down growth while he portrayed Fredrik Egerman in Bergman's "Smiles of a Summer Night."

Can I ask a question? Where are the Red Sox wives or sweetie pies in all this? Have none of them spoken up—privately or in the *Globe* or in a thousand tweets—to protest this office fad? How does it feel to wake up, night after night, in immediate proximity to a crazed Pomeranian or a Malamute or an Old English sheepdog stubbornly adhering to the once caressable jaw of the guy on the nearest pillow? Doesn't it scratch? Doesn't it itch? Doesn't it smell, however faintly, of tonight's boeuf en daube or yesterday's last pinch of Red Man? And what about the kids—how long can you keep putting them off with another recital of "The Three Little Pigs" or Edward Lear? Who does your husband/significant other think he is, anyway—Dostoyevsky? Brigham Young? Darwin? An Allman brother? Alexander Cartwright?

Come on, guys, think this over. Time to grow up. And what if you lose in the end this week, beards and all? Is this a lifetime commitment?

Hmmm. (Rubs chin.)

Post, October, 2013

PAPINESS

Game 6, 2013 World Series
Red Sox 6: Cardinals 1
Sox Win World Series

O.K., about those beards—I give up. The Red Sox took this World Series in six games, but by something wider in retrospect.

The Cardinals, ahead two games to one in the early going, led only once after that—a little 1–0 margin that held up for two innings in Game Four. In actuality, they outhit the Sox, .224 to .211, but did not draw sustenance from this gruel, because of a collective batting debility. The bottom four hitters in their order failed to deliver a single base runner in scoring position over the seven games. Their dugout was tomblike last night after Shane Victorino's three-run double, high off the wall in the third inning, and no wonder. The eight Boston batters not named Ortiz, by contrast, stayed upbeat throughout—a boys' club, you felt—despite a similar collective fatuity at the plate. Somebody or other would provide: Gomes with a three-run homer in Game Four; David Ross with a seventh-inning double the next night; that Victorino double yesterday. All this can be blamed on St. Louis pitching, of course, but there was clearly something else in play during these games—a winning conviction beyond the reach of stats. Beards did it.

Big Papi had four walks last night, three of them on free passes from the Cardinal pitchers, and struck out at last in the sixth, dropping his batting average from .733 to .688, still good enough by miles for the Series M.V.P. award. No one has ever been hotter—unless it was St. Louis third baseman David Freese, back in 2011, when he saved the Cards from extinction by the Texas Rangers in Game Six of that World Series with a ninth-inning two-out, two-strike, two-run triple, then won the game with a lead-off homer in the eleventh. Freese was present but not present this time around, striking out seven times—you wanted to look away.

Fox TV provided a nice little Ortiz vignette, with an overheard water-cooler chat between Cards catcher Yadier Molina and home-plate ump Jim Joyce as Big Papi approached the plate once again. "The guy's unbelievable," Molina said, through his mask.

"He's fun to watch," Joyce agreed.

I also appreciated a Fox shot that reprised Stephen Drew's

fourth-inning home run into the Sox bullpen, where the presiding Boston cop, Steve Horgan, again raised his arms in triumph, exactly as he had famously done in the A.L.C.S. when Ortiz's homer landed there, with Tiger right fielder Torii Hunter spinning after it, head over heels. Drew's shot put the Sox up by 4–0, and there was time for me to muse about Horgan's duties while on patrol out there: Patting down pigeons? Breaking up a deadly international ring of autograph counterfeiters?

Such are the idle between-time pleasures of baseball, but that season has now flown away, worse luck. The Red Sox have taken their third World Championship in ten years, and the first clinched at Fenway Park since 1918. No trace remains of the Curse of the Bambino and accompanying New England paranoias that filled up our paragraphs and night thoughts for so many years. Winning almost all the time has a lot to be said for it, but not quite winning, barely missing again and again, keeps you whining and breathing, and might even be more fun in the end.

Post, October, 2013

THIS OLD MAN

Check me out. The top two knuckles of my left hand look as if I'd been worked over by the K.G.B. No, it's more as if I'd been a catcher for the Hall of Fame pitcher Candy Cummings, the inventor of the curveball, who retired from the game in 1877. To put this another way, if I pointed that hand at you like a pistol and fired at your nose, the bullet would nail you in the left knee. Arthritis.

Now, still facing you, if I cover my left, or better, eye with one hand, what I see is a blurry encircling version of the ceiling and floor and walls or windows to our right and left but no sign of your face or head: nothing in the middle. But cheer up: If I reverse things and cover my right eye, there you are, back again. If I take

With Andy, Central Park, January 2014

© Brigitte Lacombe 2014

my hand away and look at you with both eyes, the empty hole disappears and you're in 3-D, and actually looking pretty terrific today. Macular degeneration.

I'm ninety-three, and I'm feeling great. Well, pretty great, unless I've forgotten to take a couple of Tylenols in the past four or five hours, in which case I've begun to feel some jagged little pains shooting down my left forearm and into the base of the thumb. Shingles, in 1996, with resultant nerve damage.

Like many men and women my age, I get around with a couple of arterial stents that keep my heart chunking. I also sport a minute plastic seashell that clamps shut a congenital hole in my heart, discovered in my early eighties. The surgeon at Mass General who fixed up this P.F.O. (a patent foramen ovale—I love to say it) was a Mexican-born character actor in beads and clogs, and a fervent admirer of Derek Jeter. Counting this procedure and the stents, plus a passing balloon angioplasty and two or three false alarms, I've become sort of a table potato, unalarmed by the X-ray cameras swooping eerily about just above my naked body in a darkened and icy operating room; there's also a little TV screen up there that presents my heart as a pendant ragbag attached to tacky ribbons of veins and arteries. But never mind. Nowadays, I pop a pink beta-blocker and a white statin at breakfast, along with several lesser pills, and head off to my human-wreckage gym, and it's been a couple of years since the last showing.

My left knee is thicker but shakier than my right. I messed it up playing football, eons ago, but can't remember what went wrong there more recently. I had a date to have the joint replaced by a famous knee man (he's listed in the Metropolitan Opera program as a major supporter) but changed course at the last moment, opting elsewhere for injections of synthetic frog hair or rooster combs or something, which magically took away the pain. I walk around with a cane now when outdoors—"Stop *brandishing*!" I hear

Carol admonishing—which gives me a nice little edge when hailing cabs.

The lower-middle sector of my spine twists and jogs like a Connecticut county road, thanks to a herniated disk seven or eight years ago. This has cost me two or three inches of height, transforming me from Gary Cooper to Geppetto. After days spent groaning on the floor, I received a blessed epidural, ending the ordeal. "You can sit up now," the doctor said, whisking off his shower cap. "Listen, do you know who Dominic Chianese is?"

"Isn't that Uncle Junior?" I said, confused. "You know—from 'The Sopranos'?"

"Yes," he said. "He and I play in a mandolin quartet every Wednesday night at the Hotel Edison. Do you think you could help us get a listing in the front of *The New Yorker*?"

I've endured a few knocks but missed worse. I know how lucky I am, and secretly tap wood, greet the day, and grab a sneaky pleasure from my survival at long odds. The pains and insults are bearable. My conversation may be full of holes and pauses, but I've learned to dispatch a private Apache scout ahead into the next sentence, the one coming up, to see if there are any vacant names or verbs in the landscape up there. If he sends back a warning, I'll pause meaningfully, duh, until something else comes to mind.

On the other hand, I've not yet forgotten Keats or Dick Cheney or what's waiting for me at the dry cleaner's today. As of right now, I'm not Christopher Hitchens or Tony Judt or Nora Ephron; I'm not dead and not yet mindless in a reliable upstate facility. Decline and disaster impend, but my thoughts don't linger there. It shouldn't surprise me if at this time next week I'm surrounded by family, gathered on short notice—they're sad and shocked but also a little pissed off to be here—to help decide, after what's happened, what's to be done with me now. It must be this hovering knowledge, that two-ton safe swaying on a frayed rope just over my head, that makes everyone so glad to see me again. "How great you're looking! Wow, tell me your secret!" they kindly cry when they happen upon me crossing the street or exiting a dinghy or departing an X-ray room, while the little balloon over their heads reads, "Holy shit—he's still vertical!"

Let's move on. A smooth fox terrier of ours named Harry was full of surprises. Wildly sociable, like others of his breed, he grew a fraction more reserved in maturity, and learned to cultivate a separate wagging acquaintance with each fresh visitor or old pal he came upon in the living room. If friends had come for dinner, he'd arise from an evening nap and leisurely tour the table in imitation of a three-star headwaiter: Everything O.K. here? Is there anything we could bring you? How was the crème brûlée? Terriers aren't water dogs, but Harry enjoyed kayaking in Maine, sitting like a figurehead between my knees for an hour or more and scoping out the passing cormorant or yachtsman. Back in the city, he established his personality and dashing good looks on the neighborhood to the extent that a local artist executed a striking head-on portrait in pointillist oils, based on a snapshot of him she'd sneaked in Central Park. Harry took his leave (another surprise) on a June afternoon three years ago, a few days after his eighth birthday. Alone in our fifth-floor apartment, as was usual during working hours, he became unhinged by a noisy thunderstorm and went out a front window left a quarter open on a muggy day. I knew him well and could summon up his feelings during the brief moments of that leap: the welcome coolness of rain on his muzzle and shoulders, the excitement of air and space around his outstretched body.

Here in my tenth decade, I can testify that the downside of great age is the room it provides for rotten news. Living long means enough already. When Harry died, Carol and I couldn't stop weeping; we sat in the bathroom with his retrieved body on a mat between us, the light-brown patches on his back and the near-black of his ears still darkened by the rain, and passed a Kleenex box back and forth between us. Not all the tears were for him. Two months earlier, a beautiful daughter of mine, my oldest child, had ended her life, and the oceanic force and mystery of that event had not left full space for tears. Now we could cry without reserve, weep together for Harry and Callie and ourselves. Harry cut us loose.

A few notes about age is my aim here, but a little more about loss is inevitable. "Most of the people my age is dead. You could look it up" was the way Casey Stengel put it. He was seventy-five at the time, and contemporary social scientists might prefer Casey's line delivered at eighty-five now, for accuracy, but the point remains. We geezers carry about a bulging directory of dead husbands or wives, children, parents, lovers, brothers and sisters, dentists and shrinks, office sidekicks, summer neighbors, classmates, and bosses, all once entirely familiar to us and seen as part of the safe landscape of the day. It's no wonder we're a bit bent. The surprise, for me, is that the accruing weight of these departures doesn't bury us, and that even the pain of an almost unbearable loss gives way quite quickly to something more distant but still stubbornly gleaming. The dead have departed, but gestures and glances and tones of voice of theirs, even scraps of clothing—that pale-yellow Saks scarf— reappear unexpectedly, along with accompanying touches of sweetness or irritation.

Our dead are almost beyond counting and we want to herd them along, pen them up somewhere in order to keep them straight. I like to think of mine as fellow voyagers crowded aboard the *Île de France* (the idea is swiped from "Outward Bound"). Here's my father, still handsome in his tuxedo, lighting a Lucky Strike. There's Ted Smith, about to name-drop his Gloucester home town again. Here comes Slim Aarons. Here's Esther Mae Counts, from fourth grade: Hi, Esther Mae. There's Gardner—with Cecille Shawn, for some reason. Here's Ted Yates. Anna Hamburger. Colba F. Gucker,

better known as Chief. Bob Ascheim. Victor Pritchett—and Dorothy. Henry Allen. Bart Giamatti. My elder old-maid cousin Jean
Webster and her unexpected, late-arriving Brit husband, Capel
Hanbury. Kitty Stableford. Dan Quisenberry. Nancy Field. Freddy
Alexandre. I look around for others and at times can almost produce
someone at will. Callie returns, via a phone call. "Dad?" It's her,
all right, her voice affectionately rising at the end—"Da-ad?"—
but sounding a bit impatient this time. She's in a hurry. And now
Harold Eads. Toni Robin. Dick Salmon, his face bright red with
laughter. Edith Oliver. Sue Dawson. Herb Mitgang. Coop. Tudie.
Elwood Carter.

These names are best kept in mind rather than boxed and put
away somewhere. Old letters are engrossing but feel historic in
numbers, photo albums delightful but with a glum after-kick like
a chocolate caramel. Home movies are killers: Zeke, a long-gone
Lab, alive again, rushing from right to left with a tennis ball in his
mouth; my sister Nancy, stunning at seventeen, smoking a lipstick-
stained cigarette aboard *Astrid,* with the breeze stirring her tied-up
brown hair; my mother laughing and ducking out of the picture
again, waving her hands in front of her face in embarrassment—
she's about thirty-five. Me sitting cross-legged under a Ping-Pong
table, at eleven. Take us away.

My list of names is banal but astounding, and it's barely a fraction, the ones that slip into view in the first minute or two. Anyone
over sixty knows this; my list is only longer. I don't go there often,
but, once I start, the battalion of the dead is on duty, alertly waiting. Why do they sustain me so, cheer me up, remind me of life? I
don't understand this. Why am I not endlessly grieving?

What I've come to count on is the white-coated attendant of
memory, silently here again to deliver dabs from the laboratory
dish of me. In the days before Carol died, twenty months ago, she
lay semiconscious in bed at home, alternating periods of faint or

imperceptible breathing with deep, shuddering catch-up breaths. Then, in a delicate gesture, she would run the pointed tip of her tongue lightly around the upper curve of her teeth. She repeated this pattern again and again. I've forgotten, perhaps mercifully, much of what happened in that last week and the weeks after, but this recurs.

Carol is around still, but less reliably. For almost a year, I would wake up from another late-afternoon mini-nap in the same living-room chair, and, in the instants before clarity, would sense her sitting in her own chair, just opposite. Not a ghost but a presence, alive as before and in the same instant gone again. This happened often, and I almost came to count on it, knowing that it wouldn't last. Then it stopped.

People my age and younger friends as well seem able to recall entire tapestries of childhood, and swatches from their children's early lives as well: conversations, exact meals, birthday parties, illnesses, picnics, vacation B. and B.s, trips to the ballet, the time when . . . I can't do this and it eats at me, but then, without announcement or connection, something turns up. I am walking on Ludlow Lane, in Snedens, with my two young daughters, years ago on a summer morning. I'm in my late thirties; they're about nine and six, and I'm complaining about the steep little stretch of road between us and our house, just up the hill. Maybe I'm getting old, I offer. Then I say that one day I'll be really old and they'll have to hold me up. I imitate an old man mumbling nonsense and start to walk with wobbly legs. Callie and Alice scream with laughter and hold me up, one on each side. When I stop, they ask for more, and we do this over and over.

I'm leaving out a lot, I see. My work—I'm still working, or sort of. Reading. The collapsing, grossly insistent world. Stuff I get excited about or depressed about all the time. Dailiness—but how can I explain this one? Perhaps with a blog recently posted on

Facebook by a woman I know who lives in Australia. "Good Lord, we've run out of nutmeg!" it began. "How in the world did that ever happen?" Dozens of days are like that with me lately.

Intimates and my family—mine not very near me now but always on call, always with me. My children Alice and John Henry and my daughter-in-law Alice—yes, another one—and my grand-daughters Laura and Lily and Clara, who together and separately were as steely and resplendent as a company of Marines on the day we buried Carol. And on other days and in other ways as well. Laura, for example, who will appear almost overnight, on demand, to drive me and my dog and my stuff five hundred miles Down East, then does it again, backward, later in the summer. Hours of talk and sleep (mine, not hers) and renewal—the abandoned mills at Lawrence, Mass., Cat Mousam Road, the Narramissic River still there—plus a couple of nights together, with the summer candles again.

Friends in great numbers now, taking me to dinner or cooking in for me. (One afternoon, I found a freshly roasted chicken sitting outside my front door; two hours later, another one appeared in the same spot.) Friends inviting me to the opera, or to Fairway on Sunday morning, or to dine with their kids at the East Side Deli, or to a wedding at the Rockbound Chapel, or bringing in ice cream to share at my place while we catch another Yankees game. They saved my life. In the first summer after Carol had gone, a man I'd known slightly and pleasantly for decades listened while I talked about my changed routines and my doctors and dog walkers and the magazine. I paused for a moment, and he said, "Plus you have us."

Another message—also brief, also breathtaking—came on an earlier afternoon at my longtime therapist's, at a time when I felt I'd lost almost everything. "I don't know how I'm going to get through this," I said at last.

A silence, then: "Neither do I. But you will."

I am a world-class complainer but find palpable joy arriving with my evening Dewar's, from Robinson Cano between pitches, from the first pages once again of "Appointment in Samarra" or the last lines of the Elizabeth Bishop poem called "Poem." From the briefest strains of Handel or Roy Orbison, or Dennis Brain playing the early bars of his stunning Mozart horn concertos. (This Angel recording may have been one of the first things Carol and I acquired just after our marriage, and I hear it playing on a sunny Saturday morning in our Ninety-fourth Street walkup.) Also the recalled faces and then the names of Jean Dixon or Roscoe Karns or Porter Hall or Brad Dourif in another Netflix rerun. Chloë Sevigny in "Trees Lounge." Gail Collins on a good day. Family ice-skating up near Harlem in the nineteen-eighties, with the Park employees, high on youth or weed, looping past us backward to show their smiles.

Recent and not so recent surveys (including the six-decades-long Grant Study of the lives of some nineteen-forties Harvard graduates) confirm that a majority of us people over seventy-five keep surprising ourselves with happiness. Put me on that list. Our children are adults now and mostly gone off, and let's hope full of their own lives. We've outgrown our ambitions. If our wives or husbands are still with us, we sense a trickle of contentment flowing from the reliable springs of routine, affection in long silences, calm within the light boredom of well-worn friends, retold stories, and mossy opinions. Also the distant whoosh of a surfaced porpoise outside our night windows.

We elders—what kind of a handle is this, anyway, halfway between a tree and an eel?—we elders have learned a thing or two, including invisibility. Here I am in a conversation with some trusty friends—old friends but actually not all that old: they're in their sixties—and we're finishing the wine and in serious converse about global warming in Nyack or Virginia Woolf the cross-dresser.

There's a pause, and I chime in with a couple of sentences. The others look at me politely, then resume the talk exactly at the point where they've just left it. What? Hello? Didn't I just say something? Have I left the room? Have I experienced what neurologists call a T.I.A.—a transient ischemic attack? I didn't expect to take over the chat but did await a word or two of response. Not tonight, though. (Women I know say that this began to happen to them when they passed fifty.) When I mention the phenomenon to anyone around my age, I get back nods and smiles. Yes, we're invisible. Honored, respected, even loved, but not quite worth listening to anymore. You've had your turn, Pops; now it's ours.

I've been asking myself why I don't think about my approaching visitor, death. He was often on my mind thirty or forty years ago, I believe, though more of a stranger. Death terrified me then, because I had so many engagements. The enforced opposite—no dinner dates or coming attractions, no urgent business, no fun, no calls, no errands, no returned words or touches—left a blank that I could not light or furnish: a condition I recognized from childhood bad dreams and sudden awakenings. Well, not yet, not soon, or probably not, I would console myself, and that welcome but then tediously repeated postponement felt in time less like a threat than like a family obligation—tea with Aunt Molly in Montclair, someday soon but not now. Death, meanwhile, was constantly onstage or changing costume for his next engagement—as Bergman's thick-faced chess player; as the medieval night-rider in a hoodie; as Woody Allen's awkward visitor half-falling into the room as he enters through the window; as W. C. Fields's man in the bright nightgown—and in my mind had gone from spectre to a waiting second-level celebrity on the Letterman show. Or almost. Some people I knew seemed to have lost all fear when dying and awaited the end with a certain impatience. "I'm tired of lying here," said one. "Why is this taking so long?" asked another. Death will get it on with me eventually, and stay much too long, and though I'm in no hurry about the meeting, I feel I know him almost too well by now.

A weariness about death exists in me and in us all in another way, as well, though we scarcely notice it. We have become tireless voyeurs of death: he is on the morning news and the evening news and on the breaking, middle-of-the-day news as well—not the celebrity death, I mean, but the everyone-else death. A roadside-accident figure, covered with a sheet. A dead family, removed from a ramshackle faraway building pocked and torn by bullets. The transportation dead. The dead in floods and hurricanes and tsu-namis, in numbers called "tolls." The military dead, presented in silence on your home screen, looking youthful and well combed. The enemy war dead or rediscovered war dead, in higher figures. Appalling and dulling totals not just from this year's war but from the ones before that, and the ones way back that some of us still around may have also attended. All the dead from wars and natural events and school shootings and street crimes and domestic crimes that each of us has once again escaped and felt terrible about and plans to go and leave wreaths or paper flowers at the site of. There's never anything new about death, to be sure, except its improved publicity. At second hand, we have become death's expert wit-nesses; we know more about death than morticians, feel as much at home with it as those poor bygone schlunks trying to survive a continent-ravaging, low-digit-century epidemic. Death sucks but, enh—click the channel.

I get along. Now and then it comes to me that I appear to have more energy and hope than some of my coevals, but I take no credit for this. I don't belong to a book club or a bridge club; I'm not taking up Mandarin or practicing the viola. In a sporadic effort to keep my brain from moldering, I've begun to memorize shorter poems—by Auden, Donne, Ogden Nash, and more—which I recite to myself some nights while walking my dog, Harry's successor fox terrier, Andy. I've also become a blogger, and enjoy the ease and freedom of the form: it's a bit like making a paper airplane and then watching it take wing below your window. But shouldn't I have something more scholarly or complex than this put away by now—late paragraphs of accomplishments, good works, some weightier op cits? I'm afraid not. The thoughts of age are short, short thoughts. I don't read Scripture and cling to no life precepts, except perhaps to Walter Cronkite's rules for old men, which he did not deliver over the air: Never trust a fart. Never pass up a drink. Never ignore an erection.

I count on jokes, even jokes about death.

> TEACHER: Good morning, class. This is the first day of school and we're going to introduce ourselves. I'll call on you, one by one, and you can tell us your name and maybe what your dad or your mom does for a living. You, please, over at this end.
> SMALL BOY: My name is Irving and my dad is a mechanic.
> TEACHER: A mechanic! Thank you, Irving. Next?
> SMALL GIRL: My name is Emma and my mom is a lawyer.
> TEACHER: How nice for you, Emma! Next?
> SECOND SMALL BOY: My name is Luke and my dad is dead.
> TEACHER: Oh, Luke, how sad for you. We're all very sorry about that, aren't we, class? Luke, do you think you could tell us what Dad did before he died?
> LUKE (*seizes his throat*): He went "*N'gungghhh!*"

Not bad—I'm told that fourth graders really go for this one. Let's try another.

A man and his wife tried and tried to have a baby, but without success. Years went by and they went on trying, but no luck. They liked each other, so the work was always a pleasure, but they grew

a bit sad along the way. Finally, she got pregnant, was very careful, and gave birth to a beautiful eight-pound-two-ounce baby boy.
The couple were beside themselves with happiness. At the hospital
that night, she told her husband to stop by the local newspaper and
arrange for a birth announcement, to tell all their friends the good
news. First thing next morning, she asked if he'd done the errand.

"Yes, I did," he said, "but I had no idea those little notices in
the paper were so expensive."

"Expensive?" she said. "How much was it?"

"It was eight hundred and thirty-seven dollars. I have the
receipt."

"Eight hundred and thirty-seven dollars!" she cried. "But that's
impossible. You must have made some mistake. Tell me exactly
what happened."

"There was a young lady behind a counter at the paper, who
gave me the form to fill out," he said. "I put in your name and my
name and little Teddy's name and weight, and when we'd be home
again and, you know, ready to see friends. I handed it back to her
and she counted up the words and said, 'How many insertions?'
I said twice a week for fourteen years, and she gave me the bill.
O.K.?"

I heard this tale more than fifty years ago, when my first wife,
Evelyn, and I were invited to tea by a rather elegant older couple
who were new to our little Rockland County community. They
were in their seventies, at least, and very welcoming, and it was just
the four of us. We barely knew them and I was surprised when he
turned and asked her to tell us the joke about the couple trying to
have a baby. "Oh, no," she said, "they wouldn't want to hear that."

"Oh, come on, dear—they'll love it," he said, smiling at her.
I groaned inwardly and was preparing a forced smile while she
started off shyly, but then, of course, the four of us fell over laughing together.

That night, Evelyn said, "Did you see Keith's face while Edie was telling that story? Did you see hers? Do you think it's possible that they're still—you know, still doing it?"

"Yes, I did—yes, I do," I said. "I was thinking exactly the same thing. They're amazing."

This was news back then, but probably shouldn't be by now. I remember a passage I came upon years later, in an Op-Ed piece in the *Times,* written by a man who'd just lost his wife. "We slept naked in the same bed for forty years," it went. There was also my splendid colleague Bob Bingham, dying in his late fifties, who was asked by a friend what he'd missed or would do differently if given the chance. He thought for an instant, and said, "More venery."

More venery. More love; more closeness; more sex and romance. Bring it back, no matter what, no matter how old we are. This fervent cry of ours has been certified by Simone de Beauvoir and Alice Munro and Laurence Olivier and any number of remarried or recoupled ancient classmates of ours. Laurence Olivier? I'm thinking of what he says somewhere in an interview: "Inside, we're all seventeen, with red lips."

This is a dodgy subject, coming as it does here from a recent widower, and I will risk a further breach of code and add that this was something that Carol and I now and then idly discussed. We didn't quite see the point of memorial fidelity. In our view, the departed spouse—we always thought it would be me—wouldn't be around anymore but knew or had known that he or she was loved forever. Please go ahead, then, sweetheart—don't miss a moment. Carol said this last: "If you haven't found someone else by a year after I'm gone I'll come back and haunt you."

Getting old is the second-biggest surprise of my life, but the first, by a mile, is our unceasing need for deep attachment and intimate love. We oldies yearn daily and hourly for conversation and a renewed domesticity, for company at the movies or while visiting a museum, for someone close by in the car when coming home at night. This is why we throng Match.com and OkCupid in such numbers—but not just for this, surely. Rowing in Eden (in Emily Dickinson's words: "Rowing in Eden— / Ah—the sea") isn't reserved for the lithe and young, the dating or the hooked-up or the just lavishly married, or even for couples in the middle-aged mixed-doubles semifinals, thank God. No personal confession or revelation impends here, but these feelings in old folks are widely treated like a raunchy secret. The invisibility factor—you've had your turn—is back at it again. But I believe that everyone in the world wants to be with someone else tonight, together in the dark, with the sweet warmth of a hip or a foot or a bare expanse of shoulder within reach. Those of us who have lost that, whatever our age, never lose the longing: just look at our faces. If it returns, we seize upon it avidly, stunned and altered again.

Nothing is easy at this age, and first meetings for old lovers can be a high-risk venture. Reticence and awkwardness slip into the room. Also happiness. A wealthy old widower I knew married a nurse he met while in the hospital, but had trouble remembering her name afterward. He called her "kid." An eighty-plus, twice-widowed lady I'd once known found still another love, a frail but vibrant Midwest professor, now close to ninety, and the pair got in two or three happy years together before he died as well. When she called his children and arranged to pick up her things at his house, she found every possession of hers lined up outside the front door.

But to hell with them and with all that, O.K.? Here's to you, old dears. You got this right, every one of you. Hook, line, and sinker; never mind the why or wherefore; somewhere in the night; love me forever, or at least until next week. For us and for anyone this unsettles, anyone who's younger and still squirms at the vision of an old couple embracing, I'd offer John Updike's "Sex or death:

you take your pick"—a line that appears (in a slightly different form) in a late story of his, "Playing with Dynamite."

This is a great question, an excellent insurance-plan choice, I mean. I think it's in the Affordable Care Act somewhere. Take it from us, who know about the emptiness of loss, and are still cruising along here feeling lucky and not yet entirely alone.

Onward and Outward, February, 2014

SPINKED

Remarks on receiving the J. G. Taylor Spink Award at the American Baseball Museum and Hall of Fame, Cooperstown, New York

Thank you—and first thanks to the Baseball Writers of America, who went out of their way to select me, a non-member and a part-timer, for this shining prize Spink! Spink! J. G. Taylor Spink! This was one of that early flood of tingling baseball names that rushed over me when I was a boy and first began hearing about and reading about baseball. Ossie Bluege! Flint Rhem! Hod Lisenbee! Mel Ott—an Oh with two "T"s! Jimmie Foxx—a fox with two "X"es! Spink—not a ballplayer but a baseball *publisher? The Sporting News*—a paper with just sports in it? Why don't we get that here at home? So this is a thrill for me as well as an honor. The roster of Spink honorees is stuffed with old heroes of mine like Red Smith and Toni Meany, and with baseball-writer friends who have also been models and heroes, folks like Jerry Holtzman and Peter Gammons and Bill Madden, who were so quick to put me at ease in the clubhouse and fill me in whenever I turned up again. A million thanks also from me to four extraordinary editors of *The New Yorker*—William Shawn, Bob Gottlieb, Tina Brown, and David Remnick—who each granted me weeks of time

and acres of space for my baseball stuff, a gift that only writers can appreciate.

My gratitude always goes back to baseball itself, which turned out to be so familiar and so startling, so spacious and exacting, so easy-looking and so heart-breakingly difficult that it filled up my notebooks and seasons in a rush. A pastime indeed. Fans know about this too. Nowadays we have all sports available, every sport all day long, but we're hanging on to this game of ours, knowing how lucky we are.

I was a city kid and I grew up on New York baseball. At Yankee Stadium, in the spring of 1930, I saw Lefty Gomez win his first game in the major leagues. A long time later he told me, "I beat Red Faber and the White Sox, 4–1, and I'd never seen so many people in one place before in my life." I was nine years old on the day of that game but had exactly the same impression. Lefty Gomez is here in the Hall, of course, still undefeated, 6 and 0 in the World Series.

In a game in 1933, I saw a pair of Yankee base-runners, Lou Gehrig and Dixie Walker, tagged out on opposite sides of home plate together—bang, bang—on a single swipe by the Senators catcher

Luke Sewell. Washington, not the Yanks, took the A.L. pennant
that fall. At Ebbets Field, eight years later—it's Game Four of the
World Series and now I'm a senior in college—I watched Mickey
Owen, the Dodgers' catcher, drop that third strike with two out in
the ninth—and the Yankees rise from the dead to win. They won
again the next day, too, for another championship.

Here's an August afternoon, in 1951, and I'm sitting up behind
first base at the Polo Grounds—still just a fan—when the rookie
Willie Mays makes the first fabulous play of his career: a full-tilt
running catch and a whirling, back-to-the-plate blind throw that
sailed from right-center field on the fly to his catcher, to nail the
Dodger baserunner, Billy Cox, at home. I can still see the Giants
players on the field and the Dodgers now coming up out of their
dugout all staring at each other and back out at Willie again—
"What! . . . What! . . . Oh, my god, did you *see* that!"—in wonder.
Well, yeah—get used to it, guys. I bring up this game again whenever I run into Willie—he doesn't quite remember me but then he
gets excited again, too. "You were there? You were there?" he cries.
"Now you tell 'em. You tell 'em—nobody here believes me!"

What's weird here and what you're all thinking, is how ancient
these games and plays are—decades old—and how clear they still
seem to be in Angell's mind. And anyway, can't we Google old stuff
like this or maybe find it on E.S.P.N., so who cares? You're right, of
course, and all I can say is yes, I care—I still do—even though this
kind of caring has gotten so much tougher for us now. What we all
have at our fingertips these days is instant replay and total recall:
the exact moment and all of tonight's other astounding moments
from all the games and all the parks, and, with them—let's admit
it—a diminishment of that moment. Let's cue Mays's throw again:
Wow! And one more time: Yes, that's it. And again: Yep. Got it.
I once asked Carlton Fisk if he still had any private memory of his
Game Six twelfth-inning home run off the left-field foul pole at

Fenway Park in the 1975 World Series—you know: Pudge dancing sideways up the line and waving at the ball, *pushing* it fair,
then raising his arms in triumph. "It's funny you ask," he said. "I
always go out of the room whenever I think that it's coming up on
the screen again, because I want to hold on to some piece of the
moment, keep it fresh in my head."

A nice quote—a line for a writer to circle in his notebook and
maybe put aside as the closer to a long piece. I collected great lines
and great baseball talkers—lifetime .300 talkers—like a billion-
aire hunting down Cézannes and Matisses. I stalked these guys
and buttered them up and got their flow into my notebooks and
onto my tapes, and, in rivers, into the magazine. Ted Williams.
Ted Simmons. Linda Kittell. Keith Hernandez. Bill Rigney. Lou
Brock. Dan Quisenberry. Roger Craig. Among others. I remember
arriving at the ballpark in Scottsdale at the beginning of another
spring training, and finding Craig, the Giants' manager, standing
with a writer out in left field—I think it was Dave Bush. "Roger
has another book out," David said to Craig after our greetings—
meaning me, this Roger—"Have you read it?"

"Read it?" Craig said. "Hell, I wrote half of it."

Funny works for me, too. The almost unbeatable Catfish
Hunter, gruesomely hammered in some game or other, smiled
afterward and said, "The sun don't shine on the same dog's ass
every afternoon." Another time, after he'd lost the second game of
the 1977 World Series, coughing up three early dingers to distant
parts of Dodger Stadium, he said, "Well, I had some folks here
from North Carolina who'd never *seen* a major league home run,
and I thought I'd give them a couple."

But let's go back for just a minute to Bob Gibson, and Game
One of the 1968 World Series, when he's just shut out the Detroit
Tigers, 4–0, striking out seventeen batters, a new World Series
record. The Tiger players have nothing to say. Asked to compare

Gibson to other pitchers he'd faced, Dick McAuliffe said, "He doesn't remind one of anybody. He's all by himself." In the clubhouse we writers gather around Gibson's locker. We're awed too. "Were you surprised by your performance today, Bob?" somebody offers at last. Gibson looks at him without smiling. "I'm never surprised by anything I do," he says.

A little later I ask, uh, have you always been this competitive? "Oh, I think so," Gibby says in his grave way. "I've played about a hundred games of tick-tack-toe with my six-year-old daughter and she hasn't beat me yet." He meant this.

Amazing men, extraordinary competitors, but there's too much winning here. Baseball is mostly about losing. These all-time winners in the Hall of Fame are proud men—pride is what drives every player—but every one of them knows or knew the pain of loss, the days and weeks when you're beat up and worn down, and another season is about to slip away. Nobody understood this better than Joe Torre, my friend and maybe my favorite baseball talker, who is part of this brilliant entering class that so honors the Hall on its 75th Anniversary. Joe Torre, the manager who never threw a player under the bus. "Oh, Paulie isn't happy with his at-bats right now," he'd say. Or: "Maybe David's not as proud of his stuff as he'd like to be"—and we writers would shift our impatient and insatiable minds a little and think about the player instead of the story. Joe Torre batted .376 as a Cardinals catcher in 1971, winning a batting title, but as a manager, he always brought up the following season with his players, when his average went down ninety points. Then he'd mention July 21, 1975, the day he became the first National League player ever to bat into four double plays in one game. His guys loved him for this. "I'd play for him any time," Mike Mussina said.

On one of his last days as the Yankees' manager, Torre said, "I understand the requirements here, but the players are human beings, and it's not machinery here. Even though they get paid a lot of money, it's blood that runs through their veins."

There was a little more like this but then he cheered up. "For a guy who never got to the postseason as a player, I'm having a whole lot of fun when you look at the whole thing."

Me, too, Joe.

Thank you, baseball.

July, 2014

EXTRA INNINGS

DEREK'S MMM

Derek Jeter hit two singles on Sunday against the Cleveland Indians, up at the Stadium, and, each time, the balls were taken out of play and handed over to the Yankees' dugout for posterity. Well, call it pre-posterity: these were Derek's two-thousand-nine-hundred-and-ninety-second and -ninety-third base hits, leaving him seven shy of three thousand. He will deliver the trimillennial bingle some time this week, no doubt, and with another Yankees home game against the Tribe scheduled for tonight, followed by three against the Texas Rangers, there's a good chance he'll oblige us by getting it done here, setting off fireworks, game-stopping ceremonials, and tears from the packed house of fans, who may be too busy tweeting (!SAWT!) to actually clap and scream. Three thousand lifetime base hits is fabulous. Only twenty-seven prior major-leaguers have attained this holy altitude, and the variety list of those who got there—Ty Cobb, Wade Boggs, Willie Mays, Honus Wagner, Rickey Henderson, Roberto Clemente, et al. (Al Kaline)—is all the more impressive because of those who didn't: Ted Williams, Lou Gehrig, Joe DiMaggio, Babe Ruth. Fabulous, yes, but, with all respect, not all that interesting, because of the wedding-anniversary blandness that surrounds the arrival of a sure thing.

Derek could add zing to the party by making No. 3,000 a home run, matching his old teammate Boggs in the feat (Paul Molitor hit the lone triple); it's less likely that he'll go in the other direction and do a Carl Yastrzemski. The eminent forty-year-old Yaz, a true Red Sox hero, was slumping and gimpy when he attained his own No. 2,999, on September 9, 1979, and then went oh-for-ten over three ensuing games before the jam-packed but deflating Fenway multitudes, at last rolling an eighth-inning single past the Yankee second baseman Willie Randolph's glove and on into right field. I was in close TV attendance that night and can testify that Randolph gave the play his professional all, and I could almost hear his murmured "Thank God" that accompanied mine and Yaz's as the ball went by.

A more vivid three-thousandth hit, the most by miles? Try Lou Brock's, at Busch Memorial Stadium, on August 13th of that very same year, 1979. Brock, the Cardinals' star left fielder, stroked a single against the Cubs' right-hander Dennis Lamp in the first inning, to bring himself one short of the mark. Facing Lamp again in the fourth, he fell behind by one and two, then got a pitch up under the chin that put him in the dirt. Brock hammered the next pitch on a low line toward center field—his hardest hit all year, he said later—and saw the ball strike Lamp on the leg, ricochet off his pitching hand, and roll off into foul territory. Lamp, injured, had to leave the game. "I was probably as big a fan of the event as anyone else there," Brock told me. "After all, I'd never seen anybody get three thousand hits, either."

Post, June, 2011

S'LONG, JEET

We know Derek Jeter by heart, so why all this memorizing? The between-pitches bat tucked up in his armpit. The fingertip helmet-twiddle. The left front foot wide open, out of the box until the last moment, and the cop-at-a-crossing right hand ritually lifted astern until the foot swings shut. That look of expectation, a little night-light gleam, under the helmet. The pitch—this one a slow breaking ball, a fraction low and outside—taken but inspected with a bending bow in its passage. More. Jeter's celebrity extends beyond his swing, of course, but can perhaps be summarized by an excited e-mail once received by a Brearley School teacher from one of her seventh graders: "Guess what! I just Googled 'Derek's butt!' "

This is Derek Jeter's twentieth and final September: twenty-seven more games and perhaps another hundred at-bats remain to be added to his franchise record, at this writing, of 2,720 and 11,094. He's not having a great year, but then neither are the Yanks, who trail the Orioles by seven games in the American League East and are three games short of qualifying for that tacky, tacked-on new second wild-card spot in the postseason. It's been a blah baseball year almost everywhere, and, come to think of it, watching Derek finish might be the best thing around.

Jeter has just about wound up his Mariano Tour—the all-points ceremonies around home plate in every away park on the Yankees' schedule, where he accepts gifts, and perhaps a farewell check for his Turn 2 charity, and lifts his cap to the cheering, phone-flashing multitudes. He does this with style and grace—no one is better at it—and without the weepiness of some predecessors. His ease, his daily joy in his work, has lightened the sadness of this farewell, and the cheering everywhere has been sustained and genuine. Just the other day, Tampa Bay manager Joe Maddon groused about the rare sounds of cheering offered up to Derek by his customarily sleepy attendees.

At every stop, there have been replays of Jeter's famous plays and moments up on the big screens—the no-man's-land relay and sideways flip to nab the Athletics' Jeremy Giambi at the plate in the 2001 American League Division Series; that horizontal dive into the Yankee Stadium third-base stands against the Red Sox in 2004. I don't expect further dramatics—he's forty and often in the lineup as d.h. these days—but closings have been a specialty of his, and it's O.K. to get our hopes up one more time. I'm thinking of the waning days of the old Stadium, in 2008, when Derek's great rush through September carried him to the top of the all-time career hits list at the famous crater, each fresh rap of his coming as accompaniment to the deep "Der-ek Je-tuh!" cries from the bleachers that the new restaurant site has pretty well silenced. The next year, up there, he passed Lou Gehrig for Most Yankee Base Hits Ever. Two years after that, he delivered his three-thousandth career hit: a home run that touched off a stunning five-for-five day at the Stadium against the Rays.

All right, I'll settle for one more inside-out line-drive double to deep right—the Jeter Blue Plate that's been missing of late. It still astounds me—Derek's brilliance as a hitter has always felt fresh and surprising, for some reason—and here it comes one more time. The pitch is low and inside, and Derek, pulling back his upper body and tucking in his chin as if avoiding an arriving No. 4 train, now jerks his left elbow and shoulder sharply upward while slashing powerfully down at and through the ball, with his hands almost grazing his belt. His right knee drops and twists, and the swing, opening now, carries his body into a golf-like lift and turn that sweetly frees him while he watches the diminishing dot of the ball headed toward the right corner. What! You can't hit like that—nobody can! Do it again, Derek.

It's sobering to think that in just a few weeks Derek Jeter won't be doing any of this anymore, and will be reduced to picturing himself in action, just the way the rest of us do. On the other hand, he's never complained, and he's been so good at baseball that he'll probably be really good at this part of it too.

Talk, September, 2014

BOGGLER

2014 National League
Wild-Card Elimination Game
Giants 8: Pirates 0

Forty thousand six hundred and twenty-nine black-clad Pirates fans tromped home last night, their summer's screaming stilled and their thoughts fixed upon the San Francisco Giants' lefty starter Madison Bumgarner, who had utterly ruined their autumn. Bumgarner threw a shutout, surrendering four singles, walking one batter, and striking out ten. The Giants won, 8–0. They will play against the Washington Nationals tomorrow to open their half of the National League Divisional Series. The Pirates won't. End of story—or almost.

Madison Bumgarner. Madison Bumgarner. What can you do with anybody like that? All night long, Pittsburgh lay sleepless, sorting out the name and the headline.

NAME GRABS OUR MIND.

Post, October, 2014

AHOY, THE SERIES!

With Derek Jeter a wisp and two wild-card teams, the San Francisco Giants and the Kansas City Royals, preparing to tee it up
in Game One of the World Series tonight, a quick tour d'horizon
of the recent postseason games could help get us in the mood
for further surprises. Let's start with Underpants. Actually, that's
Hunter Pence, the Giants' right fielder—a name misheard by my
wife, Peggy, in the next room during an announcer's introduction
of him as a batter in the early innings of the ESPN telecast of
that one-game preliminary shoot-out between the Giants and the
Pittsburgh Pirates. " 'Underpants'? 'Underpants'—what kind of
a name is that?" she cried indignantly. I murmured a correction,
but the brain-worm had been implanted, of course, and has proved
inoperable. Peggy was not much deterred. "What were his parents
thinking?" she said now, coming into the room with me. "He has
to have heard this in every grade of elementary school, you know—
every day of it, poor guy." Underpants, oddly enough, was also dis-
tinguishable by his actual pants, I'd noticed—the bottoms of his
Giants uniform are cut back to the tops of his kneecaps, a height
not seen in the majors since the White Sox briefly sported those
team Bermudas, back in 1976.

Pence or Pants diverted us from his clothing in the sixth
inning of Game Four of the National League Divisional Series, at
San Francisco's A.T.&T. Park, when the Washington Nationals outfielder Jayson Werth hammered a deep drive to the right-field corner. Pence, racing to his left, launched himself upward and outward
along the wall, stuck out his mitt and nailed the catch, saving the
one-run lead, and perhaps the game and the day, for the Giants. In
the replays, he looked like a dissected frog splayed up there, and
will remain so forever in the Bay Area unconscious, a twin specimen to Joe Rudi, the Athletics left fielder, who did more or less the

same thing against the Cincinnati Reds, back in the 1972 World
Series.

Werth, whose flowing fox-colored beard and shoulder-length
hair suggest a discarded droshky lap robe, went one for seventeen in
the Nats' wipeout loss—a miserable showing but not the worst of
this painful October. Yasiel Puig, the Dodgers' stellar young Cuban
outfielder, struck out eight times in the course of twelve at-bats
against Cardinals pitching—a crater-sized hole had developed in his
defense against inside pitches—and was benched for the last game.

Yasiel can bring us to the Giants' bearded righty reliever
named Petit (it's pronounced like the dress size), who set a record
this summer by retiring forty-six consecutive batters. The man and
the mark were unknown to me when I watched him deliver six
middle innings of one-hit ball against the Nationals, in Game Two
of the Divs, but I slowly became aware that the Fox telecasters
seemed oddly unwilling to call him by his first name, and then
familiarly shorten it, as is the custom. "Who Petit?" I muttered
once or twice. "Tell us, guys—O.K.?" Finally it showed up in a
visual: he's Yusmeiro.

So many well-regarded and heavily armed teams were going
down so quickly—the Nats, the Tigers, the Dodgers, the Angels,
the Orioles—that I had a passing flash of towering French or Spanish ships of the line blowing up or foundering with all hands in
battles taken from another Jack Aubrey novel. If that had been the
case, his fast frigate, his lightly armed but lucky and venturesome
H.M.S. *Surprise,* would be the Kansas City Royals. Possessors of the
lowest home-run total in the league, they stole thirteen bases in the
post, tied up and then won three games in which they had trailed—
including the qualifying opener against the Oakland A's—and
won four times in extra innings. The eager crew—Alex Gordon,
Billy Butler, Lorenzo Cain, Mike Moustakas, Salvador Perez, Jarrod
Dyson, Brandon Finnegan, and the rest—will be piped to quarters

very shortly, where we will come to know them and like them even better. Cain, the center fielder, and the tall, immensely talented catcher Perez will win further citations, and the Giants, because of their bullpen, will win this splendid engagement (it says here) in seven.

Post, October, 2014

THE BEST

Game 7, 2014 World Series
Giants 3: Royals 2
Giants Win Series

I missed Christy Mathewson somehow but caught almost everyone else, down the years—Lefty Grove, Carl Hubbell, Sandy Koufax, Bob Gibson, Jack Morris, Curt Schilling, Randy Johnson—but here was the best. Madison Bumgarner, the Giants' left-handed ace, coming on in relief last night in the fifth inning of the deciding seventh game of this vibrant World Series, gave up a little opening single, then retired fourteen straight Kansas City batters, gave up another hit, and then closed the deal. The Giants won, 3–2, claiming their third World Championship in five years. It was almost his third victory of this Series—the scorers had it that way for a time, then gave the W back to Jeremy Affeldt, the left-handed reliever who was still the pitcher of record when the Giants went ahead in the fourth. Bumgarner, who lost a game along the way, in the Divisionals, on a little throwing error of his own, winds up at 4–1 for his October. He had won a game in each of the Giants' World Championships, in 2012 and 2010, and now, at twenty-five, stands at 4–0 in the classic, with an earned-run average of 0.25. He was pitching on two days' rest but also on manna: possibly the best October pitcher of them all.

Sure, we can talk about this: we've got all winter. Christy Mathewson threw three shutout victories for the Giants in the 1905 World Series, and won two more games (while losing five) in the Series of 1910, 1911, and 1912, but, as Matty would point out if he were here—he was famous for his fairness—even at his best he would not fare well against the enormous, toned-up athletes of our day.

I don't know what it felt like watching Mathewson pitch, but watching Bumgarner is like feeling an expertly administered epidural nip in between a couple of vertebrae and deliver bliss: it's a gliding, almost eventless slide through the innings, with accumulating fly-ball outs and low-count K's marking the passing scenery. It's twilight sleep; an Ambien catnap; an evening voyage on a Watteau barge. Bumgarner is composed out there, his expression mournful, almost apologetic, even while delivering his wide-wing, slinging stuff. Sorry, guys: this is how it goes. Over soon.

I don't know how to bring this up, but attention must be paid, as Mrs. Willy Loman used to say. In the last line of my pre–World Series post here, I startled myself with a prediction: the Giants, because of their bullpen, would win this in seven. Yes, exactly so— and who now wants to step up with a wayd-a-minnit objection, claiming that Madison Bumgarner, though he actually emerged from there—we saw him—did not exactly represent the Giants' bullpen last night? Eat my shorts.

Post, October, 2014

THE SILENCE OF THE FANS

Security is the given reason for this afternoon's scheduled weirdness in Baltimore, where the Orioles played the Chicago White

Sox at Camden Yards, but without any fans in attendance. This is a first-ever in major-league history—one can imagine some nineteen-thirties low-level minor-league game in the Ozarks, where the ticket booths were open but no one happened by on that particular afternoon—and also a clearly missed opportunity for a struggling sci-fi screenwriter, whose attendant normal turnout of 18,462 could have been abruptly and silently transported to SpaceKlon 7 with two outs in the bottom of the third.

But what was it like there today, really? With no ushers and no vendors? With no instant replay visible in the overhead fan TV sets? Were the sounds of conversation between players in the dug-outs audible to a pigeon pausing somewhere along the silent, empty rows of seats in Section 280?

None of this matters much, to be sure, except as an unexpected reminder of the massive and relentless add-ons and distractions of modern-day ball. The Kiss Camera, the racing mascots, the T-shirt cannonades, the God Bless, the deafening rock, the home-team anthem, the infield sweepers' dance, the well-plaqued Hall of Heroes, the retired numbers, the gymnasium-sized souvenir shops, the Texas steak restaurant in right (with its roped-off waiting areas thoughtfully supplied with overhead screens), the pizzeria in left, the bleacher kiddie pool, and so on. Fans love this and eat it up, but today's silent anomaly in Baltimore is a mirror reminder that what's been taken away from the pastime isn't the crowd but the game: what we came for and what we partake of now in passing fractions, often seen in a held-up smartphone.

Some among us (I am one of them) can recall a time when the baseball and the players were the lone attractions, barring a few outfield signboards. Nothing more, not even an organist. You watched and waited in semi-silence, ate a hot dog, drank a Moxie, watched some more, yelled when something happened, kept score, saw the shadows lengthen, then trooped home elated or disconsolate. It was a public event, modestly presented, and private in recollection. If the game was a big one, with enormous Sunday crowds and endless roaring, it was thrilling to have been there, but in some fashion you'd also been there alone, nobody else in sight.

Post, April, 2015

ACKNOWLEDGMENTS

My steady feelings of thanks, which start with my children and my family and include a splendid range of cherished friends, are not reducible to a list. Elsewhere on these pages I name the five extraordinary editors of *The New Yorker* it's been my privilege to write for and work for, but I must make special mention of Tina Brown, who was so insistent that I write more about myself, and David Remnick, whose patience and generosity toward me have been exceeded only by his love and support in hard times. I send opinionated love to all my past colleagues in the *New Yorker*'s Fiction Department and to their brilliant incumbent successors Deborah Treisman, Cressida Leyshon, and Willing Davidson. I am grateful beyond measure to Ann Goldstein, Mark Singer, Pamela McCarthy, Dorothy Wickenden, Peter Canby, Ben McGrath, Betsy Morais, David Denby, Patrick Keogh, Rhonda Sherman, Bruce Diones, Eliza Grace Martin, Hannah Jocelyn, Lauren Porcaro, Amanda Urban, Bill Thomas, Rose Courteau, Angela Patrinos, Darlene Allen, and Ms. Moorman's Cathedral School fifth-grade haiku writers.

Last and first thoughts, within this book and on every day, are for my dear wife Peggy.

ILLUSTRATION CREDITS

Courtesy of Roger Angell: 6, 93, 94, 240
Tom Bachtell, courtesy of *The New Yorker:* 9
Courtesy of White Literary, LLC: 14
Courtesy of Betsy Daugherty: 43
George Shanks: 51
George Price, courtesy of *The New Yorker:* 55
Frank Modell, courtesy of *The New Yorker:* 58
William Steig, courtesy of *The New Yorker:* 58, 180, 181, 184, 193
Arnie Levin, courtesy of *The New Yorker:* 59, 95, 98
Adrian Tomine: 105
Nicholas Parker, courtesy of *The New Yorker:* 171
Ward Schumaker, courtesy of *The New Yorker:* 172
David Hughes, courtesy of *The New Yorker:* 173, 174, 175, 176, 177
© The Saul Steinberg Foundation/Artists Rights Society (ARS), New York: 203
    Untitled, 1975. Ink, pencil, colored pencil, and collage on paper, 14½ x
    11½ in. Beinecke Rare Book and Manuscript Library, Yale University.
    Originally published in *The New Yorker,* May 10, 1976.
Courtesy of Judy Tomkins: 230
Francis Barraud: 237
Courtesy of David Updike: 254
© The Saul Steinberg Foundation/Artists Rights Society (ARS), New York: 259
    Untitled, 1980. Black pencil on paper, 12⅞ x 11 in. Beinecke Rare Book and
    Manuscript Library, Yale University. Originally published in *The New Yorker,*
    November 24, 1980.
© Brigitte Lacombe 2014: 267
Courtesy of Chris Protopapas: 283

The following pieces originally appeared, some in different form,
in *The New Yorker*:

"Ahoy, the Series!" as "Ahoy, the World Series!," "Andy's Haikus," "Anna
Hamburger," "The Best," "Bob Feller" as "Rapidly," "Bob Sheppard" as "Postscript:
Bob Sheppard," "Boggler," "Class Report," "Congratulations! It's a Baby," "Chinny-
Chin-Chin," "Crying Man," "Barry and the Deathly Numbers" as "Deathly
Numbers," "Derek's MMM," "Dial Again," "Disarmed," "Duke Snider" as "And the
Duke," "Earl Weaver," as "Postscript: Earl Weaver, 1930–2013," "Greetings, Friends!"
"Here Comes the Sun," "Hersey and History," "Horse Talk," "Huckleberry Finn" as
"Huck Continued," "Jackie Robinson Again," "Joe Carroll" as "Makeup Man!"
"La Forza Del Alpo," "Life and Letters," "Lineup" as "Olden Opener," "The Little
Flower" as "Ink," "Lo Love, High Romance," "Man of Letters," "Me and Prew,"
"The Minstrel Steig," "Moose Tales," "More Time with the Britannica," "Mo Town,"
"Nothing Doing," "Off We Go" as "Catch-Up," "Over the Wall," "Papiness," "The
Crime of Our Life," "Two Emmas," "The Silence of the Fans," "S'long, Jeet," "Sox
Top Sloppy Cards," "Storyville," "This Old Man," "Three at a Time," "West Side
Story," "The Wrong Dog," "Yaz's Triple Crown," and "Zim." Reprinted by courtesy
of *The New Yorker*.

ABOUT THE AUTHOR

Roger Angell is a senior fiction editor and a longtime contributor with *The New Yorker*. His writings for the magazine include reporting, commentary, fiction, humor, film and book reviews, and, for many years, the magazine's Christmas verse, "Greetings, Friends!" His ten books include such baseball writings as *The Summer Game, Five Seasons,* and *Game Time,* and, most recently, a memoir, *Let Me Finish.* His awards include a George Polk Award for Commentary; the Michael Braude Award for Light Verse, presented by the American Academy of Arts and Letters; a PEN/ESPN Lifetime Achievement Award for Literary Sports Writing; and the J.G. Taylor Spink Award, the highest honor given to writers by the Baseball Hall of Fame. His *New Yorker* piece "This Old Man" won the 2014 prize for Essays and Criticism awarded by the American Society of Magazine Editors. He is a member of the American Academy of Arts and Letters. Mr. Angell lives in New York and Maine.